To Rayna with love

CW01507089

This Edition
copyright © Chris West 2016

ISBN 978-0-9930233-2-3

Paperback edition published by CWTK Publications
Also available in ebook format from Endeavour Press

"HELLO EUROPE!"

A History of Modern Europe in Sixty Eurovision Song Contests

by

Chris West

Author of
A History of Britain in 36 Postage Stamps
A History of America in 36 Postage Stamps

Introduction

In 1956, Europe was still struggling out of the shadow of World War Two. Its cities were pockmarked with boarded-off bombsites. In its homes, photographs stood on mantelpieces showing sons, husbands, brothers, uncles or fathers who would never return from battlefields – or whole families who would never return from death camps. Europe's thinkers pondered how such enormities could have been taken place in a supposedly civilized continent. 'Never Again,' they said, but wondered how this could be ensured.

For many Western Europeans, the reaction to this horror had been to seek out old ways: order, stability, personal respectability and duty. On Sundays, that meant a visit to church. Attendance figures, in steady decline before 1939, rose between 1945 and 1955. During the working week, it meant that most married, urban women minded the home while their husbands went off to factories or offices where they had secure jobs in large hierarchical organizations. Rural life returned to the harsh grind of tending a small family farm. Younger men did 'National Service' in their country's armed forces. Only the more raffish of such youngsters had sex before marrying. Many gay men and women hid their orientation from the world, and sometimes from themselves, all their lives.

Despite the role of militant nationalism in the previous decade's cataclysm, Western Europeans in 1956 were patriotic. The nation state remained at the heart of most people's identities. It was the centre of political power. It was where empires were ruled from: Belgium, Britain, France, the Netherlands, Portugal and Spain still had overseas dominions of various kinds. These empires were fast waning, but remained glorious in the minds of some of these nations' older citizens – and a drain on their masters' war-depleted resources.

One empire alone was not waning. Behind six thousand kilometres of barbed wire from Arctic Norway to the Black Sea, Soviet Russia held a tight imperial grip on Europe's eastern inhabitants. The driving force of that empire, Josef Stalin, had died in 1953, but his successors had yet to show any sign of changing the ruthless way it was run, with puppet regimes, secret police and relentless propaganda.

In the new, eastern empire workers were flattered and feted but didn't seem to be getting better off materially. Figures trumpeted growth, but consumer goods remained scarce or non-existent. West of the barbed wire, consumption was taking off, but still of staples: few Western European families had fridges, washing machines, TVs or cars. Few enjoyed foreign holidays. Envious eyes looked across the Atlantic at booming, consumerist America.

Six decades later…

In 2016, our economy might not be growing, but it is still vast. Almost all Europeans enjoy and expect a standard of living unimaginable to their grandparents. Cars? We have too many. TVs? Everyone has one; now we queue up for the latest iPhone or iPad. Travel? Of course we've been to other countries – though if we want to eat exotic food, all we need to do is head for the town centre. Our workplace is fast-changing, challenging and high-tech, but unforgiving: few jobs are secure now. Women are an integral part of that workplace, though still struggle for equal representation at the top. Our youngsters don't have to fight wars, but they enter the battleground of sexuality as adolescents, ever fewer of them guided by religion, which is in many countries a minority force outside immigrant communities. Most of those young people will be open-minded about sexual orientation. To many Europeans, especially the young, the safe, war-haunted values of 1956 have become comical or even creepy. Difference is something to be enjoyed, not feared, and private lives are to be governed not by respectability and duty but by the creed of authenticity: 'to thine own self be true'.

Empires? They are gone, both Soviet and European. 500 million of us live in the European Union (EU), an institution committed to democracy, diversity and individual freedom, though also criticized for being remote and bureaucratic. 335 million of us share a common currency, which is more than share the US dollar (America itself is no longer envied, with its inequality, guns, teeming prisons and own troubled sense of imperial mission).

Such huge changes raise questions. The EU is bringing Europe's old, distinct nations ever closer together: how far should this process go? Are national identities best ditched along with other old stuff from 1956 like washing machines with mangles or cars that need a starting handle on winter mornings? Or are nations still important? How large should we consider Europe to be? Does it really end at the Bosporus and the Urals, as geographers tell us, or is it bigger? Or should it be smaller? Perhaps most important of all, what does it mean to be 'European'? Are there core values that mark us out from other civilizations? Or is this a meaningless and possibly dangerous question in our post-modern, half-fractured, half-globalized world?

One way of answering such questions – the best in my view – is to look at history. Rather than debate abstractions, let's see how we have got to where we are now. I like to look at history through 'lenses', to examine things from everyday experience over time and see what they tell us.

In two earlier books I did this with postage stamps, which turned out to be tiny rectangular time-machines. For Europe, I wanted to find something different. But what? Nothing felt right...

Then one Saturday evening in May, I sat down with the family to watch TV – and there was the answer, pouting and prancing and blaring emotions in a razzle of lasers, strobe-lights, dry ice and theatricality. Of course!

You either love or hate the Eurovision Song Contest. If you hate it, you may be right from a purely aesthetic point of view. But you're missing the fun. Over 100 million fellow Europeans, in every European nation, along with fans in Australia, Brazil, China and, actually, anywhere with access to the internet, will be watching the show. (It's hard to get exact viewing figures: the EBU is oddly secretive about this, even though the show is clearly a huge – and growing – success. The EBU produces a figure for what it calls 'reach', which technically means the number of people who viewed the programme for at least one minute. For 2013, this figure was 170 million; for 2014, it was 195 million and for 2015, 197 million. Even if one assumes that quite a few people turned on Eurovision, watched for just over a minute then turned off in horror, I feel safe in deducing from these figures that 'over 100 million' people, 55% of the 'reach', watched all or most of the broadcast.)

Many viewers will been fans for years: as kids, my wife and I had sat down with our own parents and watched the contest on black and white screens in homes heated with open fires and bar heaters.

Eurovision, with its continent-wide reach and six-decade tradition, had to be the perfect lens through which to view the recent history of our home continent. Look at the costumes – the rising hemlines of the late 1960s, confident and 'liberated'; the flapping flares and lapels of the confused 1970s; the big hair and shoulder-pads of the 1980s, girding up for the pursuit of power and wealth. Look at the sets, from the creaky stage backdrops of the fifties to the hypertech virtual worlds of twenty-first century Eurovision. Look at the props and the routines, from those early Bakelite telephones and cute bird puppets to today's wheels, trapeze artists, trampolines, explosions and seesaws. And how about the subject matter of the songs, from the coy romanticism of

5

those early 1950s ditties to the in-your-face sexuality of the mid-noughties?

There's the voting. I could write a book about this on its own. There's the simple technology of it, from those early manually operated scoreboards and unreliable phone lines, to modern supercomputers flawlessly processing millions of votes phoned, texted, mouse-clicked and red-buttoned from around and beyond the continent. There are the rumours of skullduggery – did General Franco use bribery to ensure a win for Massiel's lyrically challenged *La la la* back in 1968? Above all, there's the geopolitics, the bloc voting that drove Britain's veteran Eurovision commentator Terry Wogan to distraction. Wogan bewailed this as the curse of the 2000s, but it is actually as old as the competition, with its early string of mutually supportive francophone winners.

Geo*politics*? Isn't the contest supposed to be apolitical? Isn't that why Georgia had to withdraw its 2009 entry *We don't wanna put in*?

Eurovision is, of course, political to its star-spangled, thigh-high boots. It always has been. There's politics in the songs – from Mike Moran and Lynsey de Paul's 1977 proto-Thatcherite *Rock Bottom* to Ukraine's 2005 street-fighting anthem *Razom nas bahato (Together we are many)*. Portugal's 1974 entry was the signal to start a revolution. There's even politics in the sets: Franco smuggled a fascist emblem onto the stage in 1969.

One can add to this the broader politics of race, sexual orientation and gender. The contest had to wait till 1964 for its first non-white entrant, the Netherlands' Anneke Grönloh, and till 2001 for the first black winner, Dave Benton: not a great endorsement for the supposedly liberal continent. By contrast, Eurovision has become a focus for LGBT expression, triumphantly asserted by 2014's winner Conchita Wurst but going right back to 1961, where the winning song was a hidden paean to gay love (it had to be hidden in those days). The contest has always reflected the changing role of Europe's women: as good a measure of this as any is the simple volume of female voices, from Corry Brokken quietly wishing her 1957 husband would put down his newspaper, to Céline Dion belting out *Ne partez pas sans moi* in 1988.

Talking of *Ne partez pas sans moi*, Eurovision also gives us insight into Europe's politics of language. Nine of the first eighteen winners were in French, but Dion's power-ballad was the last francophone victor. In 2014, all the national votes were announced in English apart from those from Paris, where the announcer rambled on *en Français*, just to remind us she was allowed to. France came last in that competition.

Eurovision is also about belonging, about who can join the 'Europe' club, and what do you have to do to stay in. The first 'European' song contest was essentially a domestic affair within that third of the continent interested in greater political unity. It soon broadened, showing Europe's keenness to come together culturally, if not (at that time) politically. In the 1970s and 1980s, it reached out even further, as Turkey and Israel joined the fun. At the same time, Eurovision became a symbol of freedom for those Europeans trapped behind the

Iron Curtain. A Soviet attempt to create a rival, Intervision, fizzled out. When the Berlin Wall came down, Eurovision raced to embrace the new Europe much quicker than any political institution did. In 1993 Muhamed Fazlagic risked his life to flee besieged Sarajevo and sing for Bosnia; in 2007, Maria Šerifovic made a huge step towards the welcoming of Serbia into Europe by winning.

Right now, Europe's two biggest neighbours are having a kind of dance with European identity. In 2009, Russia, eager to join the European family, spent a fortune on hosting the contest. In 2014 it seemed set on turning away – to the echo of audience boos and rocket fire from eastern Ukraine. In 2016, its entry is an early favourite for the contest. Turkey was a triumphant winner in 2003 but has been a grumpy non-participant, with its own rival contest, since 2013.

The Eurovision Song Contest has both reflected and been part of the changing social, economic, cultural and political life of the continent ever since Thursday May 24, 1956, when Lohengrin Filipello walked out onto the stage of the Teatro Kursaal in Lugarno to polite applause and announced the first contestant.

Join me on its – on our – amazing European journey.

The 1950s

Prelude

The first ever Eurovision TV broadcast was not a song contest but coverage of a giant flower show, the Narcissus Festival at Montreux, Switzerland, on June 6, 1954. Given the psychological make-up of some later Eurovision Song Contest participants, readers may find this amusing. The broadcast was a success, and the European Broadcasting Union (EBU) began looking around for other subjects on which to try out their fast-developing technology.

('Eurovision', by the way, is technically the name for the TV arm of the European Broadcasting Union, responsible for a wide range of programmes of which the song contest is just one. However most people now use the word Eurovision to mean the song contest, and from this point on, I shall follow this practice. Apologies to any pedants…)

On Jan 20 1955, Marcel Bezençon, Director of Swiss TV and President of the EBU's Programme Division, came up with the idea for an international song competition. In October the EBU announced that *Le Grand-Prix Eurovision de la Chanson Européenne* would be held in Lugano, Switzerland, next year.

Testing new technology was one reason for the contest, but Bezençon had deeper motives. Though from a neutral country, he was haunted by the war and believed that a single European nation was the best way of ensuring 'Never Again'.

Such a vision was not new. Victor Hugo, author of *Les Misérables*, had promoted it at a Peace Conference in Paris in 1846 – though he had been laughed off stage. The First World War gave it fresh momentum. The Pan-European Union was founded in 1923 by Count Richard Nikolaus von Coudenhove-Kalergi, promoting a single European state based on liberalism, Christianity and social responsibility. Many eminent individuals such as Albert Einstein, Fridtjof Nansen and Sigmund Freud became members.

After the Second World War, Winston Churchill talked of a 'sort of United States of Europe'. Churchill's Europe did not include Britain – his vision was of four great powers: America, the Soviet Union, the British Commonwealth and Europe. Other thinkers began to ponder what the boundaries of the new Europe might be, too. In 1949, former French Prime Minister Robert Schuman said it would comprise those nations who possessed what he called 'the European spirit', which he defined as a consciousness of 'belonging to a cultural family and having a willingness to serve that [family] in the spirit of total mutuality, without any hidden motives of hegemony or the selfish exploitation of others'.

During the late 1940s and early 1950s, practical steps towards European integration began with the setting up of various Europe-wide (or at least Western-Europe-wide) bodies. The Council of Europe (a human rights organization, nothing to do with the modern EU) and

NATO both date from 1949. The EBU first met in 1950. 1952 saw the formation of the European Coal and Steel Community (ECSC): six nations – Germany, France, Italy, the Netherlands, Belgium and Luxembourg – agreeing to hand over national control of these sectors, both key to waging war, to a transnational 'High Authority'. Its first President was Jean Monnet, one of the great philosophers of European integration. One of Monnet's closest friends was Marcel Bezençon. The Eurovision Song Contest was political from the start.

In 1950s Europe, there was a wide gulf between 'serious' music, essentially the western classical tradition, and popular music, which was all part of that post-war rush to untroubling conformity: the world of the German *schlager*, Italian *musica leggera*, Dutch *levenslied* or Britain's BBC Light Programme, of artistes like Freddy Quinn, Johnny Jordaan or Alma Cogan. In between these two sat jazz and a number of local musical traditions, such as the francophone *chanson*, where singers like Georges Brassens and Édith Piaf took on darker subjects: failed love, social alienation, existential disillusion. The original EBU brief for *Le Grand-Prix Eurovision de la Chanson Européenne* did not specify exactly what kind of song it wanted, only that the songs be '*originales*'.

As the 1950s drew on, a very original music began making itself heard with ever-increasing insistency from across the Atlantic, on records imported to port cities like Liverpool or broadcast by American Forces Radio or the freewheeling private Radio Luxembourg. There was nothing in the EBU brief to exclude rhythm and blues or rock'n'roll, but somehow this found itself off limits in the contest. Why? It could have been that it was deemed not European enough, but my own suspicion is that it was simply about numbers. The *Grand-Prix* was aimed at a middle-class, family audience because the EBU thought that would attract the most viewers. Oma, mama, papa and the younger kids would all watch it; if their stroppy 17-year old wanted to sneak up to their room and listen to Alan Freed on their new transistor radio, well, let them. They'd soon grow out of it.

The contest has never quite got away from this early bias. That's part of its quirky charm. But it is also what makes it such a good mirror of its times – by not seeking to present 'cutting edge' trends in music (usually a minority interest), it allows itself to reflect wider social trends instead.

1956

Date: 24 May
Venue: Teatro Kursaal, Lugano, Switzerland
Debuts: Belgium, France, West Germany, Italy, Luxembourg, Netherlands, Switzerland.
Winner: Lys Assia, Switzerland
Winning Song: *Refrain*

There are no video recordings of the first Eurovision Song Contest (except for the winner's reprise). This is oddly apt. 1956 was a watershed year in the history of modern Europe. It was the year of the Suez crisis, when Europe's two biggest colonial powers, Britain and France, suddenly found out how little clout they had in the post-war global order. Their attempt to forcibly recapture the Suez Canal, newly nationalized by Egypt's President Gamal Abdal Nasser, was halted in its tracks by condemnation from the new 'Third World', from Russia, and above all from America, which said it would effectively bankrupt Britain if that nation continued the adventure. So much for Churchill's 1948 vision of 'four great powers'. 1956 was also the year that Russian tanks seized back Hungary, killing 2,000 people and, with them, any hopes that with the death of Stalin the Iron Curtain would quietly rust away.

But both these events happened in the autumn of '56. The first, lost Song Contest was held in the spring of that year. It comes to us from a simpler, vanished world.

We have no film of the contest, but we do have sound. The first ever ESC song was the feather-light *De Vogels van Holland (the Birds of Holland)*. 'Toodle-oodle-oo' go Holland's birds – more musically than any other nation's, of course. Nothing is quite as it seems in Eurovision however. *De Vogels van Holland* was sung in the shadow of history. The singer, Jetty Paerl, came from a Jewish family that had had to flee Holland in 1940. Paerl's friends and more distant relatives would not have been so fortunate: the Netherlands had had a Jewish population of 140,000 in 1939 and of 14,000 in 1947. Most of those missing 126,000 had perished in Auschwitz or Sobibor, just over ten years before the Lugano contest. It is worth remembering that the Holocaust was closer to May 1956 than 9/11 is to us today.

The songs that followed were either *chansons* – Belgium's Fud Leclerc felt like joining *Messieurs les noyés dans la Seine (Gentlemen drowned in the Seine)* – or further light entertainment. Germany's nautical Freddy Quinn added a little swing. After they'd been sung, it was time to decide the winner. Eurovision wouldn't be Eurovision without controversial judging. There were more Swiss judges than those of any other nation – Luxembourg had balked at the cost of sending judges to Lugano and, with touching faith in pan-Europeanism, had asked two Swiss to stand in for them. Guess which nation won.

Refrain was a pleasant, reflective ballad about lost love. No other places were announced, though it is rumoured that two chansons came second and third: second, the other German entry, *Im Wartesaal des grossen Gluck (In the Waiting Room for good Luck)* (it's a *chanson*: we've got a long wait), and third Fud Leclerc.

Half the songs sung at Lugano in 1956 were in French. Modern Eurovision viewers are used to songs in English (except from France) and results announced in English (except by France), but in 1956, French dominated.

This was in line with political Europe at the time. In 1956 it was France and Frenchmen like Robert Schuman and Jean Monnet (and French-speakers like Marcel Bezençon) who were driving European integration. French was the language of the new Europe – it was, for example, the language of the original EBU brief for the Eurovision Song Contest.

More significant still is the list of Lugano participants. Apart from the Swiss, who could hardly have been denied a place given Marcel Bezençon's offer to host the event, the competitors are the six members of the 1952 European Coal and Steel Community. ECSC outsiders Britain, Austria and Denmark had applied to participate, but for various reasons did not end up on the Kursaal stage. An early federalist conspiracy? Maybe, but local incompetence is also to blame: Britain, for example, had run a contest to decide its entry – the contest was won by zither-playing Australian singer Shirley Abicair, with a song called *Little Ship* – but didn't get the admission forms in on time.

Six decades later, these remain the countries where the European flame burns most brightly. If Europe becomes 'two-speed', it is the Europe of Lugano 1956 (minus Switzerland) that will be at its heart.

Looking back not decades but centuries, the list also maps with spooky neatness onto the Holy Roman Empire of Charles the Great, Charlemagne, who was crowned its emperor on Christmas Day, 800 AD. Add Austria and Bohemia (the western half of the modern Czech Republic)and remove Southern Italy, and the roll-call of competitors at Lugano is 'Europe' as conceived 1156 years earlier. Charlemagne's empire lasted, in name anyway, till 1806, though it kept changing shape over that time (it lost large chunks of what is now France and ended up as a kind of proto-Germany). But if the emperor's ghost had been watching the contest on May 24, 1956, he would have felt totally at home with its geographical extent. This, he would have thought, is civilization. What he would have made of the music is a different matter...

Almost exactly a month after the contest, on June 26, representatives of 'Lugano Europe' met in Brussels to discuss a report form former Belgian Prime Minister Paul-Henri Spaak, which proposed they form a 'customs union', a free trade area with common external tariffs.. This is arguably the moment that the modern EU was conceived. It and the Eurovision Song Contest may not quite be twins, but they are born from the same stock and have a very narrow age-difference.

1957

Date: 3 March
Venue: Hessische Rundfunk, Frankfurt, West Germany
Debuts: Austria, Denmark, UK
Winner: Corry Brokken, Netherlands
Winning song: *Net als toen (Just like then)*

As Charlemagne's former empire planned its new, exclusive future, Eurovision opened itself to outsiders: the three failed Lugano applicants got their paperwork right this time. As a result, the 1957 contest had a more international feel to it, with ten songs in six different languages (seven if you count Flemish). The presenter was Armenian-born Anaid Iplicjian. Eurovision was reaching out to a wider Europe.

The show was more theatrical, too. Singers entered down a flight of stairs. Props were used: Germany's Margot Hielscher sang into a telephone (music by Ralph Maria Siegel, whose son would become a Eurovision legend). Italy and the Netherlands had musicians accompany the singers on stage, Dutch violinist Sem Nijveen playing a particularly attractive, jazzy solo.

The performance of the evening came from Denmark's Birthe Wilke and Gustav Winckler: dressed for the part, they sang their song, *Skibet skal sejle i Nat (The Ship must sail tonight)*, about a naval officer about to leave his new love, then concluded with a kiss that was both long (13 seconds) and passionate.

Perhaps theatrical isn't the right word. Their kiss was cinematic – Hollywood cinematic: think Ingrid Bergman and Cary Grant in Alfred Hitchcock's *Notorious*. 1957's Western Europeans were getting much of their cultural input from across the Atlantic. The great musicals of Rogers and Hammerstein – *Carousel, The King and I, Oklahoma* – had made it onto the silver screen in the mid-fifties (*South Pacific* would follow in 1958). In 1957, two lads called John Lennon and Paul McCartney met at a fete in a Liverpool suburb, and found they shared a passion for music – not *chansons, levenslied* or *schlagers* but American rhythm and blues.

In political Europe, the time between the first and the second Eurovision contests had been filled with diplomatic activity. 'Lugano Europe' had accepted Spaak's report, and then had to thrash out the details of exactly what form the new supra-national entity would take. This was not easy, as the members differed both in overall vision and specific national interests. In essence, the Netherlands and Germany wanted a more market-focused system, while France and Italy sought more social protection and regional aid. Luxembourg and Belgium stood in the middle, pressing for compromise to ensure a successful outcome.

At one point, the Dutch were on the point of quitting. Their cars, outside the Castle of Val Duchesse where the negotiations were taking place, had their engines running (cars needed to warm up before you drove them in 1957). But they stayed. After six months of wrangling, agreement was reached. Three weeks after the 1957 song contest, the Treaty of Rome was signed.

The treaty created the European Economic Community (EEC). This involved Spaak's planned customs union, but signatories agreed to take their unity further and pursue common policies in transport and agriculture. Perhaps most significant of all, the document began with the assertion that the leaders of The Six were 'DETERMINED to lay the foundations of an ever-closer union among the peoples of Europe' – surely a deliberate echo of the Constitution of the USA, with its desire 'to form a more perfect Union'.

On January 1, 1958, the EEC became a reality. Various bodies came into being along with it. These are in essence still the main bodies of Europe-level government today.

The new Community was run by a *Commission*, a kind of civil service with former politicians from Community members in charge: an overall president, Germany's Walter Hallstein, plus three vice-presidents and five other commissioners with specific responsibilities such as transport, competition, social affairs and agriculture.

The Commission's power was to be balanced by two other institutions. First of these was the *Council of Ministers*, a group of ministers from member states, which would have a new president every six months from each country in turn (Belgium had the first go). The second was the

European Parliamentary Assembly, forerunner of the modern European Parliament. This was an assembly of MPs from member states' legislative assemblies – members were not directly elected until 1979.

The *European Court of Justice* had the job of ensuring the rulings of these new entities were put into practice in member nations.

Since 1958, the main addition to these four has been the *European Council*, where heads of state meet and set Europe's overall political direction and agenda. This grew out of 'summit' meetings in the 1970s.

In 2016, there are seven formal 'institutions of the European Union'. These are the five above, plus the *Court of Auditors*, founded in 1977, which has the unenviable job of monitoring EU expenditure, and the *European Central Bank*, founded in 1998 to oversee the new economy created by the introduction of the Euro.

European political bodies were proliferating. Luckily, there was still only one Eurovision Song Contest, pure and simple (well, simple, anyway...)

1958

Date: 12 March
Venue: Netherlands TV Service Studio, Hilversum
Debut: Sweden
Winner: André Claveau, France
Winning song: *Dors, mon Amour (Sleep, my Love)*

The 1958 contest was opened by Italian cantautore (singer/songwriter) Domenico Modugno. After a slow, rather operatic intro to his song, which had the unmemorable title of *Nel Blu dipinto di Blu (In the Blue painted in Blue)*, he suddenly flung out his huge goalkeeper-like hands and launched into its refrain.

Eurovision had taken wings!

The song, retitled *Volare*, became an international hit. Modugno's words were translated into English by New York lyricist Mitchell Parish, and Dean Martin took the song to Number One in the US. *Volare* has been regularly covered ever since – by Ella Fitzgerald, Oscar Peterson, David Bowie, the Gypsy Kings and even Frank Zappa. It has found its way onto football terraces. Interestingly, when translating, Parish kept part of the song in Italian. While the elite in late 1950s Europe worried about Elvis and creeping Americanization, elite America still looked to Europe, especially France and Italy, for sophistication.

At the time, the Eurovision judges placed this classic –

in a '50 years of Eurovision' poll in 2005 it was voted the second greatest Eurovision song ever – third. The contest winner was a very Gallic ballad sung by the even more Gallic André Claveau, and second was a piece of light opera called *Giorgio*.

Volare pointed a bright way forward for Eurovision, towards making it a showcase for fresh European songwriting/performing talent that did not reject America but embraced its influences with flair and originality. *Giorgio* suggested another future, that of formulaic lowest common denominator Euro-ditties, with a dollop of la-ing and lyrics full of words recognizable all round the continent: place-names, wine, well-known dishes. *Giorgio* got 24 votes; Volare 13. The dinging and donging start here.

Luckily for its growth prospects, Western Europe's economy was following *Volare's* example, combining the best of America and Europe: US corporate organization, mass production and marketing; European taste and design. As the 1950s matured, the half-continent saw ever more consumer goods at prices ever more people could afford. Among these were TVs on which to watch Eurovision. In 1953, there was one set in France for every 1,000 citizens; by 1958, this figure was over 20 per thousand; a couple of years later, it would be 40. 1958 debutant Sweden, for whom Alice Babs sang the cute *Lilla Stjärna (Little Stars)* in national dress, showed even more dramatic growth, with less than 1 television per 1,000 inhabitants in 1953 but around 150 by 1960.

(Alice might have played it cute for Eurovision, but she was not uncontroversial in her home country. As a young jazz singer she had upset more conservative Swedes with movies like *Swing it, Teacher*. She later worked with, and was much admired by, Duke Ellington.)

For Germany, Margot Hielscher returned to Eurovision 1958 as 'Miss Juke Box', hymning the delights of music you could get for two *Groschen* (cents). Her nation was the economic superstar of the 1950s, with its economy growing at 8% a year. 1958 saw that economy become bigger than that of Britain.

There were various reasons for this: the generosity of America's Marshall Aid, the industriousness of German workers, but most of all the nation's consensus political system, the 'Social Market Economy' championed by Chancellor Konrad Adenauer and his finance minister Ludwig Erhard. In this model, private, not state, ownership of enterprises was preferred, and competition between them encouraged. The market, not the state, determined the direction of the economy: no grand planning. But the state was not inactive. A strong central bank was committed to fighting inflation. Taxes were high; the government spent them on socially useful projects such as schools, hospitals and roads, as well as welfare. In return for this expenditure, trades unions were expected to work with employers' organizations to set pay levels, not just go on strike. (1950s Britain and France lost around 2 million working days a year through strikes. Germany's annual average loss was around 100,000 days). And in return for that, enterprises were expected to invest for the future rather than pay out big immediate dividends.

This is now seen as the standard 'European way', but it was radical in 1958. France still preferred top-down *dirigiste* state planning, countered by a stiff dose of anarchy on the shop floor. Italy had the shop-floor anarchy without the dirigisme. Britain encouraged the free market but its labour relations were class-obsessed and confrontational. All over Europe, intellectually fashionable Socialist parties still talked of state ownership of 'the means of production' – i.e. of all enterprise. Behind the Iron Curtain (except in Yugoslavia), such monopoly was a fact. The nearest approach to Germany's Social Market Economy was that of the Nordic countries, with their long tradition of Social Democracy (*Folkhemmet* in Sweden: society as a large family), though these involved higher levels of state spending.

All European economies, however they were run, were benefiting from advances in technology – though this didn't always deliver flawlessly. There are few things that true lovers of Eurovision love more than voting cock-ups, and 1958 was a vintage year, thanks to hostess Hannie Lips' battles with lagging, half-audible phone lines and a rickety hand-operated scoreboard.

1959

Date: 11 March
Venue: Palais des Festivals, Cannes, France
Debut: Monaco
Winner: Teddy Scholten, Netherlands
Winning Song: *Een Beetje (A little Bit)*

The relative performances of *Giorgio* and *Volare* in 1958 did not augur well for Eurovision, and that showed in the next year's poor contest – well, that's my view anyway: other ESC fans will no doubt differ.

What cannot be denied is that France put on a fine show. It chose an elegant venue – coverage of the evening begins with a shot of the Mediterranean, then pans along Cannes' palm-lined *Promenade de la Croisette*. The staging inside the *Palais des Festivals* was adventurous. There were three ornate carousels – Eurovision meets Louis XIV – divided into quarters, and which spun round to reveal each artist against a national backdrop.

These backdrops were amusingly stereotypical: a windmill for the Netherlands' Teddy Scholten; Big Ben for Britain's Pearl Carr and Teddy Johnson; the canals of Venice for Domenico Modugno, who returned with another song, *Piove (It's raining)*, that didn't do well in the contest but went on to become a global hit. The backdrops reflect the traditional vision of Europe as a continent of

27

distinct nations.

This might seem strange coming from the home of Robert Schuman and Jean Monnet, but by March 1959, France had undergone a change of leader. In May 1958 the former wartime head of the Free French, General Charles de Gaulle, had become president. De Gaulle was a keen European, but he had no time for federalism; instead he talked of 'une Europe des patries' (the usual translation, *'a Europe of nations'*, doesn't capture the Gaullist passion of the word *'patrie'*). For the General, one *patrie* was supposed to have more power than any other. As he once told a minister, "Europe[an union] is the chance for France to become what she has ceased to be since Waterloo: the first in the world... Italy is not serious... The English console themselves for their decline by saying that they share in the American hegemony. Germany has had her backbone broken."

What had brought de Gaulle to office was the crisis across the Med from the *Palais des Festivals*. Algeria had been the most bizarre of all European imperialist ventures. It was not just a colony but a part of France; four *départements* that were supposed to be as French as Pas-de-Calais or Lot-et-Garonne. Indigenous resistance to this had been building since 1945, coalescing into the National Liberation Front (FLN) in 1954, which fought an escalating guerilla war against the colonial power. In May 1958, European *'pied noir'* settlers struck back, taking to the streets of Algiers and seizing government buildings. The

28

colonial French army joined them. Paratroopers landed in Corsica, and had plans to launch a coup in France itself – which were only cancelled when de Gaulle was made president: the army thought he would support the cause of *Algérie Française*. De Gaulle quickly visited the colony, bravely walking among the crowds and telling the *pieds noirs* that he had 'understood' them. Order was restored, but it was fragile and everyone knew it.

Unfazed, Eurovision sang on. The 1959 winner was the pert Teddy Scholten, who told her admirer she would be faithful 'a little bit'. It's a neat lyric that works best in its original Dutch, as it plays with that language's compulsion to stick the playful diminutive *je'* on the end of every noun.

Britain came second. The UK's first entry to Eurovision, back in 1957, had been a dud. The operatic *All* misjudged the feel of the contest. (The song was also extremely short – it still holds the record for the briefest Eurovision entry ever – and its conductor Eric Robinson did not get on with singer Patricia Bredin: he brought the orchestra in before she was ready.) As a result of its poor result, Britain had gone into a Euro-sulk in 1958 and not entered. 1959 saw it come back with a classic piece of camp and begin a long run of high placings.

As in Eurovision, so in political Europe, of course. Britain failed to get the point of the new EEC to start with, one diplomat reportedly telling delegates at the Messina Conference: "Gentlemen, you are trying to negotiate something you will never be able to negotiate. But, if negotiated, it will not be ratified. And if ratified, it will not work."

Third was France's *Oui, oui, oui, oui* (I shan't bother to translate this one). Sweden's Brita Borg asked her mother not to wait up for her as she went out on a date: she was 22 now, and could look after herself. Most memorable of all, perhaps, was Austria's Ferry Graf, who produced the contest's first full-on novelty number. *Der K und K Calypso aus Wien (The Imperial and Royal Calypso from Vienna)* featured calypso, swing and yodelling. The song is the first of a string of magnificently-plumed turkeys that have strutted across the Eurovision stage over the years, usually to come last, some with that ultimate so-bad-it's-good Eurovision accolade of *nul points*.

(By the way, no Eurovision judge has ever actually announced "X-land, nul points". It doesn't make grammatical sense in any European language, and even if it did, it would not be said: if you don't get any points, you just don't get mentioned. But who cares? The phrase has entered the mythology of the contest, and I shall enjoy using it.)

The 1960s

1960

Date: 29 March
Venue: Royal Festival Hall, London, UK
Debut: Norway
Winner: Jacqueline Boyer, France
Winning Song: *Tom Pillibi*

Watching Eurovision in 1960, one would have had no sense that the coming decade would end up being regarded as one of unparalleled radicalism in Europe. If anything, the competition had become more sedate than, say, 1957. In '57, most male singers had worn lounge suits; in 1960 standard masculine wear was dinner jackets and black bow ties. The theatricality of the late-fifties' contest had given way to simply standing up and singing. Lightness had conquered originality or depth. The first act on stage, Britain's Bryan Johnson, sounded like a scoutmaster trying to jolly along laggards on a cross-country hike, though his song purported to be about a man dying for love. The winner was a jaunty little piece about a boy who makes up fantasies about himself, sung by a girl who sees through them but loves him anyway (some people thought the song was about a rich show-off, but that misses its point). The most creative, experimental entry, sung in local dialect by Luxembourg's Camillo Felgen, came last.

But maybe this was what 1960 wanted. Among the

young, the great rock'n'roll revolution had lost its oomph the day Elvis was drafted into the US army. It never really recovered. Looking round Europe's seats of power on 29 March, 1960, one gets a sense of slightly exhausted conservatism. *Le Général* was in charge in France, Adenauer's Christian Democrats in Germany, the bloodhound-jowled Harold Macmillan's Conservatives in Britain, a centre-right coalition in the Netherlands, Christian Democrats in Italy. Scandinavia did different, with Social Democrat or Labour leaders – but this was traditional for this part of Europe. Norway had voted Labour since 1935. With a couple of brief breaks, Denmark had been Social Democrat since 1929. Sweden's Tage Erlander had been Prime Minister since 1946.

If there was change, it was in Europe's colonies. De Gaulle had slowly come to the conclusion that to retain Algeria was impossible, and on 16 September 1959 made a U-turn, announcing on television that its people could choose their own fate in a referendum once four years of peace had passed. This satisfied neither the FLN, who wanted independence sooner, nor the *pieds noirs*, who took to the streets again in January 1960. The violence would continue, but there was now only one realistic outcome to the struggle.

February 1960 saw Harold MacMillan give a speech in Cape Town, where he talked of 'the wind of change blowing through this continent'. In June, Belgium, terrified by what it saw happening in Algeria, hastily gave independence to the vast Congo basin it had so viciously misruled since 1885 (the new nation collapsed into anarchy almost at once). Only Spain and Portugal, still outside the charmed circle of Eurovision in 1960, seemed immune to the new mood of decolonization.

1961

Date: 18 March
Venue: Palais des Festivals, Cannes, France
Debuts: Finland, Spain, Yugoslavia
Winner: Jean-Claude Pascal, Luxembourg
Winning Song: *Nous les Amoureux (We, the Lovers)*

A wind of change blew into Eurovision in 1961. It did so literally: on the day of the contest, the *mistral* suddenly descended on Cannes, filling the usually placid sea with white horses. It did so figuratively: inside the *Palais des Festivals*, three new participants joined the show, which had been quietly expanding since 1956 and now featured sixteen European nations. Among these debutants was Yugoslavia – Eurovision had breached the Iron Curtain.

Yugoslavia was not standard eastern bloc. Its president, former partisan leader Marshal Josip Broz Tito, had no intention of letting Moscow tell him what to do. (After Stalin's death, a note was found in his papers from Tito. It read "Stop sending people to kill me. We've already captured five of them, one of them with a bomb and another with a rifle... If you don't stop sending killers, I'll send a very fast-working one to Moscow and I certainly won't have to send another." There is even a theory that Tito put this threat into action, and that he poisoned the Soviet dictator.)

In some ways, Yugoslavia shared the sinister features of Soviet empire nations – elections were rigged and it had a ruthless secret police force – but in other ways it looked west. Many factories were controlled by workers, not state planners, and were encouraged to compete commercially with rivals rather than just meeting artificial, centrally-imposed targets. Culturally, Ljiljana Petrovic looked perfectly at home in Cannes, singing her ballad of lost love, *Neke davne Zvezde (Some distant Stars)*.

There was a wider range of songs on offer than in 1960, too. Several – from the Netherlands and Sweden, for example – swung. A few others tried to. Italy produced a powerful ballad. Like *Volare*, *Al di là (Beyond)* failed to win Eurovision then went on to be a global hit. Britain's entry sounded dangerously like the kind of American–influenced music youngsters were listening to. *Are you sure?* by The Allisons was modelled on The Everly Brothers. Even more subversive – so subversive that hardly anyone noticed it at the time – was the winner. *Nous les Amoureux* is about love that is forbidden by religion and frowned on by society, though one day, the singer hopes, he and his lover will be able to carry on their relationship without controversy. The song is, surely, about a gay love affair.

At the time, sexual activity between men was illegal in nearly half the countries participating in Eurovision 1961, including Austria, Britain, Germany and (another '61 debutant) Spain. Blackmail was an ever-present threat to gay people in these countries, as two films made the same

37

year as this contest, *Victim* and *The loudest Whisper*, made clear.

Ljiljana Petrovic might have been breached the Iron Curtain in Eurovision, but 1961 is best known as the year that the Curtain became not just Iron but Concrete. There had been barbed wire between East and West Germany since 1952, but eastern citizens could cross to the West via Berlin, which, though deep in eastern territory, was partially occupied by the USA, Britain and France. As the western economy began to take off, more and more easterners took advantage of this escape route: by 1961, a sixth of the population of the Soviet-occupied 'German Democratic Republic' (GDR) had headed west. Booming West Germany had found jobs for almost all of them.

On the night of Sunday 13 August, GDR workmen began encircling West Berlin with barbed wire barriers. A few days later, concrete walls followed. On August 24, the first individual was killed trying to cross this barrier: Gunter Litfin, a 24-year-old tailor, shot by GDR border guards as he tried to swim across a canal in Spandau. Other deaths followed, including Peter Fechter, a bricklayer who took an hour to bleed to death in no-man's land. For much of that hour Fechter called out for help; the West couldn't rescue him and the East wouldn't.

In October, a trivial dispute about diplomatic passports escalated into a situation where American and Soviet tanks were facing each other across Checkpoint Charlie – armed, ready to fight, and with back-up plans involving quick escalations to nuclear weapons. If one soldier had panicked and fired… The US and Soviet leaders, John F Kennedy and Nikita Khrushchev, communicated via a Soviet agent in Washington, and the tanks inched back. Some historians argue that Berlin, October 1961, was the closest that the Cold War ever came to turning into a nuclear conflict: more dangerous, even, than the Cuban missile crisis that followed a few months later, or than the events of 1983 which will be described later.

For Europeans, this was a terrifying time but also a humiliating one. The Berlin standoff was essentially between the two superpowers. Europe was just the setting. Like Suez back in 1956, it was a sign of the new impotence of European nations that had, two and a half decades before, confidently ruled vast global empires. Whether it liked it or not, Europe was now dancing to a new *K and K Calypso*, Kennedy and Khrushchev.

1962

Date: 18 March
Venue: Grand Auditorium de RTL, Luxembourg
Debuts: None
Winner: Isabelle Aubret, France
Winning Song: *Un premier Amour (First Love)*

For lovers of Eurovision, 1962 is most notable as the first year where entries got *nul points*. It had been theoretically possible for a song to score zero under the old voting system, but nobody had (several had come close, with *un* point, including Corry Brokken in 1958, trying to follow up her 1957 victory: she is still the only artist both to win the competition and to come last). In 1962, a change in the voting method, whereby national juries could only award points to three songs, made that more likely. Four entries, including one from Eurovision veteran Fud Leclerc, ended up suffering that fate. Fortunately Leclerc didn't throw himself into the Seine as a result.

Yugoslavia continued to distance itself from the enormities taking place in Berlin and entered a sophisticated love-song. *Don't turn the Lights on at Twilight (Ne pali Svetla u Sumrak)* sang the returning Ljiljana Petrovic. Instead just let our two cigarette-ends burn in the darkness (in 1962, cigarettes were cool). It came fourth. The top three places were occupied by entries in French, the runaway winner coming from France itself. *Un premier Amour* was haunting and passionate, a classic of Eurovision's black-and-white era.

France finally separated from Algeria on July 5. Estimates of the death toll in the independence struggle vary wildly: historian Alistair Horne settles on 700,000. Violence continued after independence, with vicious Algerian reprisals on *harkis* (collaborators) and a far-right assassination attempt on de Gaulle in the south-west of Paris in August.

July 30 1962 saw the introduction of the EEC's Common Agricultural Policy (CAP). Part of the 1957 Treaty of Rome, the policy had its origins in the immediate post-war years: treaty signatories could remember hungry times, and wanted to ensure a healthy and developing EEC agricultural sector. But by 1962, it was already a dangerous anachronism. The idea was that the CAP would agree prices for basic products then manipulate the market to ensure these prices prevailed, putting tariffs on imports and buying up domestic produce if demand was too slack. This soon led to overproduction. A bizarre new European landscape of wine lakes and butter mountains appeared. Food prices to EEC consumers were kept artificially high. Third-world producers were unable to sell to relatively rich Europe. All round 'Lugano Europe', environmental damage would be caused by overfarming to produce unwanted products. Eurosceptics point to the CAP as the classic example of Brussels misgovernment, and all but the most eager federalists have to admit they have a point.

But the CAP was not going to change. France was the main beneficiary, and France had the loudest voice in the Community. De Gaulle worked tirelessly to keep it that way, most importantly by fostering Franco-German relations. He and Chancellor Adenauer had regular meetings; at one, in 1962, in Reims, they posed for pictures in the cathedral where Charlemagne's son Ludwig had been crowned Holy Roman Emperor in 816. Early in 1963, they would sign a treaty agreeing to consult one another on all major policy decisions.

Outside the EEC, seven other countries had teamed up to form EFTA, a free-trade area with no aspirations to further political unity. However, EFTA was geographically disparate, consisting of states dotted around the edges of Charlemagne's old empire. It was smaller than the EEC (its population was 92 million, compared to the EEC's 170 million) and less developed industrially. EFTA was always going to have its work cut out if it wanted to outperform its populous rival in Europe's industrial heartland.

Britain was one of the EFTA countries (along with Austria, Denmark, Norway, Portugal, Sweden and Switzerland). Eurovision viewers wouldn't have guessed it from its 1962 entry, *Ring-a-ding Girl*, but things were stirring in that nation's musical life. In February 1963, *Please please me* became The Beatles' first Number One single. The record company had wanted the four Liverpool lads to cover a *schlager* called *How do you do it?*, but they refused and

42

insisted on putting out their own song. This was a radical break from the 'Tin Pan Alley' model of popular music production, whereby professional writers wrote for passive performers (Eurovision still often follows this model, despite the fact that many of its best songs have been written by their performers). The Beatles set a trend for individual empowerment that resonated through Western Europe (and, wherever it could, through Eastern Europe). All round the continent, a new generation was stepping up to the plate, less deferential than their war-haunted parents.

1963

Date: 23 March
Venue: BBC Television Centre, London, UK
Debuts: None
Winner: Grethe and Jørgen Ingmann, Denmark
Winning Song: *Dancevise (Dance Song)*.

TV coverage of this event begins with the usual stirring *Marche en Rondeau*. Then violins swirl and the camera pans down through a dramatic evening sky to... a 1960s office block.

Nowadays we regard these things as spectacularly ugly, but in 1963, the new BBC Television Centre represented modernity and progress, two magic words at that time. Later that year, the leader of the British Labour party, Harold Wilson, would paint a picture of Britain 'reforged' in the 'white heat' of a technological revolution – and the year after would be elected to power. Wilson's vision, shared by many elite figures in Europe, was technocratic; a tidy, planned, hi-tech future imposed top-down by men (and the occasional woman) in suits, working for large bureaucratic organizations like Wilson's new Ministry of Technology, which was given the Orwellian abbreviation 'Mintech'.

Europe's relationship with technocracy would soon sour: just over five years later, students would be ripping up the cobbles of Parisian streets in furious protest at it. But this was 1963, and at the time it looked the way forward. Perhaps an inkling of its ultimately unsatisfactory nature came from this contest, where, in the name of efficiency, songs were performed in a special studio cut off from the audience, who watched in a separate part of the building. This gave the opportunity for imaginative sets which were varied, artist to artist, but took away any sense of occasion. No applause greeted the performers. Rumours persist that some or all the performances were pre-recorded – these are still denied, but it's hard to see how the sets could have been changed quickly enough between songs for this not to have been the case.

The winning entry captured the year's 'early-sixties-modern' mood perfectly. In front of a backdrop of revolving op-art circles, Jørgen Ingmann accompanied his wife Grethe on jazzy guitar; there's something rather icy about the piece (until the last bar) that is both refreshing and slightly sinister.

Dansevise nearly didn't win at all: 1963 is another vintage year for connoisseurs of Eurovision voting disasters. Norway, announcing its results fifth, initially gave Denmark two votes and Switzerland three, but did not present the results in the correct format, so was asked to resubmit them after everyone else had voted. The contest soon became a race between Denmark and Switzerland. At the end, when Norway resubmitted its results, they changed: Denmark now had four votes and Switzerland just one, giving victory to Norway's neighbour. A ripple of surprise ran round the audience. Hostess 'Miss Catherine Boyle' then rang Monaco to check a vote that had initially included too many points (cue another wonky phone line), then announced *Dansevise* as the winner.

In a final moment of comedy, an award was announced for the song's composers; the cameras cut to the stairway down which the winners would appear; the BBC orchestra played a fanfare; and... nobody appeared. "They're not here to receive the prize," said the quick-thinking prize presenter, BBC Controller – what a technocratic title! – Stuart Hood.

Hood then went on to give a short speech about the amazing achievement that was the broadcast, and how good it was that viewers were able to enjoy the results of modern science without 'that chill of fear which so often accompanies the miracles of technology today'. He was no doubt alluding to the terrible weapons of destruction being built on both sides of the Iron Curtain. Shortly after the Checkpoint Charlie face-off in 1961, the Soviet Union had tested the 'King of Bombs', a Hydrogen bomb almost 2,500 times more powerful than the devices that had obliterated Hiroshima and Nagasaki. This was, presumably, for use in Europe. West of the Curtain, Britain and France were working on smaller but still monstrous versions of similar weapons, and sporadically testing them in remote Pacific islands or in the deserts of Australia or Algeria. 1962 had been a record year for such tests, with 140, almost 100 from the USA alone. Later in 1963, the US, USSR and Britain (not France) signed a treaty banning tests above ground. But the horrific threat of these weapons did not go away.

This 'white heat of technology' Eurovision is now best known for very human failings: bloc voting, the comic non-appearance of the winning composers. The very next day, The Beatles' first album came out, recorded in one day on relatively simple equipment but bursting with raw human emotion and energy. Maybe that was the day Europe's technocratic dream began to die.

Away from the contest, Britain and Denmark had decided to abandon EFTA and had applied to join the EEC. Ireland was filing an application at the same time. The initial noises from Brussels had been welcoming, and officials had begun working on the terms of entry. All three applicants had substantial agricultural sectors and their entry into the EEC club would upset the existing CAP. But if 'Europe' were to expand, such issues needed sorting. By the start of 1963, it looked as if the door was about to open – then on January 14 General de Gaulle announced out of the blue that he was vetoing Britain's application. He came up with a range of reasons, most oft-repeated that Britain was too close to America. There was some wisdom to his arguments – Britain was not as committed to the European project as The Six – but de Gaulle sceptics argue that he was much more concerned about protecting France's interests than those of Europe as a whole. Whatever the

General's motive, Denmark and Ireland backed out at the same time, afraid that they would soon find themselves being bullied in a similar manner. Political Europe remained the world of Lugano 1956, and would do so for a decade.

Meanwhile, America – which had no desire to subvert the EEC via Britain – was busy trying to protect Europe from the Soviet Union. On June 26, President Kennedy made a speech at the Town Hall in the Berlin district of Schöneberg, where he told hundreds of thousands of people cramming the surrounding streets *"Ich bin ein Berliner"*. If one is being pedantic, this does mean 'I am a doughnut': technically, he should have just said *"Ich bin Berliner"*. But everybody knew what he meant, and felt a surge of hope that he might bring hostilities to an end.

Five months later, the President was dead. The Cold War calypso played on.

1964

Date: 21 March
Venue: Tivoli Concert Hall, Copenhagen, Denmark
Debut: Portugal
Winner: Gigliola Cinquetti, Italy
Winning Song: *Non ho l'eta (I am too young)*.

Key themes of the European 1960s bubbled to the surface in this contest. One was youth. A 16-year-old singer won the contest by a record margin. However the song, a gentle ballad, was not a standard-bearer for the teen-driven sexual revolution of the second half of the decade. Instead, lyricist Nicola 'Nisa' Salerno had Gigliola Cinquetti ask to be allowed to start playing the adult game of love in her own time.

Salerno was one of Italy's leading lyricists, noted for his creation of well-observed characters in song, especially the young. Other favourites include a wealthy young man who craves everything American in *Tu Vuò Fà L'Americano*, and *Guaglione*, another youngster on the verge of adult emotion, this time a boy in love with a woman who ignores him because he's still just a kid. Critics of Eurovision often overlook the contest's heritage of quality lyrics lurking among the dings and dongs, diggiloos and diggileys.

Other young Europeans were developing their own music and styles, too. Britain was swept by Beatlemania.

France, Spain and Italy took the Fab Four on board indirectly: youngsters borrowed the chorus from She loves you and launched their own style, calling themselves yé-yés. Yé-yé music was melodic and rock'n'rollish, its lyrics simple statements about love and sexual attraction. The Beatles would soon move on, ditching their suits and haircuts for kaftans and long hair, but the yé-yés were happy to look and stay chic: the girls (who drove the movement) kittenish, the men suave and rugged.

A second theme to emerge in Eurovision 1964 was political activism. After the third-from-last entry, a man who had sneaked backstage pretending to be a stagehand burst onto the podium and unfurled a banner that read 'Boycott Franco and Salazar'. The cameras panned away to the scoreboard; he was hustled off stage; the show went on – though maybe the judges were influenced, as Spain and Portugal between them gathered one point.

General Francisco Franco had come to power in 1939 after Spain's infamous Civil War. Dr Antonio Salazar had ruled Portugal even longer, since 1932. In many ways, the two Iberian dictators were very different. Salazar was a quiet intellectual with much less blood on his hands than Franco. He had leant towards the Allies in the War, unlike his neighbour. But both regimes used secret police and media control, and neither allowed elections or democratic parties. Though this was not the emerging European way, the two dictatorships were tolerated in mid-sixties Europe – and in Eurovision – because the real enemy lay across the

Iron Curtain. The two regimes would last another decade: the song contest will offer its usual insights into their story.

A third new theme was race. Up till then, the contest had been a whites-only affair. The Netherlands' Anneke Grönloh broke this mould, singing the poppy *Jij bent mijn Leven (You are my Life)*, which ended up mid-table, despite her coming on second, a hexed position in Eurovision.

Grönloh had been born in a small Indonesian village. Her parents had come to Holland after the war and settled in Eindhoven. In the 1950s and 1960s many former subjects of Europe's old empires made similar journeys, as the economies in the old parent countries began to take off and extra hands were needed. Algerians and Moroccans came to France; Jamaicans, Indians and Pakistanis to Britain; Indonesians like Anneke Grönloh to the Netherlands. Germany, with no old empire to tap for labour, started inviting workers from poorer countries, at first from Southern Europe then, after 1961, from Turkey. In September 1964 Germany's millionth 'guest worker', Armando Rodrigues de Sá from Portugal, was officially awarded a motorbike by the government.

Anneke Grönloh made a huge success of her adopted home: in 2000 she was voted her country's 'Singer of the Century'. Many – I believe most – other new arrivals in Europe have essentially happy stories to tell, too, of challenges met, friendships made and new opportunities taken. But they could also encounter prejudice and sometimes outright hostility. Britain's 1964 election was

51

notorious for racism: in one seat, Smethwick, Conservative Party supporters came up with the slogan, 'if you want a nigger for your neighbour, vote Labour'. While not adopting the slogan, the aspirant Tory MP refused to condemn it. The Labour party seized the moral high ground, until it was revealed that the Smethwick Labour Party club had a 'whites only' membership policy.

Non-white Eurovision entrants were rarities for a long time after 1964, and it took till the new century before a black singer stepped up onto the winner's podium.

1965

Date: 20 March
Venue: Sala di Concerto della RAI, Napoli, Italy
Debut: Ireland
Winner: France Gall, Luxembourg
Winning Song: *Poupée de Cire, Poupée de Son (Wax Doll, Sawdust Doll)*

The 1965 contest, the tenth, felt a need to modernize, but wasn't quite sure how to. The route chosen by many entrants was to add Latin percussion to their orchestrations: the bongo player in the RAI house orchestra must have had weary fingers by the end of the evening. A more radical route was chosen by Luxembourg. As usual, the Grand Duchy headed over the border to get French artistes to create its entry, but this time it called in yé-yé guru Serge Gainsbourg. Cue 17-year-old France Gall, rasping Gainsbourg's dig at young singers manufactured by the music biz who sing about love but don't know anything about it. *Poupée de Cire, Poupée de Son* is rocky, slightly discordant and totally teenage – Gall is both energetic and vulnerable. (Gall's vulnerability was genuine. Next year, she recorded another song for Gainsbourg. *Les Sucettes (Lollipops)* is full of double entendres about oral sex. Despite a comically obvious video, when she recorded the song, Gall did not understand these, and she was mortified when she later found out.)

Was Eurovision about to align itself with emerging pop trends?

An even more modern lyric came from Denmark. In *For din Skyld (For your Sake)*, Birgit Brüel sings of how she is getting fed up with her partner pushing her into a stereotypical feminine role; she wants 'to love in friendship', as an equal; she wants this for herself, but also for him, as it will make him more human, less of a gender stereotype. And if he doesn't listen, she'll be off...

Betty Friedan's *The Feminine Mystique* had appeared in America in 1963, but its message, expressed in this song, was still a minority one in Europe in 1965. It was to stay that way for a long time. Even those ultra-radical students from 1968 can sound extraordinarily sexist to modern ears, and in the 1970s men were men and wore the medallions to prove it. If anything gave Europe's women more freedom in 1965, it was not changing attitudes, fresh ideas or even Eurovision songs, but the contraceptive pill, which had been available in Britain and Germany from 1961 (take-up in these countries had been slow, but by 1965 its use was common). However this in itself did little to change stereotypes.

Most of the other songs in Eurovision 1965 were pretty standard ballads. Ireland, one day to dominate the contest, made its debut with Butch Moore's fifties-style *Walking the Streets in the Rain*. Britain's entry, *I Belong*, can be seen as having political overtones – an appeal to The Six, or at least The Five over the head of *le Général* (it had no effect, but came second in the contest).

1965 was the first Eurovision to be broadcast to Iron Curtain countries other than Yugoslavia: all the Warsaw Pact apart from Bulgaria received it. This was a sign of a thawing in relations across the Wall. Would this last?

One final feature of the 1965 show is of note: Sweden's *Absent Friend* was sung in English. Despite Britain's absence from the EEC, English was becoming ever more widely spoken around Europe – largely due to American influence, but also thanks to British popular music. French remained the language of international diplomacy and, of course, of the EEC – but in France itself, the Académie Française was gearing up to do battle with *le weekend, le parking* and *le talkie-walkie*. After the 1965 contest, the EBU responded with a new rule that all songs had to be in a native language of the country. Was this an idealistic move to protect authentic European cultures from Americanization? Or was it a move by a francophone bloc to preserve its linguistic hegemony? Five nations (France, Belgium, Switzerland, Monaco, Luxem-bourg) could sing in French; Luxembourg and Monaco often used French performers, lyricists, composers and conductors; songs in French had won six of the first ten competitions, despite less than 1/3 of Western Europe's population being francophone.

France was certainly doing its best to keep control of political Europe. In the same month as France Gall's win, the EEC was brought to a legislative halt by the Empty Chair Crisis. The long-serving President of the Commission, Walter Hallstein, had come up with a set of reforms which included the replacement of the old voting system, which had insisted on unanimity, with a more streamlined one where some measures could be passed by a majority. General de Gaulle wanted none of this, and when the five other EEC members backed Hallstein's reforms, he forbade French participation in the Council of Ministers. As it was France's turn to chair the Council, and the Council was an essential part of European-level government, such government simply stopped.

The General stuck to his guns through the rest of 1965. However in the domestic presidential election that December, he fared less well than he hoped: his brinkmanship had clearly rattled French voters, who feared it would cause the EEC to collapse, something neither French industrialists nor French farmers wanted. He returned to the negotiating table, and the Luxembourg Compromise was signed on January 26, 1966. Unanimity was retained for votes where 'vital national interests' were at stake. Exactly how these interests were to be defined – or who by – was never made clear.

The Crisis and the confusion caused by the Compromise stalled attempts to build workable Europe-wide institutions for the next decade or more – a period known as the time of 'Eurosclerosis'. During that era, EEC decisions would largely be made bilaterally and informally by France and Germany.

1966

Date: 20 March
Venue: Grand Auditorium de RTL, Luxembourg
Debuts: None (there would be no new entrants till 1971)
Winner: Udo Jürgens, Austria
Winning Song: *Merci, Cherie*

Given the new language rule, it was ironic that the 1966 contest was won by an Austrian song with a title in French. But balladeer Udo Jürgens had paid his Eurovision dues, coming 6th and 4th in previous contests.

There were more interesting entries, however. For Norway, Åse Kleveland came onstage in a trouser suit rather than the standard long dress, carrying a guitar which she then played, with the orchestra providing (by the standards of the competition at the time) minimal accompaniment. Her performance of *Inter er nytt under Solen (Nothing is new under the Sun)* was intense and honest, the lyrics poetic and the tune catchy. She came third. Kleveland went on to serve as Norway's Minister for Culture under Gro Harlem Brundtland from 1990 to 1996: no passive feminine stereotypes for her. If Serge Gainsbourg and France Gall tried to push Eurovision towards mainstream pop, Åse Kleveland leads it towards deeper, quirkier places: intelligent, sensitive, self-accompanying on guitar, she's the nearest the contest ever gets to Joni Mitchell.

The Netherlands continued its chipping away at racial barriers by fielding Milly Scott, the first black singer to perform in Eurovision. Unfortunately she was given a weak novelty song, *Fernando en Fillipo*, and collected only two votes.

France's entry, *Chez nous (At our Home)*, was all about a young man who has captured the heart of an American visitor – after which, he says, she should stay in France, as life is much better there. Dominique Walter had a point. In 1966 America was escalating its war in Vietnam and beginning to plunge into interracial violence. Vietnam would soon start having effects in Europe. No Western European nation took part in the fighting (Britain's Harold Wilson withstood strong US pressure to do so), but US spending on the conflict began to create an inflation which, initially domestic, soon became global. Vietnam also inflamed a new mood of European radicalism. Between them, these forces would begin to undercut the old economic and political models that had fuelled Western Europe's growth since 1945.

Despite these interesting entries, Eurovision 1966 is largely remembered for its bloc voting. The most blatant example came from the Nordic countries. Sweden, who fielded an arch novelty song about a 'hip' pig breeder, came second – all its votes bar one came from Denmark, Norway and Finland. Portugal and Spain swapped maximum points (neither entry collected more than one vote from the rest of Europe put together). Austria gave neighbours Switzerland maximum points; Switzerland gave Germany maximum and Austria the next best possible. Britain's Kenneth McKellar sang in a kilt and got most of his votes from fellow Celts across the Irish Sea. The Luxembourgeois audience grew restless, then laughed, then whistled as another bloc vote came in.

This neatly parallels the shenanigans in the Council of Ministers the year before, where national self-interest lurked behind the talk of greater Europe-wide concern. Robert Schuman's 1949 'European spirit' seemed a distant dream.

Away from Eurovision, popular music was changing fast. American influence was to the fore, thanks to writer/performers like Bob Dylan and Frank Zappa, but British acts were pushing the boundaries too: albums like The Beatles' *Revolver* or *Fresh Cream* by Cream (Eric Clapton, Jack Bruce and Ginger Baker), and singles like the Kinks' *Sunny Afternoon* were genuinely original. Change – and a whiff of strange-smelling cigarettes – was in the air.

1967

Date: 8 April
Venue: Hofburg Palace, Vienna
Winner: Sandie Shaw, UK
Winning Song: *Puppet on a String*

The heart of anyone who had taken *Revolver, Fresh Cream* or *Sunny Afternoon* off their turntable and turned their TV on for Eurovision 1967 must have sunk when Thérèse Steinmetz opened the show with *Ringe-dinge*. However *L'Amour est bleu (Love is blue)* followed. Singing second probably spelt doom for the song's chances of victory, but it went on to sell millions and has become bracketed with Volare as outstanding Eurovision songs that didn't win. After Vicky's classic came the usual mixture. France's *Il doit faire beau là-bas (The Weather must be good there)* is rather nice (I know, these judgements are subjective). I can't watch the Belgian entry without getting the giggles. Monaco's *Boum Badaboum* is Serge Gainsbourg's take on the Cold War: give me some time to love before we all get blown up, sings Minouche Barelli (a French singer who eventually moved to Monaco). It is arguably the most interesting lyric in the contest, and certainly the ugliest tune.

Portugal was represented by Angolan singer Eduardo Nascimento, with *O Vento mudou (The Wind changed)*. Reputedly Dr Salazar selected him to show how happy the citizens of Portuguese colonies were. But did the propaganda backfire? Couldn't the title be construed as a reference to Harold Macmillan's speech back in 1960? Portuguese songwriters became the masters of using the contest to make political points: the tradition probably started here.

Unlike Europe's other former imperialist powers, Portugal still had no intention of dissolving its empire. The nation soon found itself embroiled in colonial wars, against guerrillas who were increasingly well-armed (by the Soviet Union) and well-organized. In 1967, all young Portuguese men were required to serve four years in the army, at least two of which would be in its African colonies: Angola, Mozambique or Guinea. Portugal thus found itself on the front line of a new Cold War, where the Soviet bloc battled the West for influence in the non-aligned world. Despite its own ruthless imperialism east of the Iron Curtain, the Soviet Union managed to portray itself as a purveyor of liberation. Dr Salazar, pretending that the wind was never going to change, played straight into its hands.

Eurovision 1967 had a clear winner, Britain's Sandie Shaw. Shoeless and mini-skirted, she was a representative of Swinging London, the extraordinary cultural revolution that was sweeping a city once the global capital of the 'stiff upper lip'. Along with its music, British fashion, design and photography suddenly led the world. *Puppet on a String* went on to top charts around Europe, the first time a Eurovision winner had enjoyed such success (previous ones had all struggled to do well outside their core language markets). As such, it's a pivotal song in the history of the competition.

However it was hardly radical. Its singer reportedly hated its 'cuckoo-clock tune' and 'sexist lyrics'. I imagine the contest's *chanson-* and ballad-loving founders disliked it too. Music critics and fans of the new 'serious' rock certainly did. *Puppet on a String* marked an end to Eurovision's attempts to occupy the thoughtful middle-ground in European music. But so what? Instead, *Puppet on a String* marched off and created its own new territory: Europop. Europe's citizens loved it, defying their cultural elders and betters and buying over a million copies of the vinyl 45 rpm single.

There was never a doubt just who was pulling the strings in the EEC. A month after the 1967 contest, Britain, Denmark and Ireland reapplied to join the Community. In November General de Gaulle vetoed these applications again. Instead of expanding, 'Lugano Europe' looked inwards and concentrated on tightening its inner workings. A 1967 Merger Treaty united the three entities to which The Six belonged – the old Coal and Steel Community, the EEC and Euratom, the last of these an attempt at uniting atomic energy policy – all under the umbrella title of the European Communities (EC).

Other European boundaries were tightening in 1967, too. In September the GDR began construction of a stronger fortified wall along its western border. Concrete watchtowers replaced wooden ones; special roads were built to make patrolling easier; tripwires and electronic sensors were put in place; mines were laid. Escapes from the East fell by a factor of ten (escapes *to* the East remained constant, at zero). The division of Europe was starker than ever.

1968

Date: 6 April
Venue: Albert Hall, London
Winner: Massiel, Spain
Winning Song: *La, la, la*

The story of the 1968 winner is a bizarre one. Massiel, a yé-yé star, was not the first choice for the role. The verses, which, unlike the chorus which gives the song its title, had proper words, were originally to be sung in Catalan by Joan Manuel Serrat. Serrat was a leading performer in the Catalan *Nova Cançó* style – songs in the north-eastern language, often critical of the Madrid government. General Franco who just about tolerated *Nova Cançó* at home, would not allow such subversive regionalists to represent the country abroad, and insisted the song be sung in Castilian, the official Spanish. Serrat refused, and Massiel was brought in at the last moment. The irony of there being a row about in which language to sing a song called *La, la, la* is delightfully Eurovision, with its mixture of apparent triviality but, behind that, the serious issue of a nation's politics and identity.

There is also a perpetually humming rumour that the Caudillo bribed juries to vote for the song. This has been strenuously denied, but who knows the truth? *La, la, la* is cheerful and catchy, and most of the other entries were mediocre (*Stress* by Norway's Odd Børre was a quirky exception, but hardly winner material.) Perhaps Massiel won because she deserved to.

La, la, la didn't exactly cover the contest with glory, but 1968 is still a memorable Eurovision, as it was the first to be broadcast in colour. Britain had been the first western European nation to broadcast colour TV, in July 1967. West Germany, the Netherlands and France soon followed. (However, we Europeans mustn't be complacent here. America had had colour TV since the 1950s and Japan since 1960. Iraq started colour broadcasts in 1968, ahead of most European countries.)

Most of the artists made full use of the new technology. Dresses were day-glo yellow, turquoise or lime green. Some of the men joined in, especially Switzerland's Gianni Mascolo with his ill-fitting orange suit, and two brightly-clad mediaeval minstrels from Yugoslavia (who were one of the first Eurovision acts to employ that staple of later contests, the key change two thirds of the way through the song). Even more sedately dressed male competitors began to ditch black ties, some for nylon polo-neck shirts or, in the case of Britain's Cliff Richard, for a Regency dandy's ruff exploding out of the front of his jacket.

Colour was entering European – especially northern European – life in other ways, too. More and more northerners were heading south for holidays in bright, sun-soaked Portugal, Greece or, most popular of all, Massiel's homeland Spain, which welcomed around 17 million visitors in 1968 (the figure in 1960 had been about 5 million). Ironically, these destinations were now all dictatorships, Greece having joined the club thanks to a military coup in April 1967. Returning home to their prosperous democracies, these visitors could stay international by eating out at ever more affordable ethnic restaurants: many postwar immigrants had found this business to be a powerful source of income. Younger Western Europeans could tune in to 'pirate' radio stations, like Radio Caroline, Radio London and Radio Veronica – which offered an alternative to stuffy, cautious government-run broadcasters.

Even more challenging alternative media were on offer in northern capital cities (especially London) where underground magazines like *IT* and *Oz* began to promote the full-on hippie lifestyle: sexual experimentation, drug use and radical politics.

Outside these capital cities, sexual morality changed more slowly: historians are still arguing about how swinging the late 60s were in Clermont Ferrand, Duisburg, Karlstad, Stoke-on-Trent or Zwolle. But there was clearly change in the air. Homosexual acts, long legal in Belgium, France, Luxembourg and the Netherlands, had been legalized in England and Wales in 1967. Germany followed suit in 1968 and 1969, East Germany passing its law ahead of West.

In reaction to the new era, 1968 saw the papal encyclical *Humanae Vitae*, which forbade artificial birth control and reaffirmed the church's view that marriage was the only place for sexual activity.

France's 1968 Eurovision entry was *La Source (The Spring)* a ghostly, rural folk-tale related (beautifully, as one expects from her) by 1962 winner Isabelle Aubret. A month later, contemporary urban reality hit the streets of Paris.

The events of May 1968 began with student protests about student issues: overcrowded classes, aloof academics and sleeping arrangements in dormitories. But behind them was a deep new radicalism. France's *'soixante-huitards'* argued that Europe's growing prosperity – and behind it, that of America – had been bought at the price of sterile conformity and the exploitation of poorer nations and of the natural world. The whole system was rotten, they argued; it needed to be ripped up and power put back in the hands of the people.

On May 6, a huge demo marched through the French capital and erupted into violence, with demonstrators hurling cobblestones at the CRS riot police, who responded with tear gas. On May 10, barricades appeared in the *Quartier Latin*; the police charged in and arrested anyone they thought responsible. Public sympathy for the students rose; a General Strike was called for 13 May. Wildcat strikes and factory occupations followed – anyone passing the Berliet truck factory in Lyon would have found the sign outside respelt as *Liberte*. By May 18, two million workers were out. A week later this had risen to ten million.

On May 27, a deal was struck between employers and the official trades unions, but nobody was listening to them any longer. France looked about to collapse into anarchy – then General de Gaulle disappeared. Riots in the streets, the economy in free-fall, and no president.

He had, in fact, flown in secret to see the chief of the French Forces in Germany. (The formal occupation of Germany had ended in 1955, but French forces remained there until after the fall of the Berlin Wall, when numbers were cut back substantially. A small French force would remain in the small town of Donaueschingen until 2014.)

Apparently de Gaulle's first words to General Jacques Massu were *'C'est foutu' (it's fucked)*. Massu assured him of the military's support, promising the president he would again be able to have his breakfast on the Boulevard Saint Germain. De Gaulle flew back to Paris, announced fresh elections and probably treated himself to a *croissant* and some proper coffee. Students returned to college and strikers to work, and when the election took place on June 23, the result was an overwhelming victory for the right. Later that year, the new French government did about the least *soixante-huitard* thing it could do, test a Hydrogen bomb.

1968's wind of change soon wafted to lands unable to participate in Eurovision. Soviet-occupied Czecho-slovakia had been particularly slow to cleanse itself of the legacy of Stalin. Even the Russians had concluded that change was necessary, and in January a new Party Secretary had been appointed. Alexander Dubcek was not a freewheeling sixties radical but a loyal Party man who thought the Party should do a better job. Part of this meant liberalizing Czechoslovak life, giving people more freedoms, curtailing the powers of the secret police, abolishing press censorship and turning over more of the economy to consumer goods. He talked of elections, which he was convinced the Party would win: what could be better than 'Socialism with a human face'? Press censorship was abolished. Eurovision did its best to endorse these reforms – Austria asked Czech singer Karel Gott to represent it in 1968 (he came 12th).

However the momentum for change kept building. Articles in the newly free press took on an ever stronger anti-Soviet tone. On the night of August 20/21, the country was invaded. It was a much less grisly affair than Hungary 1956. Dubcek told people not to resist; a few did, and 75 of them died. The subsequent clampdown was gradual. Dubcek remained in office, though now with little power; when he was finally sacked he didn't suffer the fate of Hungary's 1956 leaders, execution, but was given a job as a forestry official. Some people were allowed to leave the country. But the statues of Stalin remained – and the building work continued along the wall between the two Europes.

A third European conflict area in 1968 was Northern Ireland – a topic which will soon find its way onto the Eurovision stage and so will be discussed there.

Even in Brussels, 1968 saw new voices raised. On December 21, Sicco Mansholt, a former Dutch resistance fighter now EEC Commissioner for Agriculture, filed a report that was highly critical of the Common Agricultural Policy, which was now guzzling 90 per cent of the Community's budget. Mansholt said that this had to stop. Instead, small farmers should be paid to quit the industry. This did not go down well with farmers of any size, who, in soixante-huitard style, took to the streets. Mansholt had to be protected with an armed guard when protestors came to Brussels. His report was watered down into three rather minor directives in 1972, while both the CAP budget and the lakes and mountains of unwanted produce continued to grow for the next two decades.

This remarkable year ended on a breathtaking note as American astronauts left earth's orbit for the first time, flew to the moon, took pictures of a fragile, lonely earth, then came home again. Europe watched, entranced – but was also quietly reminded which nation how held the dominant global position that Britain and France and, later, Germany had once fought to hold.

1969

Date: 20 March
Venue: Teatro Real Opera House, Madrid, Spain
Joint Winners: Salome, Spain; Lulu, UK; Lenny Kuhr, Netherlands; Frida Boccara, France
Winning Songs: *Vivo cantando (I live singing); Boom bang-a-bang; De Troubadour (the Troubadour); Un Jour, un Enfant (One Day, a Child)*.

As if in a deliberate snub to the *soixante-huitards*, the stage of Eurovision 1969 was dominated by a giant silver object unpleasantly reminiscent of the symbol of General Franco's Falangist movement, which in turn looked very like Mussolini's *fasces*. The piece was designed by Salvador Dali, which raises intriguing questions. Was he pressured into designing it the way he did? Was it supposed to be some kind of ironic comment? Or did he miss the likeness and just thought it looked nice? (An interesting thought given Dali's usual insight into the human unconscious.)

Actually the piece was a final piece of grandstanding from the old dictatorship; in July, Franco would announce that when he died, Spain's legitimate king, Juan Carlos, would become head of state. The rural/ traditionalist model favoured by both Iberian dictators had been fading for a while, anyway: Spain had begun to modernize its economy; its politics would follow. A better symbol of Spain's future than the onstage *fasces* was the interval act, which took the form of a modernist montage on the theme of the Four Elements, to the most discordant music ever heard on Eurovision (until Jemini took to the stage in 2003, anyway).

Eurovision 1969 is largely Europop, with bouncy root-fifth bass lines, but the songs are fun and some of the lyrics are original – though not Britain's *Boom bang-a-bang*. From Portugal, Simone de Oliveira sang *Desfolhada Portuguesa*, a passionate, sensual poem by Ary dos Santos, a committed opponent of the *Estado Novo* regime.

The regime had lost its former leader late in 1968, when Dr Salazar suffered a brain hemorrhage, after which he was replaced by his deputy Marcelo Caetano. (He was expected to die quickly, but lived on for two more years, during which time nobody told him he had been replaced; he was surrounded by people who pretended to him that he was still running the country).

Portugal has never won Eurovision, but in a way has got more out of it than any other nation, as the contest became a mouthpiece for the opposition before the fall of the old regime, and, as we shall see, actually played a role in that fall.

Sweden's Tommy Körberg sang a song to Judy, his friend, in *Judy, min Vän* (lyrics by Roger Wallis and Britt Lindeborg), saying he didn't want to be her partner. She loved material things ('house, TV and car' – goods that few Europeans had owned in 1956 but which by 1969 had become widely available and affordable). He wanted freedom, connection to nature and emotional intensity. Judy was a child of the early sixties; he one of the late.

The character in the song was no *soixante-huitard*, however. He was expressing a view of how he wanted to live, not a political one about how the world should be. These sentiments were probably more in line with what most people felt in Western Europe in 1969 than the opinions of the Parisian students. The far-left dreams of the Rive Gauche never became reality (except in a hideously twisted form in faraway Cambodia), but the coming decade would see many people quietly step off the rungs of the established career ladder, the way the singer wants to in this song, and 'do their own thing'.

Sadly Eurovision 1969 is now best remembered for its farcical result. In rehearsal, presenter Laurita Valenzuela had asked EBU scrutineer Clifford Brown what would happen in case of a tie, and been told that it had never happened before and never would. But as the votes came in, such an outcome looked more and more likely. Then it happened, not only with two songs but four. Valenzuela turned to Brown (who was rather bizarrely seated onstage) and asked what to do next; he brusquely told her there were four winners. She was so taken aback that she asked again, and got the same answer.

Austria, Finland, Norway, Portugal and Sweden decided not to re-enter next year. The four-way win was the major reason, though some of 1969's more thoughtful entries had come from some of these countries, who perhaps didn't fancy being in a Europop competition. Was Eurovision heading for the end of the line?

April 28 was the end of the line for General de Gaulle, who stepped down after losing a referendum. His successor, Georges Pompidou, was a technocrat who is now best known for initiating France's TGV (high speed rail) system and the modernist art museum in the Marais that bears his name. Pompidou was also keen on other nations joining The Six: Charlemagne's empire was about to expand.

West Germany also acquired a new leader in 1969. Willy Brandt belonged to a new generation. Previous German leaders, while fundamentally liberal in politics, had been personally rather starchy and formal; Brandt was warmer and more open. He had a fresh vision for dealing with his divided nation, replacing the old doctrine whereby the Federal Republic broke diplomatic relations with any country that recognized the GDR, with *Ostpolitik*, a more pragmatic approach.

Another mould-breaking leader elected in 1969 was Sweden's Olof Palme, a fierce critic of colonialism, apartheid and American policy in Vietnam, as well as the Soviet invasion of Czechoslovakia. At home, he passed a series of measures to promote gender equality, increased already high taxation and spending on the nation's welfare system, and rewrote the constitution to take all remaining power from the monarchy.

Western European life seemed to be heading in interesting new directions. But at the same time, a sinister new kind of politics was emerging: terrorism. Northern Ireland was drifting towards sectarian anarchy. In Italy, a bomb exploded at the HQ of the National Agrarian Bank in Milan, killing 17 people: 1969 was the beginning of Italy's *Anni di Piombo* (Years of Lead: lead as in bullets), which lasted into the mid 1980s. The late 1960s also saw the first deaths caused by Basque terrorists in Spain, though ETA would keep its worst atrocities for the early 1980s.

So, like Eurovision, Western Europe ended a decade which had looked to be heading for a jolly, liberated party in a more nuanced, troubled mood. Eurovision though the 1960s shows us an efflorescence of individuality and colour. Off with the bow ties and ball gowns; on with the polo-necks and mini-skirts! But as the old order crumbled, what would replace it? A gentler, more liberal, more approachable politics? Or the simple message of terrorism: violence, till we get what we want? Young Western Europeans, like Judy's friend, wanted less 1956-style 'order' and duty, and more authenticity: more individuality, more freedom to buy what they chose, wear what they chose, live as they chose. Older commentators wondered where these freedoms would take the half-continent: towards uplifting personal liberation or destructive selfishness?

East of the Iron Curtain, meanwhile, Europeans' problems were different: too little change, state violence an everyday fact of life, the future grey and static rather than colourful but uncertain.

The 1970s

1970

Date: 21 March
Venue: RAI Congrescentrum, Amsterdam
Winner: Dana, Ireland
Winning Song: *All Kinds of Everything*

Because of the low number of entrants – there hadn't been so few since 1959 – the first contest of the new decade was padded out with 'postcards', those little clips that come before each entry, and which are now an essential part of Eurovision. These stressed local rather than European identity, just as Cannes' carousels (strangely, also back in 1959) had done. General de Gaulle would have approved.

1970 also marked the debut of set designer Roland de Groot, who was to produce a string of imaginative stagings, with his trademark shifting geometrical shapes and blocks of colour: 1976, 1980, 1984. This set featured shiny spheres and floating semi-circular platforms, rearranged for each artist. Different-coloured lighting bounced off the spheres to create a perpetually changing effect. Even if its songs aren't exactly cutting-edge, Eurovision has always showcased a range of supporting skills, in lighting, in stage design, in broadcast technology, which are exactly that. De Groot has as much a place in the Eurovision Hall of Fame as Katie Boyle, Ralf Siegel/

Bernd Meinunger, ABBA, Rolf Løvland or Thomas G:son.

Male inconstancy, admitted by the singer, was the theme of two of the songs, from Switzerland via Henri Dès' eccentric Retour (Return), and from Italy. Welcome to the new 'permissive society'. Italy, true to stereotype, had touched on this topic before, back in 1963, where a flirtatious Emilio Pericoli had jokily sung about how he charmed various glamorous females. By 1970, the whole business had got more serious: Gianni Morandi, singing of the sadness in *Occhi di Ragazza (Girls' Eyes)*, had stopped enjoying his conquests. One could say that this showed a more thoughtful approach – but maybe in 1963 people just flirted but in 1970 they ended up in bed, where the emotional consequences could be much more intense (not to mention longer-lasting, especially after *Humanae Vitae*).

The winner, by contrast to all this philandering, was a young girl of radiant wholesomeness: Dana. Behind this (there is almost always a 'behind this' in Eurovision) lurked the terrible unfolding of events in Northern Ireland. Dana came from Bogside in Derry (or Londonderry, depending on your political allegiance), which in the previous August had seen a battle between largely Protestant police and Catholic residents. This had led to the British army being sent into the province. Initially the army had been welcomed, but it had not taken long for this to sour. A month after Dana's win, rioters fought a gun battle with the new arrivals. In June, six men – five Protestant, one Catholic – were murdered by terrorists. Dana wanted to show that there was another side to life in the province, and did, briefly, though events overtook her. In the long run, the winsome 18-year-old would grow into a strong woman. In 1997 she stood for President of Ireland and came third in the vote; two years later she was elected as a Euro-MP for Connacht-Ulster, a job previously held by Ray MacSharry, of whom more later.

Second came Britain's Mary Hopkin, who tried winsome too but didn't really pull it off. Germany's Katja Ebstein, a distant third, definitely didn't do winsome. This was Germany's best result in the competition so far, and a sign of that nation's continuing post-war rehabilitation. This process continued when, later in the year, Willy Brandt visited Warsaw to sign a treaty recognizing post-1945 borders. Part of his itinerary took him to a memorial commemorating the inhabitants of the infamous Ghetto, where a quarter of a million Jews had been herded into a small part of the city by the SS and murdered. Brandt laid a wreath as planned, then, unscripted, fell to his knees and remained there in silence. While it's easy to be sceptical about any 'spontaneous' gesture by a politician, Brandt seems to have been genuinely overcome by the moment. "I did what people do when words fail them," he said later. The *Warschauer Kniefall* was of great significance in Eastern and Central Europe, and helped create an impression of Germany as a modern state genuinely eager both to acknowledge and to move on from its horrific past.

The 1970 song contest was a success. The winner was a

hit all round Western Europe, a sure sign that despite continual critical tutting, Eurovision had found its niche and was entertaining people across the half-continent. It also launched the career of a global superstar. Spain's Julio Iglesias had been a goalkeeper at Real Madrid, but his sporting career was cut short by a car accident; while recovering, he began to compose songs. The bright blue suit and (nearly) matching tie he wore to perform *Gwendolyne* is probably not the best outfit he has appeared in – but his career got underway, and he is since estimated to have sold 300 million records.

Despite the *'Europe des patries'* message of Eurovision 1970's postcards, federalists kept the United States of Europe flame alight. October of that year saw a report by Pierre Werner, Luxembourg's Minister of Finance, which presented a road map towards 'irrevocable fixing of parity rates' between EEC currencies. Werner's idea was that the separate currencies would continue to exist but be completely interchangeable, the way banknotes in Scotland issued by different banks are equivalent. The aim was to have this in place by 1980. The French, despite de Gaulle's departure, still thought this too integrationist. The timing was not right, either; the world's currencies were getting less and less stable, due to Vietnam-war-induced dollar inflation and the subsequent collapse of the post-war Bretton Woods agreement which had effectively linked the world's major currencies to that of the USA. Werner's plan was quietly shelved, but the seeds of European Monetary

Union had been sown.

1971

Date: 21 March
Venue: Gaiety Theatre, Dublin
Debutant: Malta
Winner: Séverine, Monaco
Winning Song: *Un Banc, un Arbre, une Rue (A Bench, a Tree, a Street)*.

In 1971 everyone wanted to be back in Eurovision. 18 nations took to the stage, including new arrivals Malta (who came last: new arrivals often take a while to adjust to the contest). TV audience numbers kept rising. Estimates for 1971 are as high as 250 million. There was another fine set, this time with a vaguely Celtic feel – Roland de Groot had raised the bar. The only weak point was the wavering organ music over the postcards, which sounded like it had been relayed live from the local funeral parlour.

A change in the rules allowed groups, which brought in harmony vocals and countermelodies. Some of the best harmonies came from Sweden, who fielded a quartet: two female lead vocalists (one dark-haired, one fair), backed by two bearded men playing guitars. In other words…

The Family Four. They came sixth. Five places above it, *Un Banc, un Arbre, une Rue* used countermelodies to great effect. The entry was officially from Monaco, though its singer was French, as were its writers and the orchestra's conductor. Séverine claimed never to have visited the principality before the contest, and was not invited to do so after winning. It's a fine song, however, and sold well round Europe afterwards. It even made it into the UK Top Ten, in its original French. The lyric bemoans the selfishness that overcomes us as we leave childhood and start competing in the adult world: a dig from France – sorry, Monaco – at the evils of the Anglo-Saxon economic model.

After Derry-based Dana's win for Ireland in 1970, Britain chose a Northern Irish singer for 1971. Clodagh Rogers, from Ballymena in County Antrim, received death threats from the Irish Republican Army (IRA); her bravery in defying these deserved a better song than *Jack in the Box*. (After 1967, Britain spent years trying to redo *Puppet on a String*, but never quite managed it.) Meanwhile order in her home province was collapsing. In February 1971, the first soldier was shot dead in Belfast. In March, three off-duty soldiers were murdered. Later in the year, internment without trial was introduced, and in December Protestant paramilitaries let off a bomb in a Belfast bar that killed fifteen people. January 1972 saw 'Bloody Sunday', when a protest march in Londonderry was fired on by troops, killing fourteen Catholics. Was a part of Europe about to collapse into civil war?

For Germany, Katja Ebstein sung again. Her song, *Diese Welt (This World)*, had an environmental message. Influenced by the Apollo 8 mission, it sings of how the world is just a little bit of rock in space, and we'd better look after it. The topic is now staple fare in Eurovision, but not in 1971: *Diese Welt* blazed the trail.

Modern environmentalism tends to date itself from US author Rachel Carson's *Silent Spring*, a book about overuse of pesticides published in 1962, but the European response at that time was to ignore it, considering it an American problem. As the 1960s drew to a close, our confidence grew less. Trees in Scandinavia and Germany's Black Forest began to lose leaves/needles, as if struck by a mysterious illness. The oil tanker *Torrey Canyon* foundered on a reef and spewed thousands of gallons of oil onto British and French beaches – an event referenced in *Diese Welt*'s lyrics. (They were by Fred Jay, an Austrian-born writer who fled Hitler in 1938 and ended up in America: an early example of American involvement in Eurovision.)

In 1971, Friends of the Earth was founded by groups in France, Sweden, Britain and the USA. Greenpeace, originally Canadian but now based in Amsterdam, was formed the same year. In 1972 the Club of Rome, an independent 'think tank' founded by industrialist Aurelio Peccei and OECD Scientific Advisor Alexander King, would publish *The Limits to Growth*. This book painted a gloomy picture of the future, with population rising, pollution increasing and ever more strain being placed on the finite resources of the earth. 1972 would also see the UN hold a conference on the environment in Stockholm. Environmental issues would finally be taken seriously by

86

EEC leaders when they gathered for their 'summit meeting' (the forerunner of the modern European Council) in October of that year. But that was 1972: Eurovision got there before the politicians.

1971 was the biggest Eurovision yet, and the year also saw political Europe at last considering expanding to match it. Two months after the competition, Britain's new Europhile Prime Minister Edward Heath met Georges Pompidou to discuss British membership of EEC (no other European leader was present at the discussion). Denmark, Norway and Ireland also began similar talks. The new applicants would have to pay a price for admission, however. Financially, the EEC was all about agricultural subsidy, and changing that was not up for discussion. The new arrivals – especially Britain and Denmark, with their small, efficient agricultural sectors – were going to have to pay a substantial and continuing entry fee.

1972

Date: 25 March
Venue: Usher Hall, Edinburgh, UK
Debuts: None
Winner: Vicky Leandros, Luxembourg
Winning Song: *Après toi (After you)*

The most notable thing about this Eurovision was the fashion, especially for men. Hair had been getting slightly longer over the last few contests. In 1972 it broke free, cascading over necklines and suddenly matching that of female contestants for length. Lapels blossomed in sympathy; clothes began to sport glittery motifs; sleeves and trouser legs started to flare ever wider – rising to a sartorial crescendo with the last entry, Serge from Holland, who also wore various shades of poster-paint lime green. The decade that taste forgot had hit its stride (not that 'taste' and 'Eurovision' ever coincide precisely).

The contest winner was an international co-operation: a Greek singer, French, Greek and German lyricist/composers, and a German conductor. The tuba player's cousin had once been to Luxembourg. *Après toi* was a powerful ballad that went on to sell very well around Europe, keeping up the traditions of winners since 1967.

Ireland and Malta sang in local languages, Gaelic and Maltese. Neither met success, coming 15th and last respectively (Malta's his'n'hers pink polka-dot outfits probably didn't help). This reflected a new sensibility in Europe. Activists were beginning to fight to save the continent's threatened minority languages, especially on the western Celtic fringe. Welsh-speaking schools had been set up in 1971. The Gaelscoileanna, Ikastola and Diwan movements in Eire, the Basque country and Brittany respectively, would soon follow suit. Regionalist political parties began to attract votes: in 1974, the Scottish Nationalists would return 11 members to London's Westminster parliament.

Eurovision did little to follow this trend. Regional cultures added colour and interest to the competition, but, as Ireland and Malta found, were not rewarded by judges. Instead, the results reflected the overwhelming linguistic trend of the era, the continuing march of English (or, more accurately, American). It was decided that for Eurovision 1973, entrants would be allowed to sing in whatever language they wanted. This could be seen as a defeat for less populous cultures, as another sign of their being swamped by 'big' languages. However performers from smaller countries were delighted. Singing in English, surely, would heighten their chances of victory.

The language debate at this time highlights Europe's centre/periphery issue. There are various ways of dividing the continent. East/west was the obvious one before 1989. Now, people talk of the 'olive line', a north/south division below which long, blazing summers make life move at a slower pace and where Euro membership is causing appalling hardship.

But a centre/periphery divide seems the most lasting and instructive of all. There are various ramifications, but the simplest version places the old Lugano 1956 core at Europe's centre and the rest on the periphery – to start with, anyway; subtleties will emerge as this story develops. Up to 1973, Eurovision winners had largely been in 'centre' languages: French mainly, plus Dutch, Italian and German. Would the new rule allow peripheral Europe to start winning?

In 1972, Norway established its position as 'peripheral and proud of it' by voting not to proceed with its application for EEC membership. Yet the country has been a long-time and enthusiastic participant in Eurovision – one of the most interesting ones, with a fascinating variety of contributions in its 55 years, though 1972's *Småting (Small Things)* was not one of their finest.

By contrast, January 1 1973 saw the European centre open its gates to Britain, Denmark and Ireland (two of these three had been unsuccessful applicants to sing at Lugano back in '56), via EEC membership. However even these early joiners have since proven to be independently-minded. They have never cuddled into the EEC/EU system the way the original Six did. Neither Denmark nor Britain has joined the Euro, and Ireland voted against two major EU treaties in the 2000s. If not as determinedly peripheral as Norway, these nations have kept an outsider's air about them.

1973

Date: 7 April
Venue: Nouveau Théâtre, Luxembourg
Debut: Israel
Winner: Anne-Marie David, Luxembourg
Winning Song: *Tu te reconnaîtras (You will recognize yourself)*.

Along with the removal of the language rule, the 1973 contest saw another significant change, the arrival of Israel. People often ask why this non-European country is allowed into Eurovision. One suggested answer is that it was a way of testing satellite broadcasting technology with the West's main ally in the Middle East. The truth is simpler and boringly technical: the contest is open to all nations who are in the European Broadcasting Union (EBU), and eligibility for the EBU is simply determined by geography. You can join if your territory, or part of it, lies within an area bounded to the west by the Atlantic Ocean, to the east by the meridian 40 degrees E, and to the South by the parallel of 30 degrees N. North African and Middle Eastern countries, all EBU members, could have decided to sing in Eurovision; Israel got there first, after which these countries have mostly declined to exercise their right to participate.

The previous year, 11 Israeli athletes had been murdered at the Munich Olympics: security at the *Nouveau*

Théâtre was tight. Terry Wogan, on his second gig commentating for Britain, later recalled seeing armoured cars and machine guns. The audience was told not to stand up and applaud any songs, as they might get shot.

The presentation begun with a display of modern broadcast technology: modern in 1973, that is, with not a computer or a microchip in sight. Some modern (also in 1973) fashions were then displayed by Belgium's Nicole and Hugo, who both sported platform shoes, purple bellbottom trousers, and purple tops with huge lapels encrusted with rhinestones and flapping, flared sleeves. By contrast, Portugal once again produced a serious song with hidden political barbs. Ary dos Santos' *Tourada (Bullfight)* was a satire on the *Estado Novo* regime as a cavalcade of fools and crooks. Dr Salazar's replacement, Marcelo Caetano, had tried to liberalize the system a little bit – including rebranding the secret police by giving them a new name – but, like the Russians in Czechoslovakia, he then panicked and was now trying to revert to authoritarian rule.

Both Sweden and Israel used female conductors in Eurovision 1973. Up to this point, the contest podium had been a male preserve. Such exclusivity was a mirror of European life generally. In 1973 the European Parliament was 95% male, and there were no female EEC commissioners at all.

But things were changing. Women were entering the workforce in ever greater numbers, especially in Britain and Scandinavia, where for a woman to have a career became more the rule than the exception (in Southern Europe, women still tended to work up until marriage, after which many returned to the home). However these careers were usually halted by a 'glass ceiling' of male power – though not always: in Britain, Margaret Hilda Thatcher, a 48-year-old former Oxford Chemistry student, was already Secretary of State of Education and had her eye on even greater things.

More generally, sociologists began talking of the 'feminization' of European society. 1973 was the year that the number of Europeans working in the service sector surpassed those working in industry, and it was argued that these new jobs required more 'emotional intelligence', an arguably female quality, than the old muscular industrial ones.

These changes have only partially been reflected in Eurovision. Women have always done better than men in the contest, starting with Lys Assia back in 1956. But despite 1973, orchestra leadership remained an almost exclusively male preserve until orchestras disappeared. Paula Farrell (of whom more later) is one of the contest's great set designers, but that job seems to be largely male, too.

1973's new language rule actually did little to change the contest, except produce some poor songs in English by non-native speakers. The winner was a powerful ballad in French, that went on to sell well round Europe. A song in Spanish, *Eres Tú (You are)*, came second and sold even better, thus joining the elite band of classic non-winners. It has been covered by such acts as Bing Crosby, Acker Bilk and Eydie Gormé, as well as having steel-band and punk versions. A British *schlager* came third, bouncily celebrating that nation's new EEC membership: *Power to all our Friends* sang Cliff Richard. So it was Eurovision business as usual.

It looked like business as usual in 1973 for Western Europe's economy, too, despite the questions asked by the *soixante-huitards* and the Club of Rome (1973 saw German-born, British-based economist EF Schumacher add his voice to the questioning, with his book *Small is Beautiful*). Inflation might have been creeping up, but unemployment remained under 3%, a level that most economists consider to be 'full employment' and which had been pretty constant since before this story began. Western Europe, by adopting – or at least adapting – the German Social Market model, seemed to have found the formula for socially balanced prosperity, steering a middle course between the obsession with market forces across the Atlantic and the grim totalitarianism behind the Iron Curtain.

On October 6, Yom Kippur, the holiest day in Judaism, Egypt and Syria launched surprise attacks on Eurovision's latest participant with the aim of getting back lands lost in the 1967 Six Day War. The move was so successful that within three days Israel was contemplating using tactical nuclear weapons. This panicked the Americans into launching an airlift of military hardware to its ally. On October 14, a massive tank battle turned the tide. By

October 22, Israeli forces were 100 kilometres from Cairo, at which point, a ceasefire was brokered.

The Arab world was furious at what they saw as the West's meddling in a war which they reckoned they should have won – though in fact Europe had done very little meddling: America had requested permission to use its European bases for its airlift, but only Portugal and the Netherlands had said yes. On October 17, the Arab-dominated Organization of Petroleum Exporting Countries (OPEC) cut oil production and raised prices by 70%. In December, they doubled the price again, to $11.65 per barrel (at the start of October, this price had been $3).

The effect was immediate. Western Europe plummeted into recession. Car-free Sundays were enforced on the public roads of Britain, Germany, Italy, the Netherlands, Norway and Switzerland. Britain began working a three day week. Its stock market went into freefall, and electricity shortages became a part of national life. Power to all our Friends? The nation didn't even have enough power for itself. In every Western European country unemployment started rising. Inflation rose with it, confounding economists, whose theories had previously insisted that the two phenomena should be inversely correlated. A fresh concept had to be invented for this new world of inflating currencies and economic stagnation: stagflation.

Boom bang-a-bang! This wasn't just a 'recession' but the end of an era, the end of a system that had driven the world's advanced economies since Pattillo Higgins and

Anthony F Lucas had struck black gold in Texas in 1901. The cheap oil economy was dead.

The words of the Club of Rome suddenly looked frighteningly prescient. Europe had boomed since 1945. It had got used to booming; it had come to assume that growth was automatic if governments kept to a reasonably sensible set of rules. But supposing this wasn't the case? Supposing the *'trente glorieuses'* (as the French came to call the 1945 -73 era: it sounds snappier than *vingt-huit glorieuses*) was an exception, a lucky break based on cheap oil and the importation of American business methods? What was in store for Europe now that this break was over?

1974

Date: 6 April
Venue: The Dome, Brighton, UK
Debut: Greece
Winner: Abba, Sweden
Winning Song: *Waterloo*

The recession deepened. We all needed cheering up. Eurovision should have been there to do that. But could it?

The 1974 contest nearly didn't take place at all, because of a terrorist threat from the IRA: only after a thorough search of the venue was the event allowed to run, and security remained tight throughout the proceedings. Once it did start, the material seemed uninspiring. Spain (flamenco-type guitar) and debutant Greece (bazouki) provided some interesting ethnic flourishes but were short on melody. Eighth to sing was Sweden. We got a short postcard to the tune of Hugo Alfven's *Swedish Rhapsody*: viewers were probably already wondering if that was going to be the best tune they'd hear all evening. Conductor Sven-Olof Walldoff walked onto the podium dressed as Napoleon. Oh, God, not a novelty song... Then Anni-Frid Lyngstad and Agnetha Fältskog, the latter in a blue cat-suit, glitter and silver platforms, bounded down onto the stage.

Waterloo is still regarded as the best Eurovision song ever, and who am I to question that? It brought a new energy to the competition: finally rock rhythms and instrumentation had found their way in alongside the ballads and Europop (actually, *Waterloo* reinvented Europop, killing the old format). It was also a groundbreaking victory for Europe's periphery over its centre – no previous winner had been as far-flung as Sweden. Europe was a bigger place on 7 April 1974.

Yet lyrically *Waterloo* was unremarkable. British viewers no doubt enjoyed the reference to the defeat of France in 1815: especially apt in the year that English became Eurovision's *de facto* language. But Eurovision 1974 had more thoughtful and insightful lyrics on offer.

Yugoslavia, which was beginning to recant its earlier, half-western political models and to turn more hard-line (sixties Eurovision entrant Vice Vukov found himself banned from singing in the 1970s, due to his support for greater Croatian independence), reflected on the effect of war on *Generacija '42 (The Generation of '42)*. Belgium lamented the loss of late sixties idealism with *Fleur de Liberté (Flower of Freedom)*. Best of all, perhaps, was lyricist Michel Jourdan's meditation on romantic break-ups, sung by Romuald for Monaco. The francophone countries had a tradition of producing quality words. Was this tradition about to meet its Waterloo? Eurovision would surely be the poorer if it did.

Politically, the most significant song came once more from Portugal. On April 24 at 10.55 pm, the Lisbon radio station *Emissores Associados de Lisboa* broadcast the nation's

Eurovision entry, *E depois do Adeus (After Goodbye)*. This was a secret signal for a group of young army officers to launch a *coup d'état*. Early next morning, key locations – local military HQ, TV and radio stations, and Lisbon Airport – were occupied, and other institutions, such as City Hall, the national bank and the defence ministry, were surrounded. A few high-ranking old-guard loyalists escaped from the last of these and set up a rival HQ – but hardly any servicemen obeyed their orders. Instead, crowds came out onto the streets and started handing red carnations, in flower and in plentiful supply at the time, to soldiers. By the end of the day it was 'after goodbye' to the *Estado Novo*; Portugal had a new government, committed to 'three ds': democracy, decolonization and development. The change had been brought about with minimal violence (four people were shot by the secret police). This was a model example of people power – the modern European way of bringing about regime change.

Europe was still not without violence, of course. There was the threat of terrorism, so bravely defied by Eurovision in 1973 and 1974 (Brighton would be the scene of a brutal bombing a decade later). And two months after making its debut in Eurovision, Greece found itself in a virtual war with Turkey over Cyprus. Conflict between Greek and Turkish Cypriots had been escalating ever since Britain had granted the island independence in 1960. On 15 July, 1974, a military coup removed its moderate government, replacing it with one determined on *enosis*, unity with

99

Greece. Turkey responded by invading five days later, capturing a small corridor of land between Kyrenia and Nicosia. The Greek government then collapsed. Peace talks began, but these did not progress: on 14 August, Turkey launched a second invasion, and this time took over the north-west third of the country – territory that it still holds today, though most nations do not recognize the occupation. When Cyprus entered Eurovision in 1981, it would be its Greek part that did so – as all but the most unaware Eurovision watcher will know from its voting. Northern Cyprus would have to wait till 2013 to take part in a song contest – but that's for later.

1975

Date: 22 March
Venue: Stockholm International Fairs and Congress Centre, Sweden
Debut: Turkey
Winner: Teach-in, The Netherlands
Winning Song: *Ding dinge dong.*

After the best Eurovision winner ever, the contest looked poised to move up a gear and show that new-generation Europop could be genuinely original. What amazing new Abbas would emerge this time round? First to rise to this challenge was a group from the Netherlands. A blip, no doubt: their clothes were ridiculous and their song had lyrics that made *La, la, la* sound thoughtful. Never mind, something better would come along...

Many of the entries that followed had the new, post-Abba rockier feel. *Let me be the One* by Britain's The Shadows featured three electric guitars. Germany's Joy Fleming looked across the Berlin Wall and sang a blues about how *Ein Lied kann ein Brücke sein (A Song can be a Bridge).* Not rocky but lyrically intriguing was Switzerland's *Mikado.* Behind a suddenly outdated *schlager* beat, singer/songwriter Simone Drexel came up with a neat image for a selfish new age she feared was dawning – in the game Mikado (alias pick-up-sticks, jackstraws or spillikins) you mustn't show your feelings, and if someone else makes a mistake, well that's their tough luck: don't get involved.

By contrast, Portugal unashamedly celebrated its Carnation Revolution with *Madrugada (Dawn)*. Singer Duarte Mendes was a captain at the national artillery training school; he wanted to perform the song in army uniform but had to be content with a red carnation in his buttonhole. However, like many revolutions, the events of 1974 had not been as conclusive as Mendes was telling the Eurovision audience: while he was hymning his victory in Stockholm, factions were struggling for power back home, and it was still not clear who would end up the winner. On 25 November 1975, a coup would be launched by Communist paratroopers; a counter-coup would follow the same day. This effectively ended the jostling for power; elections would be held in 1976. Across Portugal's border, General Franco died five days before the two November coups; King Juan Carlos became head of the Spanish state, and set in train a cautious but ultimately effective process of reform.

After listening to this selection of interesting entries, the judges considered their options, then chose the song they considered the summit of songwriting achievement for Western Europe in the year 1975.

Oops!

Perhaps what the judges liked about the winning song was its daftness. The seventies can be seen as a puzzled decade. *Ding dinge dong* looked longingly back at the sixties and tried to recapture some of that era's lost fizz and innocence. It didn't really succeed: the musicians behind Teach-in's singer Getty Kaspers try and grin, but those beards and shaggy hairdos look more defensive than jolly.

Looking forward, things were as confusing. The old economic model was collapsing. Inflation was rising, stirring horrific memories in Germany. Nobody knew what would replace the old economy – or whether anything would.

In America, 1975 saw the first hobbyist computer, the Altair 8800, go on sale, with an operating system created by two young enthusiasts, Paul Allen and Bill Gates. Telenet, a group of linked computers that could talk to one another, became available to users in seven US cities. But, seen from Europe at that time, what relevance did these boys' toys have to serious economic activity?

Maybe the *soixante-huitards* had been right after all. Dump the system; it had failed. Eurovision 1975 was accompanied by far left protests on Stockholm's streets against the amount of money being spent on staging the contest, and, more generally, the poor quality of capitalist 'commercial' music. An *Alternativfestival* was set up, where anyone could come, sing and parody Eurovision at its worst – though could anyone have done a better job than Teach-in? Intriguingly, the anti-Eurovision argument was later to cross the political divide, and would be heard from the right, when it was the amount of *public* money being spent on the contest that came in for criticism. The moral, perhaps, is that aspirant political elites like to set themselves up as aesthetic elites, too, and that distancing yourself from Eurovision is one way of doing this. Instead, why not be a *true* revolutionary? Enjoy Eurovision and be proud of it!

Extreme left politics of a more violent nature raised its head too, with yet another terrorist threat to the show, this time from Germany's Red Army Faction. It did not materialize, but a month after the Stockholm contest, members of the faction seized the West German embassy in the city and murdered the military and economic attachés.

At the other end of the Eurovision table from the triumphant dinging and donging, with three votes, was debutant Turkey. One can't help feeling that prejudice was responsible for this, as their song was a pleasant, well-sung ballad, *Seninle bir Dakika (A Minute with you)*, that didn't deserve this fate.

Turkey had been knocking on Europe's door since joining the Council of Europe in 1949 and NATO in 1952 (where it soon became a key player: it was the presence of US missiles on Turkish soil that had prompted the Soviet Union to build bases in Cuba). In 1963 it had signed an agreement with the EEC that created a road-map to its joining. Since then, the map had not been followed – and has not been to this day. Various reasons were cited in 1975 and still resurface. Cyprus is one (Greece boycotted Eurovision 1975 due to Turkish participation). Turkey's human rights record is another (performance tables of nations' human rights are controversial, but they probably say something. Western Europe does well, especially Scandinavia. Eastern Europe is catching up. Turkey fares less well, though there are many worse places.) It has still to admit its role in the 1915 Armenian genocide. Geographically, only 3% of the country is in Europe. Is it too big? In 1975, its population was around 40 million; forty years on, that figure is 75 million; it is poised to overtake Germany, Europe's most populous country, by the end of the 2010s if current growth rates in the two countries persist. Is it too different? Many Europeans feel that the country really isn't European culturally – a feeling hotly contested by many educated Turks. Rather than get into a debate about that here, we shall follow Turkey's Eurovision career and see what light it sheds: like another outlier, Norway, Turkey's Eurovision input is particularly informative.

Across the Gulf of Bothnia from the 1975 contest venue, a truly pan-European 'Conference on Security and Co-operation in Europe', which had been running since 1973, reached its climax. On August 1, the Helsinki Accords were signed by leaders of Europe, east and west – including Turkey – and of the US and the Soviet Union.

The Accords had three principal aspects, oddly referred to as 'baskets'. One accepted existing boundaries in Europe, not good news for the three Baltic states of Estonia, Latvia and Lithuania annexed by Stalin in 1940.

West Germany's new Chancellor Helmut Schmidt – he had replaced Willy Brandt in 1974 – commented that though 'frontiers are inviolable', one 'must be able to change them by peaceful means and agreement'. East Germany's Erich Honecker was less keen on change, reminding everyone that Europe's two terrible wars had been started by 'disregard for the sovereignty and territorial integrity of other states'. *Touché*.

The Accords' second basket encouraged trade, cultural and scientific links between the two blocs. The third dealt with human rights and 'free circulation of ideas and information'. The Soviet Union saw the Accords as a win, thanks to basket one, but over time the third would become a thorn in its imperial side.

1976

Date: 6 April
Venue: Congresgebouw, Den Haag, Netherlands
Debuts: None (no new entrants till 1980)
Winner: Brotherhood of Man, UK
Winning Song: *Save all your Kisses for me.*

Eurovision 1976 saw victory with a song so middle-of-the-road that you could put cats' eyes in it. But before one sneers, *Save all your Kisses for me* then sold millions of singles around Europe, more than any other winner before or since, even *Waterloo*. The four singers, already popular in Europe, continued to enjoy success for the rest of the decade. It's also interesting that, after the previous year's lyrical inanities, the 1976 contest was won by a song whose effect relies on its lyric; everything about the winner seems ridiculously trite until the last line reveals its audience to be a three-year-old child, after which it's quite cute.

The winning nation was having less fortune with its economy. Britain's inflation level was the worst in Europe, though Italy ran it a close second. The same month as its contest victory, its currency began to collapse on world markets. By December Chancellor Denis Healey was forced to go to the International Monetary Fund, a global pot of cash set aside to rescue failing third-world economies, and beg for a bailout, a humiliation that some commentators put on the same level as Suez, two decades before. 'Goodbye, Great Britain' said America's *Wall Street Journal*.

Meanwhile in London's suburbs, an angry new music was beginning to make itself heard, about as different to *Save all your Kisses for me* as could be imagined: punk.

The other entries to Eurovision 1976 ran the usual gamut from the comical (try keeping a straight face while watching Finland's mountainous Freddi telling us to let our hips go *Hippety pump pump*) to thoughtful but not very melodic entries from Spain and Belgium. Greece bemoaned the refugees, ruins and dead bodies in Cyprus (the Greek Cypriot ones, anyway). Nonsense titles came from Switzerland and Germany – and France, though the French managed to do nonsense in style, Catherine Ferry putting pert hedonism into *Un, deux, trois*. Life, she pointed out, is not a novel by Kafka; the judges agreed – the song came second. At the other end of the table, Norway's Anne-Karine Strøm sabotaged a catchy entry about superspy *Mata Hari* by putting on some ludicrous sunglasses half way through, as if she felt 'I'm winning here: I'd better do something about that'. She is the only artist to have come last twice in Eurovision, but Norwegians don't seem to give a damn. Or do they? Such is the perpetual enigma of the land of Grieg, Munch and Ibsen in Eurovision.

A topic that did not get covered was the environment. After *Diese Welt* back in 1971, the subject had been ignored in the contest – as it had been in Europe's media: people were more concerned about stagflation. But 1976 put it right back on the public agenda. In July, six tonnes of TCCP, a gas containing deadly dioxins, escaped from a factory in Seveso, northern Italy. In the end, no human life was lost, but images of abandoned villages closed off with barbed wire and men in what looked like spacesuits clearing up thousands of tons of polluted earth went deep into Europe's consciousness. In January 1977, it was announced that the Acropolis in Athens was under threat from pollutants, largely from car exhausts. This all went to add to the worrying sense of 'game over' for the western way of getting and spending.

1977

Date: 7 May
Venue: Wembley Conference Centre, London
Winner: Marie Myriam, France
Winning Song: *L'Oiseau et l'Enfant (The Bird and the Child)*

Eurovision 1977 was due to be broadcast in April, but the host was London, and the UK plus 1970s equals strikes, in this case by BBC cameramen. UK viewers who switched on for the programme on the original planned evening, April 2, got a broadcast of the Moscow State Circus instead, which some might have found darkly significant.

Moscow was doing rather well in 1977. Russia hadn't suffered in the oil crisis, having plenty black gold of its own. Its ideology was proving attractive to the third world, where Soviet-backed guerilla fighters were filling the power gaps left by the last departing imperialists (the ideology was less attractive in Eastern Europe, where the Charter 77 movement was founded, insisting the region's governments keep to the third basket of the Helsinki Accords).

Russia even launched its own rival to Eurovision. Song festivals had long been popular in Eastern Europe, for example the Golden Stag and Golden Orpheus Festivals in Bulgaria or the Lyre Festival in Bratislava. There had been one at Sopot near Gdansk, Poland, since 1961 (the first three had actually been held in the Gdansk shipyard, after which the venue was moved to the nearby Forest Opera amphitheatre). In 1977, the Sopot Festival was rebranded as the Intervision Song Contest and broadcast all round the Soviet bloc. The competitors came from the Warsaw Pact, plus Cuba, Finland and, for some reason, Spain, to vie for first prize, the Amber Nightingale. The organizers developed an imaginative system of public voting: if you liked a song, you turned all your lights on; if you disliked it, you turned all your lights out. The electricity distributor in each country measured the change in usage during each song, and the Nightingale went to the one that used the most. In 1977 this was Helena Vondráčková from Czechoslovakia with *Malovaný Džbánku (Painted Jug)*. The middle of the Marxist-Leninist road looks and sounds remarkably like the middle of the Capitalist one.

Sadly, similar tastes in popular entertainment did not stop the two camps threatening to obliterate each other. While Helena Vondráčková was collecting her Amber Nightingale, Russia's military was deploying a new weapon, the RSD-10 Pioneer missile (known to the West as the SS-20). These could be fired quickly and easily from mobile launchers: the RSD-10 was powered by solid fuel, while previous Soviet missiles had to be slowly and riskily filled with liquid propellant at the point of firing. They were reliable and accurate: they could be used tactically, to nuke Europe's airfields and military bases rather than to obliterate whole cities – a move away from total madness, one might think, but a change which experts thought made war more likely.

1977 also saw a rise in terrorist activity in the West, which no doubt delighted Moscow, who probably supported it financially (exactly how far this went remains open to debate: one source claims that the Soviet Union was spending around $200 million a year on training and arming terrorists around this time, but this comes from the US Government, who might not be the most objective observer). The Red Army Faction (RAF) certainly received help from the East German Stasi secret police, as was discovered after 1989. 1977 saw the faction reach the climax of its activities. Germany's Prosecutor General was murdered in April; banker Jürgen Ponto suffered the same fate in July; in October, Lufthansa Flight 181 from Mallorca to Frankfurt was hijacked by Palestinian terrorists demanding the release of RAF prisoners. The aircraft ended up in Mogadishu, where the terrorists poured spirits over the hostages ready to burn them alive. But instead the plane was stormed by an elite German anti-terror squad, GSG9. Three members of the RAF subsequently committed suicide. The insanity was over – in Germany, anyway, though in Italy, further horrors, courtesy of left and right, were to follow, as were ETA atrocities in Spain.

All this reflected the continuing debate in Europe: where now? What was the way out of the mid-seventies economic mess? Sharp left? Turn right? Muddle along?

The first of these alternatives was the one argued for by

Austria's 1977 Eurovision entrants, Schmetterlinge, an agitprop group. Their previous work had been an opera entitled *The Passion of the Proletariat* ('passion' as in suffering, as in the Passion of Christ), which took listeners through events like the Paris Commune of 1871 and the 1917 Russian Revolution. *Boom boom Boomerang* was both a parody of Eurovision à la *Ding dinge dong* and an attack on the music industry as a whole, as a purveyor of mind-numbing but money-making pap. (The song's critique extended to blues, rock'n'roll, reggae and soul, which leaves one wondering what sort of music we would be allowed to listen to in Schmetterlinge's ideal world.)

The second alternative was suggested by Britain's Lynsey de Paul and Mike Moran, who lamented the economic state of their country with *Rock Bottom*, suggesting we 'rub out' the old system and start it again. Schmetterlinge might have approved of this, but not of the UK duo's intended rebuild: de Paul was an admirer of Margaret Thatcher, who was now leader of Britain's Conservative Party. Still in opposition, Mrs Thatcher was eager to introduce a strong dose of what would later be called 'neo-liberalism' into British political life. She intended to curb the power of trades unions, cut both taxes and government spending, deregulate markets, sell state assets to private buyers and encourage entrepreneurship.

Or maybe we should just forget politics, and boogie. Eurovision 1977 saw a number of entries go disco, with sixteenth beats and quacking wah-wah guitars. Germany brought in Silver Convention, a successful act in this new genre, then gave them a poor song, *Telegram*. A deliberate homage to Margot Hielscher's *Telefon* of 20 years earlier? Probably not.

Two interesting songs looked at the role of women in the new Europe. Again, different options were on offer. Italy's Mia Martini sang *Libera*, a celebration of being a modern woman, free to live life however she chooses. Belgium's *A Million in One, Two, Three* sang of a less liberated choice, reminiscent of Abba's *Money, Money, Money*.

There was also some national quirkiness on display. The Swiss entry featured an alphorn, and Finland's *Lapponia* recreated a folk tale but spoilt a potentially haunting piece with too conventional an arrangement: Eurovision would learn how to do Celtic/Norse in the 1990s.

In the end, the winner was neither political, nor disco, nor about female roles, nor quirkily ethnic, but a ballad, on the tried and tested Eurovision theme of the value of innocence and love in a potentially cruel world. It was, perhaps, a dull choice given the intriguing alternatives on offer, but Marie Myriam put in a fine performance which included singing the first verse unaccompanied. However the song did not sell well afterwards, ending the run of winners from 1967 that became hits around Europe. From then on, such breakouts would be rare.

The old rule that entries had to be in the native language (or *a* native language) of a competitor was reintroduced for this contest, and would last two decades. The problem with this rule became apparent the moment the results were announced. The table splits into two halves. Numbers one to eight are almost all in English or French; numbers nine to eighteen are almost all in other languages (there's one francophone entry down there, which had been poorly sung). The native language rule encouraged national quirkiness, which for viewers seeking to enjoy the variety of Europe's cultures was a good thing. But given the judges' obvious preference for familiar languages, it narrowed the pool of potential winners.

Political Europe's own issues are mirrored in this dilemma. How do you strike a balance between local difference, colour and control and forces that seek to centralize but impose conformity?

1978

Date: 22 April
Venue: Palais des Congrès, Paris
Winner: Izhar Cohen and Alpha Beta, Israel
Winning Song: *A-Ba-Ni-Bi*

The 1978 song contest is now probably best remembered for one of Eurovision's classic *nul points* entries: *Mil etter Mil (Mile after Mile)* from Norway's Jahn Teigen. The modern system of points allocation (or something very like it) had begun in 1975, which meant that getting none at all would be a rare event. So far nobody had endured this embarrassment. So far...

Teigen did not get off to a good start: he was allocated the dreaded number two singing slot. Then he had a very public accident on his way to perform. Instead of inter-act postcards, French TV showed pictures of the artists behind the scenes; over 100 million viewers saw the Norwegian singer head for the stage and, too busy waving at a camera, walk into a wall. Things didn't get much better during his performance, with Teigen ending up twanging his braces like a nineteenth-century dignitary giving an after-dinner speech.

But was his song that much worse than some other clunkers from 1978? Than Luxembourg's cringe-making attempt to suck up to France *Parlez-vous Français?* Than

Britain's clichéd *The bad old Days*? No. Teigen got *nul points* because he was from a peripheral country, singing in an obscure language. OK, the braces didn't help…

Nordic neighbour Bjorn Skifs decided on a different route: he'd defy the language rule and sing *Det blir alltid värre framåt natten* in English *(It always gets worse at Night)*. But he chickened out at the last moment, and ended up forgetting his Swedish lyrics.

As in 1977, the winning entries ended up largely in French and English, the bottom ones 'the rest'. Some of the latter tried language-independent titles like *Boom boom*, *Dai-li-dou* or, an Austrian song about a witch-turned-sex-goddess, *Mrs Caroline Robinson*, but to no avail.

Of course, the winner bucked this trend, by cleverly choosing a nonsense title/hook. Israel's victory created all sorts of problems for other Middle Eastern and North African broadcasters, as they did not recognize the country's existence. Most had a commercial break during Cohen's performance, and many just stopped the broadcast when it became clear who was going to win. Jordanian TV, needing to fill the time, showed a bunch of daffodils.

1978 wasn't a vintage Eurovision. Arguably, the best thing about it was the interval act, where France showed its cultural credentials by giving us Oscar Peterson, Stéphane Grappelli and Yehudi Menuhin. Perhaps we'd have had more fun watching Intervision, where the 1978 Amber Nightingale went to Russia's Alla Pugacheva, despite her making the sign of the cross at the end of her song *Vsyo mogut Koroli (Kings can do anything)*, to loud applause from the audience. Compère Jacek Bromski indulged in some anti-Soviet jokes, too: when the line to get Moscow's vote went dead, he told them to 'wake up'; when the line stayed down, hr added 'Better let them sleep' – a comment that was cut out of the actual broadcast.

Pugacheva was Intervision's Abba: she is reputed to have sold 250 million records in her career, which is still flourishing. She had some of the French *chanteuse* about her, but no self-pity; she had some of the German cabaret artiste, but no creepiness. Ebullient, sexy, emotional, unafraid to speak her mind, Pugacheva was a true people's heroine during the grey Soviet era; after that era she launched her own branded clothing, perfume, shoes as well as potato crisps and a radio station, Radio Alla.

As 1978 turned into 1979, relationships between the homes of Intervision and Eurovision grew ever more sour. In January, German and British leaders agreed to have American Pershing II ballistic missiles and Gryphon cruise missiles stationed on their territory, in response to the RSD-10s. Was Europe heading towards Berlin, 1961, again?

We were certainly headed for more economic difficulties. The Shah of Iran was overthrown in a revolution in February 1979. Oil output from the country plummeted and the price duly took off again, reaching $34 per barrel (it had cost $3 per barrel in September 1973). This price was, of course, that paid by the US and Western

Europe. Behind the Iron Curtain, the Soviet Union just kept on whistling the latest Alla Pugacheva hit producing all the oil that it and its empire needed (plus some more for export).

1979

Date: 31 March
Venue: Binyanei Ha-ouma Convention Centre, Jerusalem.
Winner: Gali Atari, with Milk and Honey, Israel
Winning Song: *Hallelujah*

Despite the missiles and the oil price, Eurovision 1979 took place in an atmosphere of optimism, because five days before the event, the hosts Israel had signed a treaty with Egypt based on 'Accords' reached at Camp David in the USA the year before. The Sinai Peninsula was to be demilitarized; autonomous Palestinian authorities would be set up on the West Bank and in Gaza; Israel's existence was formally recognized by Egypt. Peace in the Middle East at last!

The contest's broadcast intro stayed true to this optimism, showing Israel as a modern nation where different faiths co-existed. Dov Ben David's stage set reinforced this message with its futuristic, shifting steel circles: let's leave the past and move into the future. The postcards reappeared, as witty mimes having contemporary fun with outdated stereotypical national images. And then there was the winning song, building like the peace process itself, from a solo voice to four-part harmony and full orchestra, singing of simple gratitude for life itself.

It only just won: the voting was among the most

exciting ever. Spain's super-catchy, cute *Su Canción (Your Song)*, sung by graceful Peruvian-born Betty Missiego plus four children, was leading going into the last vote – from Spain itself, who awarded Israel the points that gave it victory. In third place was former winner Anne-Marie David with the enigmatic *Je suis l'Enfant Soleil (I am the Sun-Child)*, a fine lyric put across with her usual skill. And then fourth...

It didn't seem the most tactful thing for Germany to enter a contest in Israel with a song about Genghis Khan. But that's what they did – and the audience gave Ralph Siegel and Bernd Meinunger's classic Eurovision romp a hearty round of applause. That shows the mood of the time: a robust determination to move forward, not to get enmired in affront, however unspeakable the sins of the past.

All these four songs were outstanding in their own Eurovision ways. Britain's entry was rather less outstanding. It had been chosen by juries listening to tapes, because the actual televised event to select the entry had been cancelled due to an industrial dispute about which trades union the person operating the electronic scoreboard should belong to. Winter 1978 saw the nation plunged into disorder by waves of strikes, often 'wildcat' ones called at short notice. Britain's voters decided this really was Rock Bottom, and a month after Eurovision 1979 voted for Margaret Thatcher. The rest of Western Europe was watching, and a new tone of respect for the

121

marketplace and distrust of national deals between organized labour and organized capital began to enter political discourse all round the half-continent.

1979 also saw elections to the European Parliament. Back in 1957 (the year from which we have those first, black and white videos of Corry Brokken and Sem Nijveen), the Treaty of Rome had stated that a European Parliament should be directly elected by the voters of the EEC. However this hadn't happened. Instead, the body still consisted of selected members of their country's parliaments. Finally, in a bizarre piece of Euro-politics, the Parliament threatened to take the Council of Ministers to the European Court of Justice to get the Council to allow it to have proper Europe-wide elections.

Turnout varied across Europe: in Charlemagne's empire it was high, as it was in Ireland; in the more sceptical Denmark it was below 50% and sulky Britain only managed 34%. The result was a balanced house: the largest party was the Party of European Socialists (PES), but two conservative groupings came next, the European People's Party (EPP) and the more Eurosceptic European Democrats. The PES and the EPP are still the main players in the European Parliament today; the European Democrats fell apart in the late 1980s.

The new parliament held its first session on 11 July. Maybe inspired by Margaret Thatcher's victory, it elected a woman president, French Holocaust survivor Simone Veil. Veil came from a small party, the Liberals. This is the

European way: compromise, rather than simply putting the biggest beast in the biggest party in charge.

East of the Iron Curtain, people didn't bother with this messy democracy business – but at least they had Intervision. The 1979 contest took place from 22 to 25 August, and again came up with a winner who was both eminent and independently minded. Poland's Czeslaw Niemen had written protest songs in 1968. After the clampdown, he switched to progressive rock. The main track from his 1969 album *Enigmatic* was based on a 19th century work by the bohemian Romantic poet Cyprian Norwid: later he recorded with members of John McLaughlin's Mahavishnu Orchestra – as well as singing and composing, Niemen was a fine keyboard player. There is now a statue of him in the Polish city of Kielce. I can't think of any Eurovision winners from this era with similar credentials (Teach-in's plans to record with Karlheinz Stockhausen never came to anything). There was much less division between high and low culture in Eastern Europe; even the bouncy Alla Pugacheva made a hit record out of Shakespeare's Sonnet 90.

The 1970s looked to be ending on a loud, proud note for the boss nation of Intervision. Oil-rich, admired in the third world while keeping its own empire quiet – what could go wrong for the Soviet Union?

On December 27, Russian special forces stormed the Tajbeg Palace in Kabul, and captured the Afghan president Hafizullah Amin, who had only recently ousted a pro-

Soviet incumbent, Nur Muhammad Taraki. The aim of Operation Storm 333 was to remove Amin, put a new, pro-Soviet man in his place, then retreat. It would all be over by Karl Marx's birthday.

The intervention would turn into a dirty war that lasted nearly a decade: Russia's Vietnam. The Afghan campaign would sap the resources and morale of the invading nation. It would inject further poison into already deteriorating east/west relationships, once again raising the threat of nuclear conflict in Europe. In the even longer run, it would both radicalize and arm men like Osama bin Laden: the horrific mid-2000s terror attacks in Madrid and London had their genesis on December 27, 1979. The hopes of the Eurovision audience in the Binyanei Ha-ouma Convention Centre would be dashed by these events, too: instead of drawing together slowly towards a modern, amicable solution, the Middle East would split apart again as old hatreds and fanaticisms, apparently extinguished in 1979, reignited.

The 1980s

1980

Date: 19 April
Venue: Congresgebouw, Den Haag, Netherlands
Debut: Morocco
Winner: Johnny Logan, Ireland
Winning Song: *What's another Year?*

The grim economic climate brought about by the second oil price shock of 1979 meant that no-one really wanted to host Eurovision 1980. The Dutch ended up volunteering. They have been reliable, undemonstrative supporters of things European since the start, despite not getting any special goodies out of the EEC: one can argue that France got the power and the agricultural subsidies, Belgium and Luxembourg got the economic boost from new institutions sited within their borders and Germany and Italy got forgiveness for the war, but it's harder to see what special benefits the Dutch got – apart, perhaps, from a nice warm feeling of *gezelligheid.*

1980's most interesting Eurovision entries came from peripheral nations. Turkey's entry began with tabla drums and Middle-Eastern scales, and stayed that way. The singer, Adja Pekkan, talked of a difficult, love-hate relationship with her lover, *Pet'r Oil.* (The francophone nations, usually chief suppliers of intelligent lyrics, came up with nothing to match this.) Morocco made its debut – Israel was not contesting this year, as the date clashed with *Yom HaZikaron*, the nation's military Remembrance Day, so the North African nation felt able to participate. Samira Saïd sang a rather standard Eurovision entry, *Love Card*. Neither Pekkan nor Saïd did very well in the contest, but both have gone on to be superstars in their own cultures. After *Love Card's* poor performance (it came second last), Morocco withdrew from the contest and has never ventured into Eurovision since.

Norway, as often, provided the most unusual entry: *Samiid Aednan (Land of the Sami)*, based on a Sami yoik chant. The Sami, sometimes referred to as the Lapps, are the semi-nomadic inhabitants of Norway's northern regions, and the song was linked to protests about plans to build a dam and flood part of these traditional lands. The protests had come to a head with a hunger strike by activists in front of the Norwegian parliament in Autumn 1979. Behind these protests was an even deeper discontent: at the time, Oslo was still carrying out the sinister-sounding policy of 'Norwegianization', an attempt to assimilate the Sami into the national mainstream that had started in the early part of the century. At the height of this policy back in the 1930s, Sami had been unable to buy land, and even in 1970 children were not allowed to speak the language in schools (even in playtime). The new decade would see the policy abandoned; in 1997, Norway's King Harald V would apologize to the Sami for its ever having been carried out.

And then there was Ireland: 1980 was another triumph

for the periphery as Johnny Logan won with his ballad (ably assisted by fellow-Celt, Scottish saxophonist Colin Tully). *What's another Year?* sold well around Europe.

The centre's contribution to the proceedings was lightweight, except as a barometer of fashion and musical trends. The Netherlands' Maggie MacNeal introduced us to the decade's big hair and big make-up, and Belgium's Kraftwerk-inspired Telex put synthesizers centre stage: a new development for the contest. 'Synthpop' would become a major aspect of 1980s popular music, taking the focus away from the electric guitar for the first time since 1963.

An exception to the centre's poor showing was Germany. Katja Ebstein sang *Theater*, another camp classic from Ralf Siegel and Bernd Meinunger, whose second place inched Europe's economic leader one notch nearer the Eurovision winners' podium.

Siegel and Meinunger also wrote Luxembourg's 1980 entry, *Papa Pingouin*, which was a classic in a different, so-bad-it's-good Eurovision way: the song never recovered any dignity it might have had when a backing singer in a giant penguin outfit tripped over a stair eleven bars into it. So was the song a dismal failure? *Papa Pingouin* went on to sell a million copies in France. However, virtually none of the proceeds went to the two young singers, Sophie and Magaly Gilles. Sadder still, life did not turn out well for the pretty, chirpy Parisienne sisters. Sophie contracted HIV in the late 1980s, and died in 1996, after which Magaly became a recluse.

AIDS, which would overshadow the decade, was unheard-of in 1980. In 1981, the first abnormal cluster of otherwise healthy men contracting a rare form of pneumonia was noted by doctors in Los Angeles. The condition would acquire its name in 1982, and the virus responsible would be isolated by scientists at the Pasteur Institute in Paris in 1983. However public knowledge would lag behind: Britain was the first European nation to prioritize AIDS awareness, with TV advertising in 1986. France, Italy and Spain were slower to react – would Sophie Gilles have lived had they moved faster? Those countries still have substantially higher levels of HIV in their populations. A diagnosis of HIV positive would remain a virtual death sentence until 1997, when the Highly Active Anti-Retroviral Therapy (HAART) 'triple cocktail' of drugs was perfected, which successfully prevented the development of 'full-blown' AIDS. A year too late for Sophie.

Third place in Eurovision 1980 went to Britain with *Love enough for Two*. That nation's new premier did not feel that way about Europe's budget. Britain's per capita GDP was lower than that of most other EEC members, but, because the budgetary rules were skewed by the CAP, it had to make the second highest contribution to the EEC pot. The battle over this would come to a climax in 1984, and rumble on for years afterwards.

East of the Iron Curtain, August 1980 saw the fourth

Intervision Song Contest. It was won by Finland's Marion Rung, who had entered two weak songs for Eurovision in 1962 and 1973, but produced a much better one here, the ballad *Hyvästi Yö (Goodbye Night)*. Finland had a unique position in Cold War politics (mirrored, perhaps, by Yugoslavia). After a bitter war with Stalin, the Scandinavian nation had signed its own treaty with Russia in 1948. It did not accept post-war US aid (the Marshall plan) or join NATO; there were close economic ties between it and its imperialist neighbour. But it retained political and economic freedom, and acted as a bridge between east and west – it's no accident the 1975 Accords had been signed in Helsinki. Until the collapse of Communism, Finland continued to have to look both ways politically, hence its participation in both song contests. (Talking of Yugoslavia, which had not entered Eurovision since 1976, May 4 1980 saw the death of its leader, Tito, a ruthless man but one around whom the country unified. With his death, the slow countdown to the horrors of the mid-1990s began.)

1980 was the last Intervision. The reason could not have been more significant: the breakup of the Soviet empire started just down the road from Sopot, on August 14, when workers at Gdansk's Lenin shipyard went on strike.

Unrest had been bubbling in Poland (and especially on its Baltic coast) since riots about food prices in 1970 and 1976. In 1979, the newly-elected Polish pope had visited the country and given its people a new rallying-point, a reminder that there were older, deeper ethical codes than those of Communism.

On August 7 1980, Anna Walentynowicz, a former shipyard 'model worker' turned activist was dismissed for belonging to a then illegal trades union, the WZZ. Her colleagues went on strike. This soon grew into a wider protest about many issues: on August 31, the government agreed to a charter featuring 21 demands, including freedom of speech, an improved healthcare system and recognition for the union as an entity independent of the Communist Party. Getting these put into practice proved more difficult; social unrest continued, including a brief but effective nationwide strike in March 1981, by which time the Solidarity union, which had been formed in the aftermath of the 1980 strike, had millions of members all over Poland. It was as a result of this unrest that Intervision 1981 was cancelled.

Later in the year, the country's new leader, General Wojciech Jaruzelski, declared martial law, some claim in order to prevent a more draconian intervention from Moscow. Union leaders were sent to prison – but the nation's mood had changed. Solidarity's call had been heard in other Eastern European countries, too. The wind of change was blowing through the old Intervision empire.

1981

Date: 4 April
Venue: Simmonscourt Pavilion, Dublin, Ireland
Debut: Cyprus
Winner: Bucks Fizz, UK
Winning Song: *Making your Mind up*.

Johnny Logan's win in 1980 had been a triumph for Europe's periphery, and Ireland's staging of the next contest was another one. No expense was spared and the small island showed its growing potential to punch above its weight. The era of Ireland the Celtic Tiger was still a decade away, but the presentation of Eurovision 1981, especially the lighting, foreshadows that era – as does the confident Celtic rock of the interval act, Planxty, which also looks forward to the Eurovision of the 1990s.

Of course, there was plenty of Euro-comedy, too. An Austrian lady singing in an American football helmet. Reggae (of a sort) from Finland. Luxembourg singing about how wonderful it is to be French. Robotic dancers from Portugal. A classic voting moment. "Good evening, Yugoslavia." Silence. "Good evening, Yugoslavia." More silence. Finally, an answer, so Doireann Ni Bhriain asks for their votes. "I don't have it," comes the reply.

The contest belonged to Europe's big players, with the UK winning, helped by the neat skirt-removing trick half way through *Making your Mind up*. Germany came second again, again courtesy of Siegel and Meinunger. France went back to thoughtful lyrics and was rewarded with third place: looking back at the world from 3,000 AD – didn't there use to be flowers, love (and so on)? Yes, but that was before The War. The comment, courtesy of Tahitian singer Jean Gabilou and the songwriting duo behind Marie Myriam's 1977 winner, Jean-Paul Cara and José Graciano, was timely, with a new, hawkish President in the White House and nuclear weapons building up on both sides of the Iron Curtain.

The Irish trio Sheeba came fifth, bemoaning how people rely on horoscopes. Work to create your own life outcomes, they said instead – sentiments in tune with the new decade, both in their stress on self-reliance and their rejection of pseudo-science.

Back in 1963, with the white heat of technology intending to burn away the old Europe and its antiquated, unscientific ways, horoscopes had looked doomed. But the late sixties changed all that… Horoscopes stayed a part of 1970s popular culture, which was unworldly and technophobic – as the writers of *Ding dinge dong* had understood). But now it was the 1980s, and Europe seemed eager to get more real and to embrace technology again.

There was, at last, an exciting new technology to embrace. Large corporations had been using mainframe computers for a while to perform traditional clerical and complex computational functions. 1981 saw the US launch of the IBM PC, the first widely-available 'computer on a desk'. Software for these machines would soon follow, which would help small-business and private users with databases, accounts and word-processing. A new economic era was dawning; at its heart, the remorseless binary logic of the silicon chip.

Politically, the new decade seemed to be moving to the right. However this trend was not Europe-wide. 1981 saw the election of Greece's first Socialist government for nearly half a century, under the charismatic Andreas Papendreou. A month after Eurovision 1981, France voted François Mitterrand into presidential office. Mitterrand's campaign had been based on the Cartesian-sounding '110 Propositions for France'. These included newly-unfashionable Keynesian government spending to boost the economy, abolition of the death penalty, a wealth tax and a 35 hour working week, as well as odder notions such as control of the building of supermarkets. Europe did not feature greatly in the Propositions, though number 41 did call for the reform of the CAP, which was continuing to gobble the EEC's resources.

The new France would not be technophobic, however. Minitel, a unique proto-internet run by the French post office, made its national debut in 1981. The first TGV express ran on September 27, halving the journey time from Paris to Lyon. Both were, of course, the creations of an earlier administration, but France's new rulers kept faith with them. In their first full year, *Trains à Grande Vitesse* carried 6 million passengers. A decade later the figure would be 40 million.

But all was not joy in the once-again-technophilic Europe. Two months after the TGV began barrelling its way down to Lyon, the German magazine *Der Spiegel* started running articles about *Waldsterben*, the widespread deaths of trees in the Black Forest. Half the forest was in immediate danger, the articles claimed. The culprit was 'acid rain', sulphur dioxide spewed out by power plants, refineries and ironworks.

Waldsterben stayed in German headlines from then on. It hit deep into Germany's identity, which was (and still is) intricately bound up with the nation's great forests; their witchy mystery, their protection (the Germanic tribes had driven out the Romans with forest ambushes) and their opportunities for healthy hiking and fresh air. Most scary of all, acid rain ignored national boundaries. Germany could go as green as it liked, but this stuff would still come floating over from other countries. This made another powerful argument for the centralization of political power in Europe.

Just as Katja Ebstein and Fred Jay had warned us, ten years before.

1982

Date: 24 April
Venue: Conference Centre, Harrogate, UK
Debuts: None (none till 1986)
Winner: Nicole, Germany
Winning Song: *Ein bisschen Frieden (A little Peace).*

The theme of this book is that Eurovision gives us accurate snapshots of history as it unfolds, and nowhere is this more true than in 1982. Probably the gentle young woman asking for a little peace did not impress the feisty female activists then encamped round US missile bases at Britain's Greenham Common, but for many Western Europeans, Nicole's *Ein bisschen Frieden* hit the bullseye. I don't want these weapons or this warmongering; I want to live my life in peace; I'm scared; what the hell do I do?

By an elegant irony, last place – and not just any old last place, but the full *nul points* – also went to a song protesting the Cold War, Finland's Kojo with *Nuku Pommiin (Sleep till the Bomb).* The song featured a rock guitar solo, the first, I think, in the contest. Rock from Finland in Eurovision? No, it'll never work.

Russia and America were both filling their halves of Europe with missiles; Russia with newly-built ones, America bringing in existing ones from elsewhere. A new weapon was in production, too: the neutron bomb, which would kill people with radiation but do less damage to infrastructure. The western left portrayed this as a product of capitalism, but these monstrous things were being just as eagerly constructed by the followers of Marx and Lenin. Europe, as usual, was pig in the middle.

A glimmer of hope came on November 10, with the death of Russia's aged premier, Leonid Brezhnev. His younger replacement, Yuri Andropov, made peaceful approaches to the West. These were rejected by the newly elected US president Ronald Reagan. Reagan's supporters argued that words were cheap. They argued that Russia was producing ever more nuclear warheads; the destructive capacity of its arsenal had risen from just over 5,000 to 7,000 megatons between 1980 and 1982 (America's level remained constant over this time, around 4,000 megatons). Still, would a more Nicole-influenced response to the new leader have changed this?

Andropov (and Europe) didn't get one, anyway. In March 1983 Reagan would make his famous speech denouncing Russia's 'evil empire' and would announce his 'Star Wars' missile shield – over America: Europe would have to look after itself.

A war featuring a European nation was actually happening when Eurovision 1982 took place. On March 19, a group of scrap metal merchants arrived on the remote island of South Georgia in the South Atlantic. Not startling news, perhaps – but the land belonged to Britain, and the new arrivals hoisted an Argentinean flag. A week later, Argentinean soldiers joined them. The Falkland Islands were invaded on April 2, and the small British garrison had no option but to surrender. A fleet of 127 vessels was then dispatched from Britain. As Nicole sang for a little peace, this mighty armada was making its way into the South Atlantic.

The rest of Europe was not impressed by Britain's response, especially Latin Europe. Spain's Eurovision entry featured the Argentine national dance, a tango. Britain's *One Step Further* fared poorly, despite being a perfectly good song.

The war that followed was hard-fought but brief. Around 1,000 combatants died (unlike almost all other wars, there were few civilian casualties), including 323 people on the *General Belgrano*, an Argentine cruiser. The sinking of this vessel was controversial – but such, surely, is war: messy, vicious and tragic.

Another 1982 contestant also went to war shortly after the contest. Israel invaded Lebanon on June 6. This was a much bloodier business than the Falklands, with massacres at two refugee camps (largely by Lebanese 'Christian' forces) its nadir. Israel initially hoped that the war would drive terrorist organizations out of its northern neighbour and bring 'forty years of peace'. The effect was the opposite. The optimism of Eurovision 1979 at the Binyanei Ha-ouma Convention Centre was already becoming a distant memory.

Yet for many Europeans, life was getting better, largely thanks to the decade's reconnection to technology. Denmark's 1982 Eurovision entry was *Video Video*, about a young man hooked on this new invention. Basic video cassette recorders could now be bought for the equivalent of about 100 Euros. These machines subtly changed European life: gone would be the days when streets fell silent whenever popular programmes like Eurovision were aired, and with that would disappear the workplace ritual of discussing them next Monday morning. It was a tiny decoupling from a shared social ritual towards more convenient but more private experiences.

Other chip-based gadgets were appearing, too. The microwave oven began to appear in kitchens around this date. Some commentators argue that this made European men do more cooking, and thus played a role in the 'feminization' of Europe. It certainly saved time for European women, who, despite feminization, were still responsible for most domestic work. Its effect on the European diet was less beneficial.

Outside the kitchen, young Europeans could play space invaders on the new Atari 2600 console, though this was best not done on early-80's polyester shagpile carpets: static electricity caused the console to malfunction. The classic Sony Walkman WM2 had been launched in 1981, as had the world's first fully-automatic network for portable phones, in Scandinavia ('portable' by early 1980s standards: the set was the size of a small suitcase). The chip revolution was underway, and with it a new era of economic growth.

Apart from the quality of its winner, which went on to sell around Europe, perhaps the most notable thing about Eurovision 1982 was the absence of a previously regular participant, France. The new regime wanted to show its class, culturally as well as ideologically. "This so-called pop music competition," said Jack Lang, Mitterrand's Minister for Culture, "is a monument to drivel."

But it was Germany's contest, anyway. As well as being an excellent song, *Ein bisschen Frieden* was beautifully presented. Alongside his gift for melody and counter-melody, Ralf Siegel was a master stager of performances, while (usually) avoiding extravagant dance routines or irrelevant props. Many other 1982 entries tried to reprise Bucks Fizz and featured gyrating couples in primary-coloured outfits made from fabrics that one shouldn't put too close to a radiator. Nicole wore a simple black and white dress, strummed a white 12-string guitar, looked into the camera and sang with conviction. Half the juries – including Israel, the first time they had done this for a German entry – gave her *douze points*.

On October 1, the winning nation had a new chancellor, Helmut Kohl, a portly, pragmatic Christian Democrat and keen supporter of European integration. The big European national leaders of the decade, Thatcher, Mitterrand and Kohl, were now in place (Kohl would outlast the others, remaining in office until 1998). The fourth giant of 1980s European politics was currently Mitterrand's Minister of Finance, but more of Jacques Delors later.

1983

Date: 23 April
Venue: Rudi Sedlmayer Hall, Munich, Germany
Winner: Corinne Hermès, Luxembourg
Winning Song: *Si la Vie est Cadeau (If Life is a Gift…)*

The 1983 contest was held in a hall named after the former President of the Bavarian Sports Association. There's something delightfully old-fashioned-German about that: this man was an Important Official. In 2016, the venue is sponsored and called the Audi Dome, which tells its own story, too.

The show was hosted by Marlene Charrell, who made every announcement in French, German and English. This made it a long evening, and showed the practical difficulty of a theoretically admirable policy of multilingualism. It was 16 minutes into the broadcast before the first note of a competing song was heard.

The contest is not a classic, so tends to be remembered for its worst aspects: the interminable announcements; the announcer joining in the interval entertainment; two classic *nul points* entries.

Opera by Turkey's Çetin Alp and the Short Waves is often cited as the worst Eurovision entry ever – but maybe it was just twenty years ahead of its time. It was certainly bizarre: the piece segues from a tribute to Western

European opera to a Dixieland jazz middle section, then back again to Western opera. The unfortunate Alp received a barrage of criticism on return to Turkey. He had let the nation down in front of people it was eager to impress. He appears to have led a reclusive life afterwards.

If you want to be really clever about this, you can read *Opera* as a comment about Kemal Ataturk (the nation's president from 1923 to 1938) and his forcing Turkey to modernize and become a European state. Part of this involved setting up a national opera, after which Ataturk commissioned three operas about himself. Is Alp questioning the wisdom of this? Or celebrating it? Or did he just like opera and Dixieland?

1983's other nul pointer came from Spain's Remedios Amaya. *¿Quién maneja mi Barca? (Who's sailing my Boat?)* is most charitably seen as an attempt to merge Flamenco, in which Amaya was a respected artist, with Eurovision. It didn't work, but unlike poor, disgraced Çetin Alp, she went back to her roots and continued to achieve success in her chosen genre.

Hi (Alive) from Israel celebrated Jewish traditions passed down across generations – in front of an audience in a country which 30 years ago tried to eradicate those traditions in the most vicious manner imaginable, and in a city where a decade ago terrorists fuelled by similar hatred had murdered 11 Israeli athletes.

The winning song was a ballad, probably not the best winner of its kind, but well sung. There is a line in it where

143

the singer laments the child she was going to give her unfaithful lover, come the spring. I've always wondered if this was a reference to abortion; it would make the title particularly heartfelt.

It seems that abortion numbers were rising in Western Europe during the last decades of the twentieth century, though accurate figures are hard to come by. This can be used to point a moralizing finger at us, but rates were still lower here than in the rest of the world. A study done in 1995 by the New York-based Guttmacher Institute and reprinted in Britain's ultra-respectable *Lancet* magazine showed that Western, Northern and (to a lesser extent) Southern Europe had lower levels of abortion than anywhere else. Eastern Europe, by contrast, had rates above the global average (and three times higher than that in the west of the continent).

After Monsieur Lang's comments about Eurovision, one might have expected a long absence by France, but 1983 saw Marianne return to the drivel monument, with the rather old-fashioned *Vivre (To live)*. The nation had to do similar *voltes-face* in political policy. President Mitterrand found his currency under attack from global speculators. In June 1982, the Franc was downgraded 10% against the Deutschmark. In March 1983, after a defeat for his party in local elections, its value began to tumble again. Mitterrand was faced with a dilemma. He could leave the European Monetary System, the mechanism set up in 1979 to keep European currencies in step with one another, but this would mean admitting to being a second-rate European power. Or he could do a deal with the Germans, whereby they revalued the Mark and France stayed in the EMS. Germany insisted on austerity measures as a precondition of the deal, and Mitterrand accepted. This was, arguably, the moment when European leadership began passing east across the Franco-German border. Revolving sounds were heard from General de Gaulle's grave.

Not that there was much 'Europe' to lead at that time. In 1983, the EEC was still suffering from the sclerosis imposed by the Luxembourg Compromise back in 1966, with its insistence on unanimous votes on major decisions. CAP spending was spiralling out of control; Britain was clamouring for a rebate on its contribution; Spain and Portugal wanted to join the club but nobody could agree how or when. A meeting of the European Council in Athens in December 1983 found itself unable to agree even on the blandest *communiqué* to sum up its proceedings.

Meanwhile, the Cold War kept getting colder. On August 31 1983, the Russians shot down a Korean airliner, KAL 007, that had strayed over the Kamchatka Peninsula, killing all 269 passengers and crew. Three weeks later, World War Three nearly broke out.

On the evening of 25 September, Lt-Col Stanislav Petrov was manning the Soviet early warning system in its bunker south of Moscow, when a warning light went on. The US, apparently, had launched a missile. Then another. Then three more. The current Soviet plan at the time was to launch massive retaliation if attacked – but was this a real attack? Petrov had almost no time to decide, but had a gut feeling that the alarm was false: why would America just launch five missiles? He followed his intuition; the 'missiles' later disappeared from the screen. Europe woke up on the morning of 26 September with its population and cities intact, but it had been a close thing. The new K and K Calypso as *Totentanz*, as the Dance of Death.

The incident was not revealed to the world till 1990, but Europe was angry about the missiles, anyway. Across the continent October 22, 1983, was a day of protest, with huge marches in Belgium, Britain, France, Italy, Spain and, especially, West Germany, where a million people are estimated to have taken to the streets.

As Eurovision said, *Ein bisschen Friede, bitte.*

1984

Date: 5 May
Venue: Théâtre Municipal, Luxembourg
Winner: Herreys, Sweden
Winning Song: *Diggi-loo, diggi-ley*

Kooky presenter Désirée Nosbusch gave George Orwell a name-check in her intro to Eurovision 1984. The winning song would probably have brought a wry smile to the face of the great novelist, whose classic *1984* predicted, amongst other things, the existence of Prolesec, a department of the Ministry of Truth which churned out mindless entertainment for the masses, known as Prolefeed. Along with newspapers full of sport, crime and astrology, sexy films and sensational novels, Prolesec produced sentimental songs, with words composed on a machine called a versifier which combined random clichés. Both *Diggi-loo* and *diggi-ley* would no doubt have qualified for feeding into this machine.

Orwell's dystopic vision also involved three massive power blocs, perpetually at war: Eurasia, Eastasia and Oceania. Orwell's Eurasia maps spookily onto the area participating in the 21st century Eurovision Song Contest (Britain is the main exception, being part of Oceania with the Americas and the old white Commonwealth). From Charlemagne's Holy Roman Empire to Big Brother's Eurasia?

147

Like the earlier winner it is often compared to, *Ding dinge dong, Diggi-loo, diggi-ley* opened the show. It set the tone: bright primary colours (red was a particular favourite for 1984), clean-cut performers, slick performance – the three Mormon brothers put on a great show. It spoke for its era: if *Ding dinge dong* had evoked the previous decade's sense of a lost, dippy but attractive past, *Diggi-loo, diggi-ley* bubbled with mid-eighties optimism. The bad times are over; things are working well again; dream it and you can do it – as long as you have the right shoes.

The 1984 contest is best remembered for other things than the songs. The 'postcards' were quirky and imaginative. Désirée was a fun presenter, casually dressed in contrast to many of the performers, and genuinely European: she spoke four languages and solved the problem that had defeated Marlene Charrell by flowing effortlessly between them during the evening (ironically, she actually lived in the USA at the time, though she had been born and raised in Luxembourg). At the end of the show, she said 'see you next Saturday'. Many male viewers probably wished that would be the case.

And then there was the booing… Eurovision audiences have sat politely through *Boom boom Boomerang* and *Opera*, but the Motown-influenced UK entry *Love Games* proved too much for a section of the crowd at the *Théâtre Municipal*. The main reason was memories of the previous November, when English football hooligans had run riot in the Grand Duchy (not for the first time: back in 1977, England fans had damaged the Luxembourg national stadium). Maybe the booers were also protesting Margaret Thatcher's dogged insistence on her CAP rebate. Or perhaps they didn't like Motown. The boos certainly reveal a cultural clash: Luxembourg regularly wins polls for being the most European-minded nation in the EU, while Britain usually comes last.

The battle of Britain's EEC budget contribution was finally settled in 1984. François Mitterrand had taken over the six-monthly Presidency of the European Council at the beginning of the year, and decided to get political Europe moving again. Sorting out the rebate was part of that. The process of admitting Spain and Portugal to the club was put in motion. Some attempt was made to tackle the CAP and its mountains and lakes. CAP spending actually continued to grow in the late 1980s, but this was because of the new members. Less cash ended up in France, which made Mitterrand unpopular back home. However he stuck to his guns on these essential reforms.

The Cold War remained intense during 1984 – but on December 10, a senior Soviet politician called Mikhail Gorbachev gave a speech to a Communist Party conference on ideology, calling for *glasnost* (openness) and *perestroika* (economic reform). Shortly after that, he visited Britain, and in March 1985, he was elected General Secretary of the Party.

1985

Date: 4 May
Venue: Scandinavium, Gothenburg, Sweden
Winner: Bobbysocks, Norway
Winning Song: *La det swinge*

The peripheral, Eurosceptic Nordics always go to town on Eurovision. The 1985 contest was the most spectacular to date. 8,000 people attended: the capacity of the previous year's venue had been less than 1,000. Another contrast with 1984 was the announcements. Lill Lindfors – dressed and made up to the nines – introduced most of the songs in English (beneath a large sign reading 'Eurovision Song Contest'). The songs (by and large) had a modern, professional edge to them. Even the one that came last, *Laat me nu gaan (Let me go now)* by Belgium's Linda Lepomme, was pleasant and well sung, just a bit dull. When the results were announced, there were no French-language entries in the top five (or, actually, the top nine). These differences all go to make 1985 feel like the first modern event.

This new-look Eurovision was a northern affair. Britain's Vikki came fourth, telling us what *Love is*. She is now better known as New Age artiste and composer Aeone – a journey many people were to make once the material-girl 1980s gave way to the 1990s. Above her came Sweden's Kikki Danielsson with *Bra Vibrationer* (the title actually just means

150

Good Vibrations) and Germany's Wind, with *Für alle (For everyone)*, one of those let's-all-be-nice-to-each-other ESC specials. Bouncing up to the winner's podium were Norway's female duo Bobbysocks, with Rolf Løvland's Abba-ish jive. The Land of the Midnight Sun and of Jahn Teigen's Braces had finally won!

By contrast, political Europe remained a centre project. 1985 saw Jacques Delors, a former banker, trades unionist, state planner and MEP, become President of the European Commission. Like his countryman's presidency of the European Council the previous year, this gave 'Europe' a new energy. Delors was to stay in the job for ten years, during which political Europe effectively became the EU we now know and love (or hate, or – the most common reaction according to polls – feel mildly positive about). He oversaw the implementation of the Single Market and of EU citizenship, worked to introduce social legislation, and expanded Europe's two 'Structural Funds' (the European Social Fund, set up back in 1958, which largely funds training, and the European Regional Development Fund, founded in 1974, which helps finance job creation). Most significant of all, he drove the move to the creation of a common currency.

On June 14, five of the seven original contestants from Lugano (Italy and Switzerland were the non-participants) signed an agreement at Schengen in Luxembourg to remove all borders between each other. Like the EEC/EU, this zone would later be expanded. The agreement would become part of EU law in 1999.

All EEC nations were involved in drafting the Single European Act, the text of which was finalized at a European Council meeting in December 1985. This was essentially about creating a true Common Market in Europe, the 'Single Market', with free movement of goods, services, capital and labour. The Act was extremely thorough, specifying 282 measures needed to bring this about. The aim was to have these in place by 31 December 1992, and a special '1992 Programme' was launched to push them along the obstacle course of national and Europe-level legislative change they would face. The decision-making apparatus of EEC-level government was also speeded up, with more majority voting and less Gaullist insistence on unanimity. Britain, usually lacking in Euro-enthusiasm, was an eager participant in this process. Margaret Thatcher was keen to increase trade, and the man who did most to both write and implement the act was Arthur Cockfield, a British commissioner.

1985 also saw political Europe formally adopt its flag, the twelve gold stars on a blue background (the flag had been used by the Council of Europe since the 1950s), and its anthem, Beethoven's setting of Schiller's *Ode to Joy* (Eurovision fans still think Charpentier's *Marche en Rondeau* would be a better one).

The rest of the decade can be seen as a high point of European federalist idealism, on a par with those idealistic, late forties/early fifties days of Jean Monnet and Robert Schuman. Delors worked tirelessly to turn the long-dreamt-of European currency into a reality. A committee would be set up in 1988 under his leadership, to work out how this should best come about. In 1989 it would report, suggesting three stages towards complete monetary union. There would be a common currency issued by a European central bank, and rules on national government borrowing to ensure no one nation could devalue the currency by mismanaging its finances. Sadly, little attention was paid to cultural differences in this technocratic report.

Part of the motivation behind the monetary union project was a desire to get away from the inconvenience of national exchange rates, which made both commercial and 'Eurocratic' planning difficult (and sometimes embarrassed good loyal European nations whose economies weren't as robust as that of Germany). But the quiet driver of it all was the conviction that monetary union would lead to political union. Once nations share a currency, how much control can their governments have over interest rates, levels of borrowing or even tax regimes? Monetary union was never just about economics.

In November, the new K and K, Mikhail Gorbachev and Ronald Reagan, met for the first time. There was a high level of suspicion on both sides, but the two leaders began to develop a personal understanding. Both agreed 'a nuclear war cannot be won and must never be fought'. The missiles remained on Europe's soil, however.

1986

Date: 3 May
Venue: Grieghalle, Bergen, Norway
Debut: Iceland
Winner: Sandra Kim, Belgium
Winning Song: *J'aime la Vie (I love Life)*

Like Sweden, Norway welcomed Eurovision with great enthusiasm. The host city of Bergen was *en fête* for the entire week before. The Norwegian Royal Family attended the contest, which took place in a mythological 'ice palace' that glowed with the various pastel shades shone into it. And Åse Kleveland sang her famous 'Soon we will know who'll be the best…' version of the Eurovision theme.

1986 saw another move towards the modern competition, with the orchestra playing less and less a part in the proceedings. Some acts dispensed with it altogether, replacing it with lead and bass guitars, keyboards (including a transparent grand piano), saxophones and white hexagonal syn-drums – 1986 was the year of the syn-drum.

1986 was also the year of the francophone fight-back, with the three top songs in French. Not France's however, for whom Cocktail Chic sang of being modern *Europiennes*, moving between Paris and London and enjoying '*Musique USA*'. *Non!* said the judges, and put them 17th.

The north made its presence felt visually, without

greatly impressing the judges musically. Sweden's Lasse Holm and Monica Tornell sang in black, possibly out of respect for Olof Palme, who had been assassinated on February 28th.

The identity of Palme's killer remains a mystery. A loner convicted of the crime in 1988 was freed on appeal. Conspiracy theories abound. The South African government is in the frame, due to Palme's support for the African National Congress. Other suspects include Kurdish separatists, the Yugoslav Secret Service and Chilean fascists. The most bitterly ironic theory is the one that suggests his killing was a mistake: Palme was mistaken for a local drug dealer. As with JFK, we will probably never know the truth.

Norway's Ketil Stokkan sang about his failures as a *Romeo* with two dancers behind him from the Great Garlic Girls, a drag act founded, initially as a joke, by three members of Norway's gay community in 1981. This was the first drag act in the contest (unless you count Charlie Rivel, the bizarre clown/pantomime-dame interval entertainment from 1973). Iceland made its debut, the first new nation since 1981, with the imaginatively named trio Icy singing about *Gledibankinn* or *The Bank of Happiness*. Don't take out too much in one withdrawal, they recommended.

Such financial prudence was not on the menu in Britain, where October 1986 saw radical changes in the City of London, the most powerful financial centre in Europe. In what was called the 'Big Bang', fixed brokerage commissions were abolished, the old stock exchange floor was replaced by electronic trading, and regulations were relaxed. This set in motion a process whereby the world's major financial centres competed with one another to attract global capital by deregulating – which would have disastrous effects twenty-two years on. But in 1986, it just gave us the 'yuppie', that model 80s aggressive, acquisitive young professional. In many ways he or she was the polar opposite of the *soixante-huitard*, but both archetypes shared youth, arrogance and ideological certainty.

Yuppies weren't just to be found in London, but in Frankfurt, Paris, Milan... Their neo-liberal ideology was fast becoming the dominant one in Western Europe. Yuppies also believed in globalism, trading capital from around the world: the EEC, which looked a behemoth to old-fashioned nationalists, seemed too small to the globally-minded City young.

This change is often represented as a move to the right, but it was to a new liberal, anarcho-capitalist, global-minded right, not the old authoritarian/nationalist one. Yuppies believed strongly in individual freedom of choice. The old right had not gone away, however. France's 1986 elections saw Jean-Marie le Pen's right-wing *Front National* win 35 seats in the National Assembly. Austria was about to elect a man with a questionable Nazi past as its president. That country's Eurovision entrant, Timna Brauer, who was Jewish, was pressurized to pull out of the contest in protest at this, though she participated in the end – and came 18th out of 20.

In contrast, Germany's 1986 Eurovision entry was – as its entries often are – about building bridges between peoples and nations. Especially, of course, in its own split country: *Uber die Brüke gehen (Go over the Bridge)* also recommends the listener to open his or her mind by looking behind a wall. The wall that Ingrid Peters had in mind showed little sign of weakening, though the two sides that eyeballed one another across it looked ever less likely to obliterate each other. 1986 was the year of the explosion at the nuclear reactor at Chernobyl, an event which sapped the Soviet Union's already fading confidence even further. At a second summit, in the capital of Eurovision debutant Iceland, Messrs Reagan and Gorbachev found more personal chemistry. The idea that Germany might soon unite seemed a dream, however. Fine for a Eurovision song, but hardly realistic…

The contest was rounded off by *Não sejas mau para mim (Don't be mean to me)*, a pleasant, contemporary song from Portugal's Dora, in a ra-ra skirt and Doc Martens boots. Her home nation was now a member of the EEC, having joined on January 1. So had Spain, whose entry, *Valentino*, shared with Romeo and Switzerland's *Pas pour moi (Not for me)* the topic of men's attempts to seduce women and their lack of success. Eighties women had become more tough-minded than the sad-eyed girls of 1970. The Swiss entry came second, beaten only by Belgium's teenage Sandra

157

Kim, who purported to be 15 but later turned out to be 13. Switzerland tried to have Kim retrospectively thrown out, like an Olympic gold-medallist found guilty of taking drugs, but this came to nothing. Probably for the best: Kim's song, poppy, high-tech and a-bubble with *Diggi-loo diggi-ley* optimism, suited the era better. Switzerland and its song's composer, Attila Sereftug, would have their moment later.

As she introduced the voting, Åse Kleveland said she wished we could all participate in it, but at the moment this was not technologically feasible. However, technology was driving the new economic boom, filling people's homes with ever more gadgets and yuppies' wallets with ever more cash. Would it really enable us all to vote in Eurovision one day?

1987

Date: 9 May
Venue: Palais des Expositions, Brussels, Belgium
Debuts: None (no more till 1993)
Winner: Johnny Logan, Ireland
Winning Song: *Hold me now*

The contest took another leap forward in 1987, thanks to the magnificent laser show. A giant globe shimmered behind the singers; beams of multicoloured light cut through smoky air, creating different patterns for each singer (the home representative, Liliane St Pierre, had a particularly spectacular backdrop). Look back to only a few years before, let's say 1983, and consider the sea-change in the look of the show.

However 1987 is probably best remembered for Johnny Logan's victory, which made him the only person to win the contest twice – a record that still holds today. He has also written two winners, including this one. *Hold me now* remains popular with fans: in the 2005 poll of all-time contest favourites, it came third, behind *Waterloo* and *Volare*. It says something about the wonderful oddness of Eurovision that Logan's unparalleled achievement didn't really lead to success anywhere else. However he continues to sing professionally and has a couple of gold discs to put on his wall thanks to his wins. He is often referred to as

'Mr Eurovision'.

Elsewhere in the contest, Cyprus produced one of its better entries: *Aspro marvo (Black and white)*, where Alexia Vassiliou finds solace after a failed relationship by playing the piano. Belgian punk Plastic Bertrand reinvented himself as a Luxembourgeois Eurovision contestant, and got four points. *Nul points* went to Turkey, though with a much less bizarre offering than *Opera*. This was not a good omen for that nation's application to join the EEC, which had finally been filed a week beforehand. Brussels then took two years to say 'Non', or at least 'not yet'. By contrast, in July, former Eurovision contestant Morocco applied to join the Community but was quickly turned down on the grounds that it was not a European state.

1987 saw a crisis in funding for the new, expanding political Europe. The Brussels budget had doubled since 1980, and old ways of raising money – tariffs on imports from America, Japan or the Third World, plus a proportion of each nation's VAT – were no longer up to the job. Next year would see a new system introduced whereby nations contributed sums commensurate with their GDP. The richest nation, Germany, was happy to sign up to this because of its enthusiasm for the European project (Germany remains the biggest overall contributor to the EU, though if you look at contribution per member of the population, it is Europhile Luxemburgers and loyal Dutch who fork out most.)

Commercially, the eighties boom continued. October 19

saw a stock market crash around Europe (and the rest of the world) – spectacular at the time, but short-lived. A few traders tore out a few fistfuls of expensively coiffeured hair on the day itself, but capital markets soon regained lost ground and continued their relentless rise.

Behind the dominant materialism of the era, there was a more caring side: no decade is totally one-sided. The cause of AIDS awareness was greatly boosted by Princess Diana, who in 1987 shook hands with victims at the Middlesex Hospital: previously many, maybe even most, people had thought that the disease could be transmitted by such contact. 1987 also saw Domenico Modugno, of Volare fame, elected to the Italian parliament, where he became a fierce campaigner for the handicapped, physical and mental. He became particularly famous for his exposé of conditions in the psychiatric hospital at Agrigento in Sicily, and later performed a concert to raise money for former inmates.

1988

Date: 30 April
Venue: Simmonscourt Pavilion, Dublin, Ireland
Winner: Céline Dion, Switzerland
Winning Song: *Ne partez pas sans moi (Don't leave without me)*

The updating of Eurovision's look was effectively completed here, with the old-fashioned scoreboard getting a makeover: the new, computerized one flashed up onto a giant 'video wall' at the flick of a finger from co-presenter Pat Kenny. The set, designed by Paula Farrell and Michael Grogan, was as spectacular. Over the next few years, Irish broadcaster RTE would create a series of stunning sets, courtesy of Farrell (1988, 1994, 1997) and Alan Farquharson (1993, 1995). If Roland de Groot represented the second generation of Eurovision staging, Farrell and Farquharson are the stars of 3G, the stage no longer so much a 'set' as a three-dimensional world of its own, a fantasy kingdom of light and colour.

1988 is the year of Céline Dion. She went on to sell 220 million records worldwide, but she only won Eurovision by one point, after losing an early lead in the voting to UK singer Scott Fitzgerald then staging a late come-back. Turkey also won in 1988: not its own rather lame *Sufi*, but via the composer of the winning song, Atilla Sereftug. Sereftug is a perfect counterexample to the argument that

Turkey is incapable of being European. Trained in western classical music, he later got into jazz, especially the piano of George Shearing, and then – this was back in the late 1960s – rock. He moved to Switzerland in 1975. After his 1988 win, he worked in both Europe and his original homeland.

It is sometimes said that Eurovision did little to boost Dion's career. But she had just turned 20 when she won the contest. Her win enabled her manager to renegotiate the budget for her first anglophone album, Unison, quadrupling the record company's investment in her. That album went platinum in Canada and the USA, and she hasn't looked back since. *Merci, Eurovision.*

There were some other pleasant songs on offer (as well as a few clunkers: Eurovision wouldn't be Eurovision without these). Ralf Siegel and Bernd Meinunger's *Lied für einen Freund (Song for a Friend)* was, perhaps, now sounding a little old-fashioned, but, as always with these writers, professional. Norway's Karoline Krüger sang *For vår Jord (For our Earth)*, about a wild female spirit protecting the world, a theme that looked forward to the 'New Age' that was on its way. Austria's Wilfried Schütz was unlucky to pick up nul points – in my view, anyway, though a poll carried out in 2003 asked which *nul points* song least deserved the fate and put Schütz last, thus effectively voting *Lisa, Mona Lisa* the worst Eurovision song ever!

For the history-lover, the most intriguing thing about Eurovision 1988 was the interval act. The Irish group Hothouse Flowers were sent on a trip around Europe, to show the unity of the continent. The video actually showed the unity of half the continent: it did not occur to anyone to send them across the Iron Curtain. It would probably have been difficult to do this, though the contest was broadcast to the Soviet Union and its empire – but it's significant that in 1988 people said 'Europe' and thought of Western Europe. A whole Europe, united, with no barbed wire or watchtowers? Dream on…

One person who did dream on was Margaret Thatcher. In September 1988 she gave a speech to the College of Europe in Bruges, an elite postgraduate academy, many of whose students go on to become senior Brussels officials. The speech is often cited as a piece of venomous Euroscepticism – by people who haven't read the text. Sadly, it was spun as this to suit the prejudices of the UK media by her press secretary, Bernard Ingham, and some people in Brussels chose to pick up on the spin rather than the substance.

The speech is, of course, anti-federalist and anti-Socialist – it was at least partially given as a response to a speech by Jacques Delors, when he told British trades unionists that he envisaged Europe-wide social legislation as well as a Single Market. But it is not anti-European: it is 'intergovernmentalist', promoting a Gaullist '*Europe des patries*'. To say, as Mrs Thatcher does, that "We shall always look on Warsaw, Prague and Budapest as great European cities" was radical and prescient at the time, and remains a statement more of European idealism than of scepticism.

The Iron Lady later became much more critical of the European project. Like many leaders, she lingered in power too long and rather lost the plot at the end of her time (she was the first of the 1980s 'big three' to leave office, in November 1990). But it is odd that her speech is now so often misunderstood. Committed enthusiasts for a United States of Europe will not like it, of course. Maybe it blows the British trumpet louder than some might find tasteful. But it expresses a clear, positive vision of a view of Europe, both in what 'Europe' means and how its transnational institutions should work. Much of that vision subsequently became reality.

The dream of belonging to a truly continent-wide Europe was certainly not dismissed behind the Iron Curtain. Instead, it began to express itself in startling new ways. One of them was musical. Estonia – still a part of the Soviet Union – had a long history of song festivals, where thousands of people would gather to sing traditional tunes. There was even a purpose-built venue for these near the capital, Tallinn. Stalin had tried to change these events into Soviet propaganda-fests, but his censors oddly missed a song called *Mu ismaa on minu arm (Land of my fathers, land that I love)*, which everyone sung with much more gusto than the *Internationale*. (It was finally banned in 1969 – but people sang it at that year's festival anyway, despite attempts by a Russian military band to drown it out.)

Singing became a unique expression of optimism and pride in this small, occupied nation. Two weeks after

165

Eurovision 1988, a pop festival was held at its second city, Tartu, and the crowds began to sing patriotic songs by young composer Alo Mattiisen. The moment is regarded as the start of Estonia's 'signing revolution'. In June, people started gathering at the Tallinn venue during the long summer evenings to sing these and other, more traditional songs. Estonian flags were unfurled and flown. In September, a staggering 300,000 people, about a third of the population, attended a Festival of Estonian Song, where they sang again – and heard the head of the Estonian Heritage Preservation Society, Trivimi Velliste, call for national independence. Song as visionary politics: Marcel Bezençon (who had died in 1981) would have approved.

On December 7, Mikhail Gorbachev gave a speech to the UN General Assembly where he announced radical cutbacks in his armed forces. Did this mean a green light to Eastern Europe to break free? The stage was set for a remarkable year.

1989

Date: 6 May
Venue: Palais de Beaulieu, Lausanne, Switzerland
Winner: Riva, Yugoslavia
Winning Song: *Rock me*

Eurovision did its best to provide a barometer for its times in this game-changing year. The winning song was unmemorable, probably one of the weakest winners ever – but it came from the one Iron Curtain nation allowed to compete in the contest. Giving victory to Riva was a signal from Western Europe to the countries behind that once-impenetrable wall. Join us!

Yet in another way, the contest was mute on the great events of the year, as those events took place in nations still unable to compete in it. However, one can't tell the story of modern Europe without telling the 1989 stories of East Germany, Poland, Hungary, Bulgaria, Czechoslovakia and Romania – none of whom took part in Eurovision 1989 – so for this chapter I'm going to change the rules and leap across to the former land of Intervision.

By May 6 1989 the Iron Curtain already had a small crack in it. A few days before the contest, the Hungarian government had begun dismantling the fortifications along its border with Austria. This was partly an economic decision: the wall needed upgrading, and Hungary didn't have the money. But it wasn't just cash: an Interior Ministry spokesman commented, "Not only do we need the world, but the world needs us. An era will be closed with the removal of this fence, and we hope that such systems will never be needed again." At the same time, Hungary assured its eastern bloc critics that the border would still be policed.

Next month, (largely) free elections were held in Poland. Solidarity won 99 of the 100 seats in the nation's Senate, and all the 35 seats on offer in the second house, the *Sejm*, where a majority was still reserved for the Communist Party.

As summer drew on, many East Germans went to Hungary for their holidays. This was nothing new – scenic Lake Balaton had become a popular destination – but in 1989, when their tourist visas expired, thousands stayed on in a refugee tent city, convinced that a chance to escape west would soon present itself. It did. On 19 August, a 'pan-European picnic' was held at Sopron, a Hungarian city right next to the border, to which all Europeans were invited. (Central to organizing the picnic was the old Pan-European Union founded back in 1923.) For three hours, the nearby crossing-point was opened. Around 600 East Germans attended the event, then walked or drove to freedom (many more had stayed in their tent city, believing the picnic was too good to be true and was actually a Stasi trap). The border was then closed again. The Hungarians were still nervous about what Moscow would do. Two days later, a young East German architect, Kurt-Werner Schulz, was shot trying to smuggle his family to the West. The Hungarian Prime Minister, Miklós Németh, decided this was intolerable: the border had to be opened. He consulted with Helmut Kohl (not Mitterrand or Thatcher), who in turn contacted Gorbachev, who hinted that no action would be taken. The gates opened on September 10.

Protests were spreading to East Germany itself. Pastor Christian Führer had been conducting 'services for peace' at Leipzig's St Nicholas church since 1982. In September 1989, attendances began to skyrocket. The services would be followed by peaceful demonstrations. The Stasi tried to stop these with roadblocks and random arrests, but failed. Demonstrators began taking to the streets in other cities. Then on October 2, East Germany sealed its borders. Next Monday, the 9th, the country's leader, Erich Honecker, ordered security forces to open fire on the demonstrators.

This approach was not new. Back in June, China had come up with its own way of dealing with democracy protestors, killing around 2,000 people in Tiananmen Square. Was the German Democratic Republic about to have its own version?

Local Party leaders – unsung heroes of this story – refused to pass these orders on, and the demonstrations went ahead peacefully. Honecker was sacked and his place taken by Egon Krenz, a man a generation younger. Krenz tried to reform the existing system, but it was too late. November 4 saw a protest meeting fill Berlin's vast

Alexanderplatz with an estimated one million people. On the evening of the 9th, it was announced that visas would be issued to East Berliners wanting to visit the West. Crowds immediately gathered at the crossing-points. The press soon became so great that the guards let people through, to be welcomed by partying West Berliners. The wall had been breached.

The very next day saw the downfall of Bulgaria's leader of 35 years' standing, Todor Zhivkov. This was more due to internal Politburo politicking than 'people power', but a month later, that nation's Communist Party renounced its right to rule and announced elections for June 1990.

Czechoslovakia also had a hard-line leader, Miloš Jakeš. Would he resort to violence to preserve the old order? On November 17, a peaceful protest meeting in Prague was broken up by baton-wielding police (reports that a young student had died turned out to be false). More and more people took to the streets. It is rumoured that Jakeš summoned special forces to Prague on November 21 to quell the unrest, but he did not order them into action. Next day, a vast gathering of people filled Wencleslas Square, and within a week Jakeš had resigned, along with the rest of the politburo. By the end of the year, dissident playwright Vaclav Havel would be the nation's president.

Romania's dictator, Nicolae Ceausescu, had no compunction about going down the Tiananmen route. Protests in the western city of Timisoara were met with a military crackdown. But even this old monster's days were numbered. On December 21 he addressed a rally in Bucharest. Cheering Party goons lined the front, but behind them people started booing and chanting 'Timisoara'. The army was ordered to shoot, but the Minister of Defence refused to pass on the order – and died in suspicious circumstances immediately afterwards. His death destroyed any loyalty the army might have had to Ceausescu. Next day, the dictator tried to flee his white marble palace and was arrested and executed, along with his Lady MacBeth wife, Elena.

This leaves the winner of 1989 Eurovision, Yugoslavia. Arguably it didn't need a revolution, peaceful or otherwise, to leave the Soviet bloc, as it had always been half-in, half-out. But it had protests, anyway, 'anti-bureaucratic' marches in Serb-dominated parts of the country. However, these were not spontaneous 'people power' but were orchestrated by Serb leader Slobodan Miloševic, whose agenda was not liberation but Serbian nationalism. Their end result was not fewer pen-pushers but new leaders in three previously semi-autonomous provinces, Vojvodina, Macedonia and Kosovo, all of whom called for closer integration with Serbia.

Historians still argue about what caused the sudden collapse of Communism. I'd like to put forward a new thesis. It was the Eurovision Song Contest. Riva won, and shortly afterwards down came the wall!

Sadly, I'm not sure this would convince many people. Nevertheless it can be argued that popular music in general played a huge part in the downfall. Many young Eastern Europeans – and young Russians – listened to western music and wanted both the fun and, at a deeper level, the personal authenticity it talked of. Eurovision, especially in the 1970s when watching it was illegal in some Communist countries, did its bit in this subversive process. If it didn't bring the wall crashing down on its own, the contest certainly helped undermine it.

The collapse of the Iron Curtain was a fitting end to a tumultuous decade for Europe. If the missiles were still on our shared soil, nobody now had any intention of using them. In the West, anyway, 1970s stagflation had turned to 1980s growth, fuelled by a new economic paradigm and based on a resource that seemed able to grow exponentially – throughout the decade computer chips just kept on getting smaller, cheaper and more powerful, following the 'law' formulated back in the 1960s by Gordon Moore, whereby affordable chips double in power every two years. To the east, nations were emerging from behind the Curtain, blinking in the light of democracy and freedom. The decade saw the end of 'Euro-sclerosis' and the creation of real Europe-wide governmental institutions. It arguably saw the casting of the main roles in modern political Europe: Germany the leader, France the shrewd follower, Britain the bolshy outsider. (The next four biggest Eurovision economies are, in order, Italy, Spain, Turkey and the Netherlands. Italy is, perhaps, Europe's magician, perpetually appearing to be on the edge of chaos but actually doing rather well. In the 1980s Spain was still a 'dark horse', rediscovering itself after the Franco years. Turkey remained the outsider; the Netherlands the loyal European team player. I'm talking about national political roles here, of course, not fixed 'essentialist' national identities or the character of individuals from these countries.)

The decade saw a new, entrepreneurial attitude in business, replacing the old corporatism. It saw burgeoning opportunities for women. Right at its close, it saw legislative progress in gay rights – the first civil partnerships came into being in Denmark in 1989.

A darker side? Of course. Not everyone shared in the growth. Unemployment steadfastly refused to drop below 6%. There was a prevailing tone of brashness, harshness and crude materialism. There was the spectre of AIDS and, among many people still, the prejudice that came with this.

In Eurovision, the 80s created a song contest that in most ways looks and sounds like it does today. The decade did the same for political and economic Europe, putting in place a template with which we are still living, working, and in some ways now struggling.

The 1990s

1990

Date: 5 May
Venue: Vartroslav Lisinski Hall, Zagreb, Yugoslavia
Winner: Toto Cutugno, Italy
Winning Song: *Insieme: 1992 (Together: 1992)*

Eurovision 1990 began with the now-mandatory travelogue, which stressed the cheerful diversity of the host nation. Later, co-presenter Helga Vlahovic (already famous in Eurovision lore as the voice who had finally answered the phone, resultless, back in 1981) enthused about Yugoslavia being like an orchestra, where the strings, woodwind and percussion sections all sit next to each other and combine to create beautiful music.

Sadly, things weren't that harmonious in reality. The original, planned presenter had been Dubravka Markovic, a Serb, but she had started to receive anonymous phone calls threatening to kill her if she hosted the show (the event was being broadcast from Zagreb, capital of Croatia). Vlahovic replaced her. The Serb slated to direct the event was also suddenly replaced by a Croat. Yugoslavia's bubbly entrant for the contest, Tajci, was also from Croatia. If the show meant to represent the Yugoslav orchestra, it ended up showing just one section.

One might have expected the 1990 contest to celebrate the collapse of the Iron Curtain – but the Eurovision judges didn't feel this way. Norway's (perfectly good) *Brandenburger Tor*, about the once-blocked gateway in the centre of Berlin which had been formally reopened on December 22, 1989, came equal last: neither Germany nor Austria gave it any points at all. Austria's *Keine Mauern mehr (No more Walls)* ended up mid-table, with no votes from newly wall-free Germany. Germany's *Frei zu leben (Free to live)* suffered a similar mediocre fate.

Two songs, neither about the wall, tied for second place. Guadeloupe-born Joëlle Ursull's *White and black Blues* marked a new direction for France, ditching the ballads and chansons and looking to its old empire and new immigrant populations for musical inspiration. The song sold well in its home market: French popular taste was opening up to new sounds like Ursull's Caribbean *zouk, raï* from North Africa and hip-hop (France's first rap star, MC Solaar, emerged at this time; his parents had come to France from Senegal when he was six months old).

Second equal was a much more forgettable Irish entry, *Somewhere in Europe*, one of those old-style Eurovision songs that just lists loads of internationally recognizable words, in this case, place-names. By contrast, Ireland itself was modernizing fast: 1990 saw it elect its first female president, Mary Robinson, who had

178

campaigned for the right of women to serve on Irish juries and been legal adviser to the Campaign for Homosexual Law Reform.

1990's winner, from Italy's Toto Cutugno, hymned the upcoming uniting of *Western* Europe via the Single Market in 1992 – an event that had been planned back in the mid-80s and would have come about whether the Berlin wall had been bulldozed flat or built twice as high with extra guns and watchtowers. It's interesting to speculate why the judges felt as they did. Maybe it was just musical: the winning song was catchy, well sung and nicely arranged. Its singer/composer was well-known around Europe. But maybe Europeans were also ambivalent about the end of the wall. Germany seemed eager to reunite, but how overpowering would that new nation be?

Initially, there had been no rush to recombine the two Germanys – a professor at the London School of Economics was confidently predicting reunification in 50 years' time. But the process developed a momentum of its own (helped by an extra push from the portly Herr Kohl). The old DDR economy, weak in the first place, went into freefall. Kohl concluded that action had to be taken fast, and visited Moscow to check that Gorbachev would accept reunification. He would, as would US President George HW Bush. Kohl then turned his attention to Europe, where misgivings were stronger. Margaret Thatcher, a child of World War Two, and former resistance fighter François Mitterrand did not want unification; Italy's Prime Minister Guilio Andreotti said he loved Germany so much he preferred to see two of them. However Mitterrand was bought off with a promise that Germany would support French plans for monetary union; Thatcher and Andreotti were ignored. Meanwhile, an election was held in the old GDR in March 18, 1990, and won by the 'Alliance for Germany', whose manifesto called for speedy reunification.

Two weeks after Eurovision 1990, East and West Germany signed a treaty on 'monetary, economic and social union', which came into effect on July 1. East German citizens were allowed to exchange 4,000 old eastern marks for new western ones (a gift, essentially: the GDR marks were worth a fraction of this), and to swap further 'Ostmarks' at generous rates. Tons of old currency were carted away: the coins to be melted down, the notes stashed in a cave. (After an attempt to steal some of the notes, the remaining ones were burnt. The last Ostmark note outside private collections went up in flames in July 2002.). On October 3, less than a year after the opening of the Berlin wall, East Germany simply ceased to exist: it was quicker to simply admit its five provinces (*Länder*) to the *Bundesrepublik* than create a new, united Germany.

The old West Germany had been, along, perhaps, with Belgium, Luxembourg and the Netherlands, the nation most true to Robert Schuman's 1949 'European spirit', happy to write out a large annual cheque in order to be one of the Europe club. But now, rather like a young man who suddenly falls in love and stops spending all his evenings with his mates, would Germany's enthusiasm for club membership wane? It had found its perfect partner, its 'other half', and had other things on its mind. Not old dreams of conquest, but, like many newlyweds, a shiny new home.

The dream home would not come cheap. Initial optimism that privatizing East German industry would pay for reunification soon vanished: nobody wanted to buy old technology. Instead, money had to be poured into the East's inadequate telephone lines, crumbling autobahns and noxious power stations. Kohl insisted on honouring the pension obligations of the old DDR government, placing a huge (and lasting) burden on the more productive west. Unemployment soared in the uncompetitive east, necessitating yet more government assistance. According to some estimates, in the first three years after reunification, the exercise cost the new, expanded Germany 350 billion Deutschmarks. Ill feeling between 'ossies' and 'wessies' resulted: the marriage turned out to be stormier than had been hoped. But it was still a marriage.

Iron Curtain technology also dogged Eurovision 1990. Croatian TV had a small budget (though the expenditure still horrified people in Zagreb, where wages were well below Western European levels). Spain's song had to be started twice due to a mix-up with the backing tape, and there were phone problems during the voting – worst of all, prophetically, with the line to Belgrade.

But elsewhere in Europe, technology marched on. The previous year, Tim Berners-Lee, a British scientist working at the European Organization for Nuclear Research (CERN: the acronym comes from the French) in Switzerland, had suggested creating a 'world wide web' of sites that other academics could access via their computers to make research easier. In 1990, this came about. The world's first webpage went live.

1991

Date: 4 May
Venue: Cinecitta Studio 15, Rome, Italy
Winner: Carola, Sweden
Winning Song: *Fångad av en Stormwind (Caught in a Storm)*

It had originally been planned to hold Eurovision 1991 at San Remo, the home of the song festival that had inspired Marcel Bezençon back in 1955, but security concerns meant it was switched to film studios near Rome. These concerns were caused by the outbreak of the first Gulf War. Iraqi dictator Saddam Hussein had invaded Kuwait; the United Nations told him to get out or face the consequences; he stayed put. A global coalition of troops, led by the US but featuring many European nations, liberated the small oil state. The main European participants were Britain and France, with backup from Italy, the Netherlands, Sweden, Spain, Poland, Czechoslovakia, Greece, Denmark, Hungary and Norway.

Perhaps because of this late change of venue, Eurovision 1991 is now treasured as a vintage one for connoisseurs of Euro-cockups. Choose your favourite! The phone ringing offstage as the second song is announced. The awful sax solo in the Greek entry. The mysterious twang half way through Luxembourg's song. The venue's PA conking out half way through *Fångad av en Stormwind.*

The lights going out before the (rather good) interval act. Or maybe it was just the presenters. Gigliola Cinquetti and Toto Cutugno chatted away in Italian between the songs (Eurovision announcements are supposed to be in English or French), testing to the limit the boundaries between charming informality and self-indulgent amateurism. The show went on way beyond its planned time – and then two songs tied for first place. Chaos threatened to engulf the whole proceedings: luckily EBU scrutineer Frank Naef stayed calm and a winner was quickly announced.

It wasn't a vintage year for songs: Carola's victory was more a reward for her gutsy delivery than the quality of the material. Her French rival for the top spot, Tunisian-born Amina Annabi, continued that nation's new self-presentation as *la France mondiale* with the elegant eastern-influenced *C'est le dernier qui a parlé qui a Raison (The last one to speak is right)* – a dig, perhaps, at the ever more vociferous right in France. The result was the closest ever, apart from the 1969 farce: Carola won by virtue of having more second places than Annabi, both having got 146 points and maximum votes from five countries.

At the other end of the table, Austria's Thomas Forstner was unlucky to get *nul points*. One point clear of him was Yugoslavia's Bebi Doll with *Brazil*, a bland song covering up the fact that the singer's nation was about to implode. Looking behind the scenes at Zagreb 1990, we had seen the seeds of this. These were now sprouting. During that year, whenever free elections were allowed in

184

the different parts of the country, separatist politicians won. Serbs in the Krajina region of Croatia began to prepare for an uprising should Croatia declare independence. A month before Eurovision 1991, a shootout took place between Croatian police and Serb rebels. Croatia and Slovenia did formally declare independence two months later. Slovenia was at once invaded by the Yugoslav (now, essentially, Serb) army, but the half-hearted invasion was not a success: after ten days the army pulled out. Slovenia, the northernmost part of Yugoslavia and an area with little history of ethnic conflict, was essentially left alone to get on with making itself a modern nation. (A good sign of its success is the fact that since 1993 it has been a regular, if not hugely successful, participant in Eurovision, missing only two years.)

In Croatia, however, things just got nastier and nastier. In July 1991, Serb forces invaded, this time with more resolve – and more brutality. On August 1, Croat prisoners of war were murdered at the border village of Delj. Later that month, the bloody siege of Vukovar began: more massacres followed the city's fall in November. This was the old, riven Europe that the Song Contest had been created to transcend, a place of World War Two hatreds, still haunted by memories of pro-Nazi Ustasha atrocities and post-war partisan reprisals.

In January 1992, a peace treaty brokered by the USA was agreed to – upon which the tension moved to Bosnia. Both Serbs and Croats began to eye up chunks of this

185

province, which was ethnically divided (about 45% of the population were Muslim, 40% Serb and 15% Croat).

1991 also saw the break-up of another state composed of cobbled-together nationalities: the Soviet Union. It seemed at the beginning of the year that Moscow was going to stamp on separatism within the Union. In January, two waves of Russian troops had stormed public buildings in Vilnius, Lithuania, killing 18 people. But at that point Gorbachev realized where this was leading and backtracked, condemning the 'brutality' of these events. This was probably the moment he realized he couldn't both hold the Soviet Union together and retain his moral principles. After this, various republics started voting to leave: Estonia, Latvia, Georgia.

However on the morning of August 19, 1991, Russian citizens awoke to the news that Gorbachev was 'unwell' and that martial law had been declared. A group of high-ranking conspirators had seized power. In the Baltic states, the Soviet army moved in on key targets, ready to use maximum force. Helmut Kohl's haste to reunify Germany suddenly seemed extremely prescient. But Moscow's citizens took to the streets, led by the President of the Russian Federation, Boris Yeltsin. The coup plotters did not do a Tiananmen/Timicoara: they were reactionary old men, but not Stalin or Ceausescu. By August 21, the coup had failed.

One could regard this date as the final fall of Communism and thus the sputtering end of Cold War.

Bizarrely, two days afterwards, Tim Berners-Lee's 'world wide web' became officially available to non-academic users – though there were few takers to start with. One era ends, another begins…

On December 8, the presidents of Russia, Ukraine and Belarus signed a treaty ending the Soviet Union and replacing it with a 'Commonwealth of Independent States'. The Supreme Soviet finally voted itself out of existence on Boxing Day.

Two and a half years later, the nation that had spent forty years dominating Eastern Europe and threatening to obliterate the rest of the continent with nuclear missiles would be singing in the Eurovision Song Contest.

1992

Date: 9 May
Venue: Malmö Ice Stadium, Sweden
Winner: Linda Martin, Ireland
Winning Song: *Why me?*

The 1992 contest was held on Europe Day, the anniversary of the announcement of the plans for Jean Monnet's European Coal and Steel Community back in 1950. This was appropriate: earlier in the year, the Maastricht Treaty had been signed, marking a huge step forward for European integration. At Maastricht, 'Europe' got its new name, the European Union. Jacques Delors' timetable for the new currency became official: a new Europe-wide currency (it still had no name) was to be in place by January 1999 – in the financial world, at least, though not on the streets. The rules for joining the currency were formally put in place: 'convergence criteria' were supposed to ensure that no nation could participate if its economy wasn't in shape. Britain and Denmark were allowed to opt out of the new currency.

As a sop to old-fashioned de Gaulle/Thatcher inter-governmentalists, a concept known as subsidiarity was written into the treaty, which held that European government was supposed to interfere in national government as little as possible: if a decision could be made at a regional or national level, it should be. Quite how this would be interpreted was up for debate – and still is. But Maastricht was essentially a triumph for the federalists – its official name is the Treaty on European Union (TEU), not the Treaty on Subsidiary. It showed just how far the European project had advanced from the doldrums of the early 1980s. Historians see Maastricht as the third major agreement in modern European history, alongside the 1957 Treaty of Rome and the Single European Act of 1986. Subsequent EU treaties (Amsterdam, Nice, Lisbon) have largely been about tying up loose ends of Maastricht.

Oddly, in the year of such forward-looking Euro-triumph, there was a retro air to the 1992 contest. The set was elegant – designed around the prow of a Viking ship – but static, unlike the shape-shifting laser kingdoms of the 1980s. Alongside the electric guitars and Yamaha DX7 synths, we saw accordions feature in several numbers. Belgium's Morgane sung that her generation was, beneath its confident appearance, afraid, because it lacked emotion and connection to the past. Switzerland's Daisy Auvray wanted an old-style song with some tenderness from *Mister Music Man*.

She got it in the winner, an unassuming ballad where the singer wonders, as many self-doubting people do when they finally find love, '*Why me?*' Back in the eighties, one feels, few people would have asked such a question, confident that their romantic success was due to their charisma, hard work, businesslike attitude and giant shoulder pads. The new decade was already assuming a gentler, more thoughtful tone. The composer of the winning song was Johnny Logan, a man it seemed impossible to keep off the winners' podium.

If Linda Martin's win was the start of Ireland's run as darlings of Eurovision, 1992 also saw an Irishman come to the fore in political Europe. That man was Ray MacSharry, who had once been MEP for Connacht-Ulster (a role later performed by 1970 Eurovision winner Dana) and who was now European Commissioner for Agriculture.

In the 1980s, both François Mitterrand and Jacques Delors had tried to do something about the Common Agricultural Policy (CAP). They had briefly succeeded, but by 1991 the money was haemorrhaging out again. MacSharry was the man who finally grabbed the highly subsidized bull by its highly subsidized horns. The programme of price support was cut back and new measures were introduced to encourage farmers to look after land, rather than just overproduce, and to retire if their farms were no longer financially viable. Eurosceptics point out that *overall* EU expenditure continued to grow as fast after MacSharry as before, but it was no longer largely vanishing into wine lakes and butter mountains: the two Structural Funds and, after 1994, a new 'Cohesion Fund' created especially to improve transport links began to take up more budget, and what remained in the agricultural pot was more wisely invested.

The top three songs of 1992 were all in English. Britain, represented by stage star Michael Ball, came second: Linda Martin's gentleness seemed to suit the times better than Ball's grandiose power ballad. Malta, the only other competitor allowed to sing in English, came third.

Britain did not rule in political Europe, however. It was a grudging signatory to the Maastricht Treaty: its unfortunate Prime Minister, Conservative John Major, found himself under attack from ever more assertive Eurosceptics in his own party. In September 1992, the British pound crashed out of the European Monetary System (EMS) in a day of financial high drama with UK interest rates flying through the roof and money pouring into the pockets of speculators (one of whom, George Soros, is reputed to have made $1 billion from 'shorting' sterling that day).

Other nations were cagey about European integration, too. In June, Danish voters refused to ratify the Maastricht Treaty. In September, France voted for ratification – but only just: 51% of votes cast were in favour (the referendum became known as the *petit oui*). In the same month the Swedish krona, which had been 'shadowing' the EMS currencies with the intention of joining them, got savaged by speculators: in 2016, it has yet to join the Euro.

Shadowing – when governments pull various economic levers such as tinkering with interest rates or rushing into currency markets to buy or sell, in order to keep its currency level with another one – is a risky business. Once speculators work out that you are doing it, they can milk you, and the interest rate changes make life difficult for domestic businesses and home buyers

Eurovision 1992 saw the last appearance of Yugoslavia – though technically this was no longer the old Yugoslavia but a new state that had come into being a month before the contest, consisting of Serbia and Montenegro. Snežana Beric, a.k.a. Ekstra Nena, sang her Alla-Pugacheva-ish *Kissing you with Songs* with flair and grace. One line in the lyric talks of two broken glasses: the lovers in the song had had too much wine that evening. It's a neat flashback to those two cigarette ends from 1962. This was a much classier way to bow out than with Bebi Doll. *Nul points* for Beric's political awareness, however: at the pre-contest press conference, she insisted that her government and president (Milošević) were "against all kinds of violence and armed conflict".

Bosnia had declared independence a month before Eurovision 1992, and was soon invaded. The notorious siege of Sarajevo began on May 2. Hills ring the Bosnian capital, and these were occupied by Serb forces who, after initial failed attempts to storm the city, blocked its main access routes, cut off its utilities and began shelling it. Sarajevo's main street became impassable due to snipers who would shoot at anyone trying to cross it. Only the airport, which was held by United Nations forces, kept the city connected to the world – but you had to go up 'sniper alley' to get to it.

So much for that happy orchestra.

1993

Date: 15 May
Venue: Green Glens Arena, Millstreet, Ireland
Debuts: Bosnia Herzegovina, Croatia, Slovenia
Winner: Niamh Kavanagh, Ireland
Winning Song: *In your Eyes*

The evening that Linda Martin won Eurovision 1992, entrepreneur Noel Duggan wrote a letter to RTE, the Irish broadcaster, offering to host the 1993 event for free. The venue would be his equestrian centre in Millstreet, a small town – it had around 1500 inhabitants – half way between Cork and Killarney. Cue, one suspects, laughter at RTE headquarters. But Duggan meant what he said. He began lobbying influential people. A local committee was set up to co ordinate the bid and convince visiting RTE officials that Millstreet could really deliver. The officials agreed, and it got the gig.

There's a lot to be said for small Eurovision venues: they generate a special enthusiasm. As in Bergen in 1986, Millstreet went Eurovision-crazy; visitors can still see where one local resident decorated the wall of his house with the flags of the 25 contestants. Such venues generate good PR: the world's media descended and gave the contest a fresh injection of publicity. They do, of course, pose logistical challenges – the local railway station had to be enlarged for the event – but these were triumphantly met by RTE. Alan Farquharson's set was back to the standards of the late 1980s. Millstreet put on a great show: the mouse roared.

Such was the spirit of the times. Two weeks before the 1993 contest, CERN made the software for participating in the world wide web freely available for anyone to use. Soon the new 'internet' would be providing ever more opportunities for nimble entrepreneurs like Noel Duggan, with big ideas and can-do mindsets.

1993 was the start of a new Eurovision era, as entrants from Eastern European nations began to appear. The undoubted heroes of Millstreet were the six musicians from Bosnia, who had to run the gauntlet of snipers to get to Sarajevo airport to attend the event (their conductor wasn't able to make the flight out). Muhamed Fazlagic, the vocalist, sang that *Sva Bol Svijeta (All the Pain of the World)* was in Bosnia at that time, and got a rousing reception from the crowd. Croatia and Slovenia also made debuts that year. Croatia sang a lament for a young man killed in the war. Slovenia's entry, *Thi deževan Dan (Rainy Day)*, is least remembered of the three debuts, but arguably the best musically. It's a dreamy song featuring acoustic guitar and a strange middle section where the singer seems to be recalling an unpleasant past – some kind of internment camp? Or was it just school? Sadly, none of these songs got much respect from the judges.

To be fair, they faced strong competition: 1993 was a

good year. The periphery was on particular form. Iceland, Portugal, Greece and Norway all came up with attractive entries. Spain's Eva Santamaria sang of the egotism of men – sentiments one would not have heard in Eurovision a few years back.

The centre, by contrast, was more out of touch. Several songs sounded dated. Denmark's Tommy Seebach sang a rather sweet lullaby, *Under Stjernerne på Himlen (Under the Stars of the Sky)*, for his infant daughter. It came 22nd. Denmark, freshly opted out from the Euro, was much less happy about a probable exit from Eurovision (in 1993, the bottom countries were threatened with expulsion from next year's contest). Seebach was assailed by the Danish press on his return from Millstreet, found solace in alcohol, and died in his early 50s. His son re-recorded the song in 2003, and it was a hit in the country that had been so vicious about it first time round.

Seebach's story highlights one of the less attractive features of the new decade, the rising power of the media – and with it, rising arrogance. Back in April 1992, Britain's populist *Sun* newspaper had claimed it had won the election for John Major ('It's the Sun wot won it', the paper crowed in its headline). Later that year, a cabinet minister who tried to curb media power, David Mellor, was exposed by the press for having an affair with an actress. He lost his job. Eurovision will see the media harpie in action again later in the decade.

Amongst other centre losers, Luxembourg came 20th

and left the competition, never to return. Their last two entries were wholly or partially in Luxembourgeois – and fared badly. Respect to the Grand Duchy for this: having prospered as France B for many years, they decided to return to their roots and to hell with the consequences. Belgium's Barbara Dex came undeservedly last, then suffered the added insult of having an annual award named after her for Eurovision's worst dressed contestant.

The 1993 results were influenced by language again, with English-speaking entries taking the top two places. Again, too, an Irish song beautifully sung from the standpoint of an unconfident, understating female beat a brassier UK entry by a big name. Welcome to the 1990s. The song that came third was in the other official EBU language, French, and the fourth-placed entry a mixture of French and Corsican.

Croatia and Bosnia may have shared a stage at Millstreet, but the two nations were already at war. Croatia had initially sided with Bosnia when the latter was invaded by Serbs, but soon turned on its new ally, eager for territory. In April 1993, Croat forces killed over 100 civilians in Ahmici, a largely Muslim village in Central Bosnia. The sinister term 'ethnic cleansing' was beginning to enter the vocabulary: the removal of ethnic groups from territory by violence (or at least by the threat of it). Croat forces also besieged the city of Mostar, 100 miles south west of Sarajevo; in November its 500-year-old bridge, a masterpiece of Ottoman architecture, was blown up; it became a symbol of resistance for the oppressed Bosniaks. This oppression did not go unnoticed in the wider Islamic world.

While this was going on, the newly-powerful European Union did little. It was split: Germany had traditional links with Croatia; France and Britain feared the spread of German influence (they still hadn't really got used to reunification). Nobody wanted to drag Russia, keen supporters of fellow Slavs in Serbia, into a war. But critical voices were raised at this inactivity: this was a European tragedy, not some trouble in far-away Vietnam or Kuwait. One of the 'pillars' of the post-Maastricht EU (it had three; they lasted till 2007) was supposed to be a 'Common Foreign and Security Policy'. In 1994, US President Bill Clinton came over and gave us a nudge. But the killing went on and Europe did little to stop it.

1994

Date: 15 May
Venue: The Point, Dublin, Ireland
Debuts: Estonia, Hungary, Lithuania, Poland, Romania, Russia, Slovakia
Winner: Paul Harrington and Charlie McGettigan, Ireland
Winning Song: *Rock 'n'roll Kids*

1994 was the great year of eastern accession to the contest. Four former Soviet satellites joined: Hungary, Poland, Romania and, recently split from the Czech Republic, Slovakia. Two Baltic states: Estonia and Lithuania. And, of course, Russia itself: the old enemy, now singing along with us on Paula Farrell's stage based on 'Dublin by night'.

Other European institutions were way behind Eurovision. Eastern bloc nations would not be admitted to the EU until 2004. Germany and Austria were worried about immigration, France about the watering down of its agricultural subsidy. Spain, Portugal and Greece feared they would get less Structural and Cohesion Fund handouts as even poorer nations joined. Talks didn't even start till 1998. Sadly, the idea that the EU immediately welcomed these nations and thereby guaranteed freedom and democracy in them does not stand up to scrutiny: these nations chose freedom and democracy, then joined the EU when they were finally allowed to. NATO was only a little speedier, admitting the Czech Republic, Hungary and Poland in 1999, but nobody else till 2004. Eurovision alone opened its arms at once to these nations and said, "You are European: welcome!"

The contest itself was a triumph for Ireland. It was superbly staged. Technology marched on: 1994 saw satellite links to each nation's announcement of their votes. The host's entry was a runaway winner. For *Rock'n'roll Kids*, the orchestra was not used: two men sat on stage, played piano and guitar, and sang a wistful ballad. In the 1980s, it would probably not have featured in the top ten, but this was the 1990s, and quiet reflection was the order of the day.

Several other songs featured a quiet, confessional tone. Best of all was Hungarian singer Friderika Bayer's *Kinek mondjam el vétkeimet? (Who can I tell my Sins to?)*. Hungary has rarely bought into the *Diggi-loo diggi-ley* approach to Eurovision, preferring intelligent, sometimes troubling songs. The answer to Bayer's question in 1990s Europe – especially Northern Europe – was increasingly 'a therapist'. The decade saw a boom in counselling and therapy courses. Therapy itself became a gentler practice, influenced more by Carl Rogers' 'person-centred' approach than the old experts-know-best Freudian psychotherapy. Eurovision can't be accused of lacking emotion, but in many European countries – like my own – there still was a big difference between relating to a song and actually admitting to emotions, especially ones involving

199

vulnerability. But this was beginning to change.

We heard twenty-five songs from all round an expanded Europe – but the best of Eurovision 1994 was yet to come. Interval acts in the contest have, let's say, varied in quality over the years. Particular clunkers include Britain's 1974 Wombles (a kids' programme not shown anywhere else in Europe) and the 1989 William Tell act where the arrow was clearly seen missing the apple, though moments later a pre-pierced apple was held up for our admiration. But 1994 gave us *Riverdance*, a stunning display of traditional Irish dancing presented in a totally modern way by Jean Butler, Michael Flatley and a troupe of dancers, to the music of Limerick-born composer Bill Whelan. The 6-minute piece began with a haunting vocal section from soloist Katie McMahon and the group Anúna. Butler and Flatley then took solo turns, performed a *pas de deux*, then were joined by the ensemble for the finale. It brought the audience to its feet. *Riverdance* was turned into a stage show and ran for years. It's up there with Abba and Céline Dion.

It was also a perfect symbol for the Ireland that was arising at that time. Entry to the EEC had benefited that nation in several ways, widening the market for its products and allowing it to receive money from the Structural and Cohesion funds. In addition, the Irish government had provided a low-tax environment for both business and, true to its soul, artists. The results were startling. In 1994, unemployment was 14.7%; by 2001, that would have fallen to 3.8%. GDP would grow by 8% annually over the same time-frame. People began talking about the Celtic Tiger, by analogy with the booming Asian Tiger economies of South Korea and Taiwan. Critics say this was false growth based on bribing foreign companies to invest in Ireland, but it takes energy and enterprise to attract and retain such investors, and Eurovision 1994 shows that Ireland had these aplenty.

Right now, the new arrivals to Eurovision could only look on and hope their economic turn would come. If Eurovision was anything to go by, Poland would be the next Tiger – Edyta Górniak stormed to second place, showing off her remarkable vocal range in *To nie ja (That's not me)*. This barometer is not false: the newly-liberated nation had restructured its economy after 1989, and by the mid-1990s was reaping the benefit. Growth for the five years after 1994 would average 6% a year.

Less tigerish musically were the Baltic states, who came last and second last, with *nul* and *deux points*. They were still recovering from escaping the Soviet Union – there had been 150,000 Russian troops in the three nations in 1991; by the time of the contest, withdrawal was still incomplete – and had a lot to learn about Eurovision. Lithuania's nul pointer Ovidijus Vyšniauskas was only belatedly asked to provide a song, and claimed to have written the tune of *Lopšine Mylimai (Sweethearts' Lullaby)* in three minutes. Economically, however, these nations were modernizing fast. Estonia, in particular, looked at Ireland's success and began courting overseas investment. It reformed its currency, cracked down on corruption, stopped subsidies to old Soviet-era enterprises and began looking at the potential of the fast-developing internet.

The arrival of new states gave a new shape to both the Eurovision and the political maps of Europe. Arguably there was now a new, eastern periphery, out beyond the old periphery, which in turn was looking if not like the old centre, at least more like a half-way house. Peripheral Britain was now directly linked to core France by a tunnel which opened a week before Eurovision 1994. Austria was preparing to join the EU. Scandinavia was signing up, too, with Finland and Sweden becoming members on January 1, 1995.

Norway, as usual, did different and voted to stay out: an oil-rich nation, it has much less to gain from EU membership than other peripherals. At the same time, Norway has a love-hate relationship with Eurovision. Some years it doesn't give a hoot (or the twang of a pair of braces). Others... Sitting in the audience during *Riverdance* was composer Rolf Løvland. He'd already won back in the bouncy 80s with Bobbysocks. A shrewd judge of *zeitgeist*, Løvland heard the haunting vocal and the lone Celtic violin accompanying Jean Butler's solo dance, and knew the kind of piece he had to come up with.

1995

Date: 13 May
Venue: The Point, Dublin, Ireland
Debuts: None (none till 1998)
Winner: Secret Garden, Norway
Winning Song: *Nocturne*

In 1995's dark, brooding, beautiful set, a dark, brooding, beautiful tune walked away with the competition. Not everybody approved, however. *Nocturne* has only 24 words; Fionnuala Sherry on violin features a lot more than singer Gunnhild Tvinnereim. Sweden said the piece should not have been allowed to participate, and gave it no votes. Norway's response was probably unprintable – rivalry between the two nations runs deep (Norway was once part of a Swedish empire). Denmark only gave *Nocturne* one point, too: so much for the Nordic bloc vote. Almost everybody else loved it. If you're watching the Youtube video, the many-stringed instrument is called a Nyckelharp and the player is Åsa Jinder – who is Swedish: national grudges aren't held by everybody.

The New Age had arrived in Eurovision. Back in the 'white heat' early 1960s, it was assumed that religion would quietly wither away, as we Europeans all became scientific and rational. The *soixante-huitards* ditched the science and rationality, but wanted no truck with religion. That old stuff, all thoughtful people seemed to agree, was on its way out. The stats support this. Between 1960 and 1990 the number of practicing Catholics in Belgium fell by 31% and in France by 23%, while the Dutch Catholic and Reformed churches lost 24% between them. The percentage of Scots taking communion halved between 1960 and 1995. If one assumes that most older people kept their faith, these figures show a very low take-up of established religion by the younger generation. Some of these defectors became, as expected, technocratic atheists (a classic example being Richard Dawkins, whom 1995 saw being appointed Professor for Public Understanding of Science at Oxford University).

However many more Europeans took a third route, looking for new, more personal ways of pursuing the spiritual life. Some of these ways were, and still are, delightfully daft (or sinister, in the wrong hands), but for many, the New Age brought a sense of personal power and significance. One can imagine Judy's friend from Sweden, 1969, following this route.

Eurovision mirrors this change from orthodox religion to non-orthodox spirituality. The 1995 winner is full of the New Age's yearning and sense of mystery. A song with a more conventional religious message, Germany's *Verliebt in dich (In Love with you)* ('You' in this song is God), came last, only escaping *nul points* thanks to one vote (the award came near the end of the voting, and got a loud cheer from the sporting Irish crowd).

Of course, the nineties weren't one long hug. Eurovision 1995 also saw another musical genre debut in the contest: an angry import from America, rap. Critics of Eurovision say this is a rather late take-up, as people had been rapping since the mid-1970s. But that was in the South Bronx. The genre took a long time to go mainstream. If the cynics who say that 'go mainstream' means 'get taken up by white artists' are right, then Eurovision was ahead of its time, as the great white rapper, Eminem, had yet to make it big by 1995. Britain's *Love City Groove* was a relatively gentle introduction to the genre; it came mid-table, but rap did not take root in the competition.

Russia participated for the second time, courtesy of the wild-haired Philipp Kirkorov, who had recently married Alla Pugacheva. Kirkorov's song, sung sixth, was poor and came 17th – but in Russia, where the programme was not broadcast live, the running order was edited and *Kolybelnaya dlya Vulkana (Lullaby for a Volcano)* appeared to be sung last. The voting was then not shown, leaving viewers left with the impression that Kirkorov had won. The Soviet Union might have vanished, but old habits die hard.

For Bosnia, Davor Popovic sang about *The 21st Century (Dvadeset i Prvi Vijek)*. The words were gloomy, but the tune quite upbeat. Tragically, words trump music here. 1995 saw the Bosnian war hit new lows and reach the crisis point that finally forced the international community to sort out the mess.

205

The city of Srebrenica in the far east of Bosnia was one of three Muslim enclaves in that part of the country, which was otherwise now held by the Bosnian Serb army (VRS). It had been under siege since 1993. UN forces had been struggling to keep it a 'safe area' since that date, but the force was under-resourced and only allowed to actually fight 'in self-defence'. By the time of Eurovision 1995, the situation was drastic, with ever fewer supply convoys getting through and ever more VRS troops in place around the city.

The final attack began on July 6. It met little resistance; on July 11, General Ratko Mladic was filmed walking through the deserted town centre. The town's Muslim residents had all fled to the UN headquarters, an abandoned battery factory at nearby Potocari and were camped around it. The next day, VRS forces came to this place and walked through the encampment, separating out men of military age. Some tried to escape to Bosnian-held territory, but these columns of already hungry and weakened refugees made easy targets. In the end, over 6,000 men and boys were rounded up. Over the next week, these people would be systematically murdered by the VRS. Small groups were taken out to remote fields, shot, then buried in mass graves.

UN forces did little to prevent this, so the war continued. What finally prompted decisive action was the more visible siege of Sarajevo. On August 28, a Serb mortar attack killed 37 people in a crowded marketplace.

Two days later, NATO began air strikes on the besiegers. These lasted three weeks, after which a joint Bosnian and Croat force was able to begin driving the VRS from their positions. Basic facilities were slowly restored to the city, but the siege was not officially declared over until February 1996.

In the meantime, an agreement had been thrashed out at a US airbase near Dayton, Ohio. Bosnia in theory retained its former boundaries, but was effectively divided into two similar-sized 'Entities': the Federation of Bosnia and Herzegovina (largely inhabited by Bosniaks and Bosnian Croats) and the Serb-dominated 'Republika Srpska'. Hostilities ceased. Had peace finally arrived in the land of Ljiljana Petrovic's sophisticated late-night lovers?

In April 1996, four army patrols were attacked in the southern Serbian province of Kosovo. A little-known group called the Kosovo Liberation Army (KLA) claimed responsibility.

1996

Date: 18 May
Venue: Oslo Spektrum, Norway
Winner: Eimear Quinn, Ireland
Winning Song: *The Voice*

30 nations were now eager to participate in the contest, so a pre-final was organized, whereby the juries listened to recordings of all the songs and put 22 through to the live event (to join the hosts, who qualified automatically). One of the nations not to make the cut was Germany, the largest single TV audience and a major financial contributor to the show. All seven fallers at this fence had the disheartening experience of winning their national heats then not competing in a live competition. This unsatisfactory system was not used again. (A system based on recent past performance was introduced instead. In 2000, the four biggest financial contributors to the contest were allowed to skip this. A semi-final, the only really fair system, followed in 2004, though the 'Big Four' exemption remained, with Italy making it a 'Big Five' in 2011.)

Norway put on a stunning show, in front of 8,000 people. A range of material was on offer. Austria brought us gospel, courtesy of blind pianist/singer George Nussbaumer. Poland's Kasia Kowalska took us to a smoky intellectuals' bar with her dark, intense *I want to know my Sin.*

We went clubbing with Britain's Gina G and her saucy, techno *Ooh, aah, a little bit more*, Eurovision's answer to a Donald McGill seaside postcard.

New Age was still the dominant genre, however, floaty and ethnic. France's entry was sung in Breton. France had once ruled the contest, thanks to its creative power and its dutiful satellites, Luxembourg and Monaco. But now the satellites had crashed to earth and music had moved on. Since Joëlle Ursull back in 1990, the nation had been on a fascinating Eurovision journey of self-discovery, looking to its minorities and regions for inspiration. From 1996 onwards, it would struggle in Eurovision, with long runs of poor results broken by the occasional single-figure placing.

As in Eurovision, so in European politics. The reunification of Germany – a few months after Ursull took to the Eurovision stage – had been the *coup de grâce* for lingering Gaullist dreams of French supremacy in Europe.

France remained committed to the European project, however: being number two is, after all, not the worst fate in the world – some Eurovision second-placers are remembered as classics (*Su Canción, Theater, All out of Luck, Never ever let you go, Sanomi, Lane moje* and *Madness of Love* are my personal favourites; you will no doubt have others). The project appeared to be coalescing even better than expected. Experts had forecasted that only a few centre countries would initially meet the Maastricht criteria for membership of the new shared currency – named the Euro at a meeting of the Council of Europe in Madrid in

209

December 1995. However as the nineties progressed, the 'Club Med' nations – Italy, Spain and Portugal – made unexpected progress in sorting out their public finances. The three nations that had joined the EU in 1995, Austria, Finland and Sweden, all seemed eligible, too (though Sweden was not keen to join).

Critics of the single currency argued that what was now happening was that potential members were fudging their figures to fit the criteria – even centre ones: France, Italy, Germany and Belgium. But such criticisms were brushed aside: the Euro was on its way. It even had a physical form: 1996 saw a competition to design the banknotes, which was won by young Austrian, Robert Kalina. The coins – the one, shared side of them – would follow next year, when Belgian Luc Luycx won another contest (look closely at Euro coins and you can see his signature, interlocking Ls).

Critics also pointed at the huge differences between the economies of different part of Europe. Could they really all be squeezed into one monetary system? To be fair to Euro enthusiasts, there was little agreed knowledge on what makes a currency union work. Economists talked rather vaguely about 'Optimal Currency Areas' (OCA), but there seemed a limited agreement about what these exactly consisted of, and even less empirical evidence. The Euro was in many ways a leap in the dark. Such leaps require, above all, faith.

However there was not a complete absence of evidence.

Europe had witnessed several goes at creating shared currency areas, albeit back in a previous century.

In 1872, Sweden and Denmark had merged their currencies. Norway joined them in 1875. Initially the Scandinavian Currency Union worked well, but in 1905 Norway sought more political independence from Sweden, and Denmark decided to follow different economic policies to the other two nations. The Union, now under stress, lumbered on till the First World War, when the different experiences of the three countries (Norway was linked to Britain; Denmark shared a border with Germany and traded extensively with it) created such different economic conditions in the three nations that it finally collapsed.

By contrast, German monetary union had been a success. At the beginning of the nineteenth century Germany didn't exist; it was a mass of states, mostly small but with two big players, Prussia and Austria. In 1818 Prussia began to set up a customs union, and over the next few decades more and more states joined it. Austria didn't want to participate, and in 1866 ended up at war with Prussia, where it was quickly defeated, after which it went its own way, forming a joint Balkan empire with Hungary. Prussia set up a North German Federation, which in 1870 went to war with France and won. South Germany (Bavaria and Baden-Württemberg) joined the Federation soon after, and the new nation became the *Reich* (Empire). A central German bank was only founded in 1876.

Looking at these examples, the prognosis for the Euro did not look good. Monetary union had worked where, politically, one state ended up effectively taking over the others – and where this take-over was generally accepted: the German statelets became Prussian when they wanted to; Austria, unwilling to join the party, was excluded. It had worked where participants shared a language and a sense of national and cultural identity. It had, in other words, worked where there was already a high, agreed level of political union.

Ah, but maybe that was old stuff. Would this material from over a century ago have any relevance to our own post-modern, post-national continent? This was 1996, not 1876…

Eurovision 1996 was won by Ireland, which gave the once-peripheral nation a record-busting sequence of four wins out of five (or four and a half wins, given that Secret Garden's Fionnuala Sherry had come from County Kildare). The Voice was sung by former Anúna member Eimear (it's pronounced Ee-ma) Quinn and written by Brendan Graham, who joined the elite double-winners group as he had also written *Rock'n'roll Kids* in 1994. The lyrics talk of past pain, and the need to both remember that pain and transcend it if one truly wishes to find peace. The message was extraordinarily timely.

When this narrative last visited the UK province of Northern Ireland, it was to reveal an atmosphere of hatred and violence, psychotic in the 1970s, simmering in the

1980s. The nineties finally saw change. In 1993, a joint declaration had been issued by the British Prime Minister, John Major, and the Irish Taoiseach, Albert Reynolds, renouncing both nations' theoretical claims on the province: its future was, instead, up to its inhabitants. In 1994, first Catholic then Protestant paramilitaries announced ceasefires. The much-discussed 'peace process' was becoming a reality. However it then got bogged down in arguments about verifying the decommissioning of weapons. 1996 saw backsliding; the Provisional IRA detonated a bomb in London's docklands, after which Sinn Fein, a party with links to them, was excluded from talks. *The Voice* was a much-needed call to get the peace process moving again.

Meanwhile, European technology marched on. The results for Eurovision 1996 were beamed into a virtual studio. Presenter Ingvild Bryn was able to walk 'behind' a scoreboard that seemed to hover in space, while behind her was a virtual window into the 'Green Room', where we could see artists reacting to the latest allocation of points. Direct video links to the results announcers around Europe were shown on another part of the studio 'wall'.

More generally, the internet, whose public era had dawned back in 1991, was beginning to impact on ordinary citizens' lives. Nine million Europeans now had access to it. This figure was still overwhelmingly made up of business users, but 1996 saw AOL open up the net to private subscribers in Britain, Germany and France. And if you didn't have your own computer, you could go to a cybercafé: by June 1996, Paris had fifteen of these.

1997

Date: 3 May
Venue: The Point, Dublin
Winner: Katrina and the Waves, UK
Winning Song: *Love shine a Light*

Eurovision 1997 saw a runaway winner, Katrina and the Waves, from Britain (Katrina Leskanich, the lead singer, was the daughter of a US airman stationed in East Anglia). *Love shine a Light* is an anthem, the kind of song you stand and sway to while holding up a cigarette lighter. (Assuming, of course, you have a cigarette lighter. Over the last three decades, smoking has declined in Western Europe, especially Scandinavia – though not in Eastern Europe, where the habit has gained popularity: lovers can still turn the lights out and watch their cigarettes glow in the dark. In Britain, when Abba won Eurovision, 50% of men and 40% of women smoked; by 1997, the level for both sexes was 30%; in 2016 it is around 20%.)

Love Shine a Light is often cited as the UK's best-ever Eurovision entry. It's certainly my personal favourite. The song was the performers' own, rather than chosen for them by the public or 'experts'. The powerful arrangement was by a friend of the band, Don Airey. Authenticity works in Eurovision.

Ireland's Marc Roberts came second with a rather tame

ballad, prompting more mutterings about the unfairness of insisting on national languages in Eurovision: English was now the *lingua franca* of Europe – even the EU had dropped French as its main language – and entrants who could sing in it had an ever-increasing advantage. Having said this, *Love shine a Light* was the outstanding song of the contest. From the fifth sung bar in, Leskanich is clearly loving the performance, the way Agnetha and Anni-Frid did back in 1974.

When asked to comment on her victory, Leskanich observed that it was the second landslide in a week. Two days before Eurovision, Tony Blair's 'New Labour' party had trounced John Major's Conservatives in the UK general election, gaining 41% more votes than their rivals (Katrina and the Waves got 44% more points than Marc Roberts).

The Blair victory marked a radical change in British life. New Labour was inclusive – there were twice as many women in the new parliament as the old one, and its approach to gay and other minority rights was much more liberal than its predecessor (the previous incumbents had passed a law in 1988 preventing local authorities from 'promoting homosexuality'). New Labour was pro-Europe (though still cagey about the Euro). It was business-friendly but also seemed caring and compassionate. *Love Shine a Light* resonates with this new mindset: it was originally written for the Samaritans, a charity that provides phone support for the suicidal.

Britain couldn't keep out of the headlines in 1997. On August 31, Princess Diana was killed in a high-speed car crash in Paris: the outpouring of national grief, symbolized by the millions of flowers left at Buckingham and Kensington Palaces, caught the nation's stiff-upper-lip old guard totally by surprise. Blair, by contrast, understood the new national mood perfectly.

Books paying tribute to Diana came out at once. If you went into a London bookstore to buy one, you might also have seen a newly-published children's story called *Harry Potter and the Philosopher's Stone* – though you might also have missed it, as it was the first book by an unknown author and the initial print run was 500 copies. Over the next decade, the book and its six follow-ups would sweep Europe more fully than almost any other popular cultural phenomenon (The Beatles had been minority tastes in France and east of the Iron Curtain). Almost? No individual Potter book has come near the viewing figures for Eurovision: it is estimated that the seven books in the series have, in all, sold around 450 million copies, so that's about 64 million per book; audience estimates for each song contest are over 100 million.

Elsewhere in Eurovision 1997, Russia was represented by Alla Pugacheva, who was showing her years visually though not vocally: *Prima Donna* was dated, but still a *tour de force* of showmanship.

Austria's Bettina Soriat came up with a line that probably wouldn't have got into contest a decade earlier, complaining that her lover was too quick in bed. (Lyrically, the 1990s saw Eurovision getting more daring. In 1994 France's Nina Morato had sung – or rather howled – putain, which can mean a range of things but in context clearly meant 'fuck'.) Holland's 'Mrs Einstein' sang how nobody had any time any longer. *Zeit* (Time) was also on the mind of Germany's Bianca Shomberg.

The pace of life seemed to be accelerating all round Europe, with economies growing and stock markets booming (a 'mini-crash' in October was soon reversed). Darlings of the market were new internet businesses. None of these was actually making profits, but the argument ran that this was a race into uncharted but incredibly valuable territory; whoever rushed in most vigorously and staked out most ground (in terms of 'brand awareness') would later be able to reap huge rewards. Interest rates were low at the time: borrowed money flowed into what became known as 'dotcom' start-ups.

Katrina and the Waves sang second last; last to sing in Eurovision 1997 was Iceland's Paul Oscar. *Min hinsti Dans (My last Dance)* was a dramatic farewell by a wealthy pleasure-seeker to that life, or maybe even to life itself. This was unusual enough for Eurovision, but the staging completely rewrote the contest's script. While a techno beat thumps away, Oscar, Eurovision's first openly gay contestant, is surrounded by four gorgeous but doped-looking women in PVC, boots and fishnet stockings, posing and re-posing with a suggestiveness that makes

Gina G look positively homely. We are suddenly in a new world of sexual fantasy and fetishism, sex as power-play and transgression rather than just good old-fashioned 'naughty but nice' Euro-fun. Katrina and the Waves were the old post-Abba Eurovision at its best; a two-minute postcard later, here is a Eurovision that will emerge in the next decade.

Anyone familiar with the contest fan-base may be surprised that an openly gay artist had not appeared before. But even in 1997 most competing nations still reckoned that fielding such a competitor would damage their chances. In the host nation, Ireland, sex between consenting male adults had only been legal since 1993. In 1995, the highly-respected annual BSA (British Social Attitudes) survey had shown that 44% of the UK population still thought that sex between people of the same gender was 'always wrong', while only 22% said 'not wrong at all'.

However, things were finally changing. 'Not wrong at all' would overtake 'always wrong' in the 2003 BSA survey, and by 2006 the figures would show 24% condemnation and 38% 'not wrong at all'.

Similar changes were taking place around Europe, though at different speeds. By 2005, when the European Social Survey asked for responses to the question 'Do you agree that gay men and lesbians should be free to live their own lives as they wish?', Holland and Scandinavia (excluding Finland) said a resounding 'yes' (over 85%);

most other Northern and Western European countries came in around 75%; Finland, Czech Republic and Portugal around 60%; Slovenia, Greece and Hungary above 50%; the rest of Eastern Europe around 45% and only about one third agreed in Ukraine and Russia.

After Paul Oscar had sung, it was time to vote. 1997 saw the first Eurovision televoting: five nations – the UK, Germany, Austria, Switzerland and Sweden – dispensed with juries and instead asked the public to phone in their chosen winners. Intriguingly, only one of these nations was an original 'Lugano 1956' EEC member, but four had belonged to the ill-fated EFTA. Make of this what you will: it can be argued that the centre countries tend to have a more top-down, experts-know-best culture – let the judges decide – while peripheral Britain and Scandinavia are more individualistic and democratic. What cannot be denied is the sheer technological achievement: in the UK, 250,000 votes were cast in the five minutes the lines were open. For viewers in these countries, another part of modern Eurovision was now in place.

The year 1997 ended with the signing of a new EU treaty in Amsterdam. This gave new powers to the European Parliament, putting it on an equal footing with the previously more powerful Council. In theory this made 'Europe' more democratic, though this is really only meaningful if people bother to vote in European elections and are given a genuinely broad range of political views to choose from. The treaty opened EU borders (with opt-outs for Britain and Ireland) and tried to simplify decision-making in EU institutions, with an eye to the future where new, eastern nations – already part of Eurovision – would be joining.

1998

Date: 9 May
Venue: National Exhibition Centre, Birmingham, UK
Debut: Macedonia
Winner: Dana International, Israel
Winning Song: *Diva*

The 1998 contest was much hyped in the media – or rather three contestants were, sharing different fates. Most memorable was Israel's Dana International, a transgender singer (she had undergone sex reassignment surgery in London in 1993). Her nomination as Israel's representative had been controversial back home, with members of the ultra-Orthodox Shas party calling her an 'abomination' and trying to prevent her being sent to Birmingham. She went, anyway, and on arrival received death threats. She defied these, sang her hi-NRG anthem *Diva* and won. Israelis of all sexual orientations celebrated: her win was clearly a boost for gay culture, but Dana had stressed her national identity, too. The win gave Israel much-needed PR, reminding the world that there was more to it than its by now usual embattled, defensive image. However that nation's political troubles remained: the Wye Deal, yet another attempted peace initiative between it and its Palestinian neighbours, was signed later in 1998 but quickly collapsed.

If Dana's win 'queered' the contest, using it to subvert conventional gender roles and narratives, Germany's Guildo Horn simply took the mickey out of it, ripping off various items of clothing, running into the audience, tousling Katie Boyle's hair and ending his set half way up a gantry. His song *Guildo hat euch Lieb (Guildo loves you)* had *nul points* written over it – but came 7th, beating a number of strong singers with reasonable songs.

Both participants were shrewd users of media – which mattered in Eurovision 1998, as televoting was now used by all participants except Cyprus and Hungary. A third contestant was not so shrewd. On winning her country's qualification heats, Switzerland's Gunvor Guggisberg had been feted by *Blick*, that nation's bestselling newspaper. But in the fortnight before the contest, *Blick* started running articles ripping her reputation to shreds. These increased in unpleasantness; on the very morning of the contest, it ran a piece accusing her of having worked in a brothel. One has to admire her courage in going out to sing that evening, but it was in vain. *Lass ihn (Let him go)* was not a great song and Gunvor was no Céline Dion, but it and she didn't deserve the *nul points* they got. Such was the emerging power of the media, to take naïve, ostentatious people from obscurity, to build them up as 'celebrities', then to rip them down again in a vast, public and, of course, money-making (for the media) circus of humiliation.

There had, of course, always been 'celebrity' figures in European life – leaders, famous artists, movie stars – and media like *Paris Match, Bunte, Se og Hør* or *Oggi* to feature them. But the new era was generating a new type of celebrity, 'famous for being famous'. Such individuals are much easier to put through the build-'em-up, knock-'em-down mill than people of genuinely exceptional gifts, who always have their talent or achievements to fall back on. New ways of generating willing fodder for this mill were emerging: next year would see the start of Dutch company Endemol's *Big Brother* TV show, where 'ordinary' people are confined in a house and spied on by cameras, 24/7. The mill was ever busier, too: a survey of news media (in the US, but Europe followed this trend) showed that in 1985 coverage of news took 35% of space and coverage of celebrities 4%, but that by 2000 the figures were 29% news and 8% celebrity.

Yet maybe that was what Europe wanted. The era also saw the consolidation of media ownership into fewer hands: hands that were ever less concerned about standards and ever more about profit. But profit means giving people what they want... So is democracy of taste a liberation from stuffy old elitism, or a new servitude to lowest-common-denominator mediocrity? In 1998 Eurovision was hurtling towards democracy, with the old, potentially elitist juries disappearing and continent-wide phone voting taking over. What would this experiment reveal?

The initial answer seemed to be 'not much'. Maybe the top-of-the-table songs were a bit more modern. There were two black artists in the top four: did this show that the public were less prejudiced than the juries had been, or was this just the case of two good songs with good singers? The UK's Imaani Saleem was particularly impressive, producing that nation's third strong entry in a row. (After this, the Brit-rot would set in. Before 1998, the UK had only twice finished outside the top ten. After 1998, it would only have two top ten placings, one of them 9th, and would soon start racking up an embarrassing list of last or nearly-last places.)

Phone voting did little to change 'language bias', with English lyrics at positions 2, 3 and 9, and Diva's winning chorus sung in fluent internationalese (though older British listeners did appreciate the reference to Queen Victoria).

Amid the media noise, a new nation made its debut in 1998: Macedonia, with the brooding *Ne zori zoro (Somebody stop the Dawn)*. Macedonia was not allowed to call itself that, however, as Greece objected to the name, and Greece had got its foot into European institutions first. So Vlado Janevski sung for the 'Former Yugoslav Republic of Macedonia'. Parts of what used to be 'Macedonia' lie in the modern country of Macedonia and parts of it lie outside, largely in Greece. The Greeks object to the modern use of the name because they think it implies a territorial claim on their bit of former Macedonia. Modern Macedonian politicians deny this claim: they just want to use their country's name.

North of Macedonia, in Kosovo (still then a province of Serbia), the political situation was deteriorating. There had been tension in the region between ethnic Serbs and ethnic Albanians for centuries. In the 1990s the Serbs, despite being only around 10% of the population, had the upper hand, controlling the media and education. In 1997, the collapse of order in neighbouring Albania led to an influx of weapons into the province: the stage was set for violent rebellion, and by 1998 this was escalating fast. By the time of the contest, the once-obscure KLA controlled around a third of the province: three weeks after, Serbs launched a counter-attack. In September the bodies of an extended family of Albanian Kosovars was discovered near the village of Gornje Obrinje: a blood-spattered doll found with one of the murdered children became the defining image of the conflict. NATO threatened air strikes; a cease-fire was agreed, but that soon broke down; by the end of the year fighting had broken out again. In the new year, more talks took place at the beautiful *Château de Rambouillet* near Paris: more ceasefires, more subsequent breaches, more killing. In March 1999, NATO had had enough, and a bombing campaign against Serbia was begun.

In the same month, a 'Committee of Independent Experts' appointed by the European Parliament published its report on the European Commission, which since the retirement of Jacques Delors in 1995 had been led by Luxembourgeois Jacques Santer. Tension between Commission and the Parliament had been rising for a while, with the Commission refusing to share information with the Parliament and the Parliament accusing the

Commission of arrogance and corruption. In 1998 a Commission official, Paul van Buitenen, blew the whistle on financial irregularities – and suffered the usual fate of such brave, conscientious individuals: dismissal and personal defamation. But he had been heard: the Parliament commissioned the report in January 1999, and two months later it appeared. It was damning, saying of the Commission at one point: "It is becoming difficult to find anyone who has even the slightest sense of responsibility". The Commission resigned shortly afterwards.

The farce of the Santer Commission was another turning point in the history of political Europe. The federalist glory days of the late eighties and early nineties – of Jacques Delors and the Maastricht Treaty – were over. Those days had given the European project such momentum that it was still moving ahead, with monetary union – and thus political union – firmly in its sights. But new doubts were emerging. How popular was the project? In the first European election, in 1979, turnout had been over 60% across the (then) EC. In 1994, that had slipped to 57%, but in 1999 it would fall to 49.5%. Defenders of the project could point to the Parliament's positive role in exposing the Santer Commission, but overall, the events gave 'Europe' a bad name.

The concept of 'Europe' had changed since the glory days, too. Before 1989, it had meant Western Europe, essentially Charlemagne's empire plus some outliers tagged on. Now political Europe was following the lead of

Eurovision, and becoming much bigger and more inclusive (and thus harder to corral into a unified federal state). On April 19, 1999, the German *Bundestag* (Federal Parliament) met for the first time in Berlin, making official the move of the new nation's capital from sleepy little Bonn. Europe's centre of gravity made a huge move to the East.

A month after that, it was time to celebrate the whole of Europe, via its song contest, the last of the millennium...

1999

Date: 29 May
Venue: Binyanei Ha-ouma Convention Centre, Jerusalem, Israel
Debut: None
Winner: Charlotte Nilsson, Sweden
Winning Song: *Take me to your Heaven*

The 1999 contest saw two major changes in the rules. Singers were now allowed to use any language they wished, and they could also perform with no orchestra, just a pre-prepared backing track (Johnny Logan commented that this second change had reduced the contest to karaoke). The removal of the language rule opened the door to non-periphery winners, but removed some of the quirkiness and authenticity of the contest   a baton which would soon be taken up by the Liet Festival, of which more later.

A pre-contest poll was also taken on the now-booming internet to identify favourites – though it did not prove very accurate: it selected two songs, one of which came second last with two votes. But the net was here to stay. There were now over 60 million users in Europe, with Germany leading the way, followed by Britain, Italy and France. This represents an astonishing take-up since 1996: essentially, Europe had caught up with the USA. In 2014, some smaller European countries have over 90% 'internet penetration' (that means percentage of people with access to the net, not what some of those people end up watching on it).

The 1999 contest was not a classic. Several singers had trouble with the feedback system which meant that they wandered off key. The English lyrics of many of the non-native English songs were banal (as were the native-speaking English ones, but there was nothing new in that). But the new language rule did allow new nations to appear at the top of the table: Sweden was back in business, and Iceland's techno *All out of Luck* earned the far-northern island, and the lovely Selma Björnsdóttir, second place. Germany and Bosnia experimented with mixing languages – something the judges liked, putting these entries third and seventh.

The German entry, which had lyrical fun with their term for the game of 'musical chairs', *Reise nach Jerusalem (Journey to Jerusalem)*, broke that country's mould by featuring Turkish performers. This reflected a new national mood: in 1998, a Social Democrat /Green coalition, led by Gerhard Schröder, had replaced the last of the eighties/ early nineties titans, Helmut Kohl. Marieluise Beck from the Green Party was made Commissioner for Migration, Refugees and Integration, and took a more positive, welcoming line with that nation's immigrant population, many of whom were second- or third-generation Germans, but still found it hard to get formal German nationality.

France's entrant, Nayah, was a member of the

Mouvement Raëlien, a cult whose members believe that humans were created by extraterrestrials who now come back and visit us in UFOs: a true citizen of the New Age. French officialdom has always had an uneasy relationship with alternative religions, and calls were made for her to be replaced as the national representative. She was – rightly, surely – allowed to sing on, though *Je veux donner ma Voix (I want to give you my Voice)* did not do well.

Songs in Eurovision 1999 were largely presented in a conventional way, with singers singing at us, sometimes with backing support discreetly tucked away behind microphones (Iceland winged out a bit and gave us two manic dancers in macs). It was left to Dana International to put on a truly extravagant show as the interval act.

On the 25th anniversary of Abba's victory, the eventual winner was, perhaps, fitting. The backing track to *Take me to your Heaven* could have been borrowed from *Waterloo*. Less fittingly for the anniversary of a runaway winner that became a Europe-wide hit, bloc voting was a feature of 1999. Academic treatises have been published on the subject – for example biologist Dr Derek Gatherer's, which coins the phrase 'eurovisiopsephology' (the study of Eurovision voting), in which, surely, Terry Wogan should have been given an honorary doctorate. Gatherer points out – and demonstrates mathematically – the formation of voting blocs in the late 1990s. The most notable ones are a 'Viking Empire' (Scandinavia and the northern Baltic states), a 'Balkan bloc', and those old favourites Greece and

Cyprus. The start of the next decade would see the arrival of a 'Warsaw pact' group, initially featuring Latvia, Lithuania, Poland, Russia, Estonia and Romania, and later expanding to include other parts of the former Soviet Union. Eurovision shows that national and regional identity matters to people, as do surveys that we will look at later.

The final act of the contest – once Charlotte Nilsson had received her prize and Dana International had tried to steal the show by falling over when presenting it to her – was for all the contestants to join in singing 1979 winner *Hallelujah*, as a tribute to all the victims of the Balkan war.

That war was still going on as the contestants sang. Serbia was still refusing to quit Kosovo, and NATO was still carrying out airstrikes to persuade it to change its mind. It would be another month before Slobodan Milošević accepted a peace plan to end the fighting.

Once he had done this, a joint NATO/Russian peacekeeping force entered Kosovo. There was little harmony between these new allies. Russia wanted autonomy and its own sector to occupy; NATO wanted overall command of a province-wide operation. This led to a race to control the airport at Pristina, the province's capital, which was won by the Russians. American NATO general Wesley Clark then ordered British forces to block the runway. The officer leading these forces queried this order, and was supported by his commander, General Mike Jackson. This officer was James Blount, who later became singer James Blunt, and is thus the only person to avert a Third World War and have a platinum-selling album.

The decade ended with relative peace in the Balkans. It ended with shares in dotcom companies booming on Europe's stock markets. A 'millennium bug' that was supposed to wreak havoc on the continent's computers at midnight on December 31 had no effect at all, though the fuss about it did highlight how dependent on information technology our lives had become. The Euro was now a reality, though not on the streets. It had been traded on global financial markets since January 1, 1999, as mandated by the Maastricht treaty. The currencies of eleven nations were locked to its value: the old centre countries of Lugano 1956 (less Switzerland) were joined by Austria, Spain, Finland, Ireland and Portugal (the Vatican and San Marino also participated).

Despite the east/west confrontation at Pristina airport, academics, especially in America, began to talk about 'the End of History'. Neo-liberal economics and democratic government were now going to spread out across the world, Taking us to their Heaven slowly but benignly and inexorably.

The 2000s

2000

Date: 13 May
Venue: Globe Arena, Stockholm, Sweden
Debut: Latvia
Winner: The Olsen Brothers, Denmark
Winning Song: *Fly on the Wings of Love*

Eurovision opened the new millennium with ambition: the stadium was the biggest venue yet for the contest, with an audience of 16,000. It was also the first Eurovision to be broadcast on the internet, though this was not a success: Europe's IT infrastructure was not yet up to the job. The bubble in internet-related stocks had popped a few months earlier, but figures for internet use around Europe kept rising: the net was here to stay.

Eurovision 2000 began in a youthful, albeit out of tune, manner, with a hi-NRG entry from Israel's Ping Pong, telling us to *Be Happy* (the singers unfurled Syrian flags at the end of their song). Most of the other contestants were young, too: Ines from Estonia sang of the adventure of being seventeen, Russia's Alsou, eager to go Solo, was a year younger. By contrast, Denmark's Olsen Brothers, Jørgen (aged 50) and Niels (47), had been performing together since before most of the contestants were born – their first band, The Kids, had supported The Kinks when the UK sixties supergroup played Copenhagen. In 2000 the likeable Danes had won their national heats with a song, written by themselves, called *Smuk som et stjerneskud (As beautiful as a Shooting Star)*, in praise of a woman who 'gets more beautiful year after year'. This beauty-in-middle-age theme was toned down for the new, English lyrics used in the final. A shame, in a contest that is often obsessed with youth.

Fourteen of the 24 songs were in English. Sadly, this meant overtime for George Orwell's 1984 'versifier': the clichés flowed thick and fast, and the subject matter of far too many songs was 'I fancy you', with no reflection, irony or poetry. All part of life, of course, but after the sixth repetition it gets a bit samey. Add to this odd phrasings and pronunciations from singers for whom English is not a native language, and you have a recipe for mediocrity.

Between the songs, postcards neatly stressed the interconnection of modern nations: after recording a scene of Swedish life, the camera would zoom in on some item in that scene that actually came from the country about to sing – an Amos Oz novel from Israel, lighting from Denmark, clocks from Switzerland (and so on).

When voting began, the Olsen Brothers stormed into the lead, and they kept it, pulling ever further ahead of the opposition. Jørgen became the first competitor aged over 50 to win. Beneath them was a scoreboard that would have looked bizarre five years before. The north and east of Europe ruled (the top five entrants all had coastline on the Baltic Sea, as did the nation that came seventh). The old centre was slipping down the chart – the two entries in French were last and second-last. The most impressive singer in the contest was probably Switzerland's Jane Bogaert – who came 20th. Germany alone defied this, with Stefan Raab taking the Guildo Horn route of poking fun at the contest (he had co-written Horn's 1998 entry) and coming fifth with *Wadde hadde dudde da* – the title comes from a comment overheard by Raab by an old lady to her dog which had just messed on the pavement. Dutch viewers did not see this turnabout, as that evening, an explosion killed 23 people at a fireworks distributor in the eastern town of Enschede, and NOS, the nation's broadcaster, pulled the show, feeling it was too light for such a solemn moment.

Two representatives of the old Yugoslavia sang in the contest, balladeer Goran Karan from Croatia and the bouncy but not very tuneful XXL from Macedonia. The terrible drama of that region was coming to its end. Elections in what was effectively Serbia (though it still called itself Yugoslavia) had been announced for September 24th. The main opposition parties teamed up to challenge the incumbent President Milošević. On August 25th, one of the main opposition figures, Ivan Stambolic, a former ally of Milošević turned reformist, disappeared – it later turned out he had been murdered on the president's orders. The opposition went on to win the election but with less than half the votes, which would mean a rematch. Complaints were made, of vote-rigging…

Serbia had had enough. People took to the streets, chanting *"Gotov je!"* (He's finished!). A construction worker drove a heavy vehicle into the State TV building: the events of October 2000 became known as the Bulldozer Revolution. Milošević resigned two days later and Serbia began its journey towards modern nationhood – one that would soon include participation in Eurovision. In April next year, the ousted president would be arrested for war crimes.

One nation absent from Eurovision 2000 was Greece. But that nation had other things on its mind: on January 1, 2001, it became the twelfth member of the Euro club. Critics of this move pointed out that both Greece's inflation and its public sector debt were way beyond the official 'convergence criteria' that had been designed to keep unstable economies out of the new currency. But optimism was the order of the day. Greece met some of the criteria, and, more important, it was eager to join.

In the same upbeat mood, 2000 saw the European Council produce its Lisbon Agenda: "the Union has today set itself a new strategic goal for the next decade: to become the most competitive and dynamic knowledge-based economy in the world, capable of sustainable economic growth with more and better jobs and greater social cohesion."

While producing a number of sensible policy ideas – better education, more expenditure on research, less 'red tape' for business (especially smaller business) – the agenda

240

didn't really explain how these would make Europe overtake the USA, Japan or China, who were also busting a gut to be biggest and best. More worrying still, it didn't explain what Europe had to do if faced with a choice between social cohesion and competitiveness: the agenda simply assumed that such a trade-off shouldn't be necessary.

A serious lack of realism seemed to be creeping into the European project. But maybe mood is all. Let Ping Pong set the tone. Be happy!

2001

Date: 12 May
Venue: Parken Stadium, Copenhagen, Denmark
Winner: Tanel Padar and Dave Benton, Estonia
Winning Song: *Everybody*

Literal-minded people had spent much of 1999 and 2000 pointing out to the rest of us that the millennium really began on January 1, 2001. For them, *this* was the first Eurovision of the new era.

Eurovision 2001 certainly had more of a 'start-of-an-era' feel to it than 2000. It was the biggest yet (and is still the biggest ever): Denmark stuck a roof over their national football stadium and made a venue for 38,000 fans. The first song of the contest, *Out on my own*, by the Netherlands' Michelle, was about walking away from the past in a new spirit of freedom, though the song's restrained tone carried a measure of sadness: freedom, we infer, comes at a cost.

Michelle later put her words into practice by marrying her girlfriend in 2006. The month before Eurovision 2001, the Netherlands had become the first nation in the world to allow same-sex couples formally to marry (the contest's host nation, Denmark, had instituted something similar, a 'registered partnership', back in 1989). Belgium would be next in 2003; the rest of Europe is still slowly catching up.

Twenty-two songs followed, many with soaring vocals

242

over punchy, techno beats: Slovenia, Malta and Greece stand out. Russia's Mumiy Troll, from distant Vladivostok, went down a different route, indie rock (or 'rockapops' as the band, still big in Russia and the Far East, called their style). Lead singer Ilya Lagutenko brimmed with adolescent attitude. France also eschewed techno, and returned to its traditions with *Je n'ai que mon Ame (I have only my Soul)*. Natasha St-Pier did the song proud, putting herself up there with the contest's classic francophone power balladeers: Anne-Marie David, Marie Myriam, Corinne Hermès, Céline Dion (St-Pier is also from French Canada). Unlike them, she sang the last verse of her song in English. *Mon dieu!* Popular with the crowd was the final act of the night, Denmark's own Rollo and King, with their catchy *Never ever let you go*.

Denmark, France and Estonia featured well in the early voting, and Estonia eventually came out the winner. Tanel Padar and Dave Benton had also avoided techno, preferring to go back to late 1970s funk. The song was not that special, but it was performed with gusto, especially by Benton. His spontaneity was a contrast to the heavily choreographed stage-shows of some other entrants, and voters seemed to warm to this. He took Jørgen Olsen's record for the oldest victor, and also became the first black contestant to win. About time, too, given the contribution of black artists to European popular music.

The win was a triumph for the small Baltic state (it has a population of 1.3 million: on the list of European countries

243

ranked by population, it comes 41st). Ten years earlier Estonia had been an occupied 'republic' of the Soviet Union; in 2001 not only was it competing in Eurovision as a free, European nation, but it was winning. Centre, and even old-peripheral, nations can easily take their European identity for granted. Estonians do not. People partied all night in Tallinn after the win; Padar and Benton were welcomed by the country's president, Mart Laar, when they returned from Copenhagen. The premier commented, "We freed ourselves from the Soviet empire through song. Now we will sing our way into Europe!"

2001 is one of my favourite contests, with exciting, energetic songs. This is despite the presenters, whose arch rhyming couplets sent people demented (Terry Wogan treated them with particular derision but he'd long since stopped enjoying Eurovision). Technologically, another attempt was made to stream the contest live, but Europe's infrastructure was still not yet up to it. There were also facilities for viewers to go online and chat with the contestants: there is something both modern and ironic about the apparent intimacy of such chats and the actual impersonal vastness of the stadium where the contest was held.

Later in the year, three events took place that would define Europe's new era. Maybe the pedants were right about 2001 being the start of the millennium.

Enough has been written of the September 11 attacks in New York; I don't need to add anything here, except,

244

perhaps, to point out that nationals of 20 Eurovision contestant nations died in them, almost half (67) from the UK. A great feeling of solidarity with America swept over Europe – *Nous sommes tous Américains* (We are all Americans) commented Paris newspaper *Le Monde* the next day. (More revolving sounds from a grave at Colombey-les-deux-Églises?)

Three months later, China joined the World Trade Organization. That nation's exports to the West had been quietly growing since it liberalized its economy back in 1978. These stalled a bit at the end of the 1990s, but the new decade would seem them skyrocket. With seemingly boundless supplies of poorly-paid labour and a currency kept cheap by its government, China began to drive European manufacturers out of business. That Lisbon Agenda aim of being both the world's most competitive economy and its cuddliest society was already beginning to look unachievable.

Finally, at the stroke of midnight on December 31, the Euro became the everyday currency in twelve European nations. In Germany, it became the only currency, though you could still take your old Deutschmarks to banks and change them (you still can). Elsewhere there was a two-month period when you could use both, though ATM machines only dispensed Euros and traders of all kinds were expected to give all change in the new. Despite complaints about prices being rounded up, the change was essentially trouble-free.

The new currency was justified on various economic grounds, such as ease of transactions and cross-border price comparison. But it had always meant more. On the day the new money hit the streets, Wim Duisenberg, the Governor of the European Central Bank, observed that the change was "not only the completion of economic and monetary union... but one of the major, if not the major, steps forward in the history of European integration".

2002

Date: 25 May
Venue: Saku Suurhall Arena, Tallinn, Estonia
Winner: Marie N, Latvia
Winning Song: *I wanna*

When the post-victory partying in Tallinn had died down, Estonian TV was left with a headache: could they afford to stage the 2002 contest? After some national soul-searching the answer was yes, Estonia could and must put on the show. It was all part of their new European status and pride in that status. The decision was, surely, justified from the moment two presenters walked out onto the stage of Estonia's brand-new and largest venue and shouted "Hello Europe!"

The contest's 'theme' – an innovation in 2002 – was 'A Modern Fairytale'. Fairytales have happy endings, and Eurovision 2002 was a celebration of one such story.

The contest produced some interesting controversies. A campaign had been launched to get Israel, represented in 2002 by a big star, Sarit Hadad, banned. It failed, but on the night, TV commentators in Sweden and Belgium actually asked people not to vote for *Light a Candle*. "She may be wearing white, but don't be fooled into thinking that Israel wants peace," said the Belgian. Tension between Israel and Palestine had been mounting since late 2000, when the peace process between the two nations had broken down. The tragic but oft-repeated cycle of atrocity and counter-atrocity had been ratcheting up since then, with youngsters killed by both sides, then suicide bombings, then Israeli military action. May 2002 saw both the second Palestinian *intifada* and Israel's reaction to it in full swing.

Slovenia was less used to controversy. But its 2002 entrants – selected by local juries – were Sestre, a drag act. When this was announced, anti-gay protestors took to the streets of Ljubljana. Slovenian TV changed its decision, and it was the turn of gay activists to hit the streets, flying a huge rainbow flag outside the TV station. The issue was raised in both the Slovenian and European parliaments. Dutch MEP Lousewies van der Laan commented that homophobia could not "be deemed acceptable in a candidate to join the European Union". The broadcaster reversed its decision, and Sestre went to Tallinn, where they came thirteenth.

As a sign of the times, both Britain and Spain featured artistes selected through televised talent contests: *Pop Idol* in the UK and, from Spain, a special series designed to find the year's Eurovision contestant, *Operación Triunfo*. Both selections appeared to pay off: Britain's Jessica Garlick came third: no British entry has done as well since. Rosa López' performance was watched by more Spanish TV viewers than any other event, until that nation played in (and won) the 2008 European Cup Final. Plucked from obscurity by the contest, she went on to have a successful singing career. Talent contests, once regarded as cheesy, would loom big in European media from then on.

The contest was won by Marija Naumova, a Latvian jazz singer. *I Wanna* often appears in polls of worst-ever Eurovision winners. Like the previous year's top song, its victory was more about the performance than the material: Naumova produced an immaculately choreographed show whereby she came on in a tuxedo and ended up in a long, flame-red dress. During the song she flirted with both female and male backing singers. The lyrics, especially the last line of the chorus, show the danger of singing in non-native languages. She wants to be the last what in my eyes? No, it's 'love spark', apparently. (Most Eurovision fans have their favourite easy-to-mishear lyrics. My personal fave comes from the previous year, when Malta's Fabrizio Faniello spent the second verse of *Another Summer Night* summoning up a picture of a scorching hot summer beach, then appeared to end it with 'And a snowman passing by'.)

France stood up for older traditions with a power ballad about peace, *Il faut du Temps (It takes Time)*, and did well, coming fifth. But English did seem to be engulfing the competition. As a welcome contrast, a new contest for songs in European regional and minority languages was held around the same time as Eurovision. The first Liet International Festival took place in Leeuwarden in Friesland, near the northern coast of the Netherlands. Competitors sang in Catalan, Frisian, Breton, Sami, Basque,

Gaelic, Kashubian (a Polish dialect), North Frisian, Occitan (from southern France / northern Spain and Italy) and Welsh; the winners were a duo from Catalonia. The contest was a success, and has been held annually from then on, apart from a break in 2013.

The Netherlands were not competing in Eurovision 2002, having finished too low in the previous years' contest. That was perhaps painful enough to this long-standing, eager competitor, but May saw the nation suffer another blow to its identity, when a Dutch politician was assassinated. This is not the Dutch way: you say what you think, to the point of tactlessness if necessary; you take similar criticism if it comes your way; you never doubt the other person's right to speak, however wrong they seem. Pim Fortuyn's anti-immigrant views were unattractive to many, but his silencing by the gun horrified Europe's arguably most liberal nation. Conspiracy theories bubbled up briefly, but the assassin, as often happens, turned out to be a loner.

Violence was an underlying theme of the year 2002. Events in Iraq were drifting towards war. American president George W Bush was determined to remove Iraqi dictator Saddam Hussein, incorrectly believing he was in some way implicated in the 9/11 atrocity. Would Europe get embroiled in this conflict? America was stepping up the pressure. There was doubt that the United Nations would sanction an invasion, the way it had done in 1991: instead, Bush sought to build a 'coalition of the willing'. However, in Europe, only Britain seemed seriously willing. The rest of the continent was split between half-hearted support and no support at all. Transatlantic relationships, warm after 9/11, were fast deteriorating.

This was not a good time for European-level government. There was no common position on Iraq, and fresh accusations of corruption were leaking out of Brussels. Were we going to see another Santer Commission? Earlier in the year, the EU had appointed Marta Andreasen as its Chief Accountant. Andreasen soon found out that the accounts were a mess. Attempts to sort the matter internally failed, and she finally went public with her criticisms, which led to her being dismissed. Her tale, of corruption, smugness, sexism and bullying, did not reflect well on an institution that was supposed to lead, and thus instantiate the best values of, Europe.

Eurovision was coming in for criticism, too. The last two winners had been weak and had failed to sell on the streets. Was it, like the European Commission, losing touch?

2003

Date: 24 May
Venue: Skonto Olympic Hall, Riga, Latvia
Winner: Sertab Erener, Turkey
Winning Song: *Everyway that I can*

The 2003 contest took place in the shadow of a war. Militarily, the second Iraq war had been won by the time Marie N and Renars Kaupers welcomed Europe to Riga. But the real battle, to win the 'hearts and minds' of Iraqis, had only just begun.

The early part of 2003 had seen America pressing ever harder for European nations to join its coalition, but to little avail. George W Bush is reputed to have phoned French president Jacques Chirac and told him that events were the fulfilment of a prophecy from Chapter 38 of the Book of Ezekiel. Even despite this, Chirac did not alter his refusal either to participate in the coalition or vote for war in the United Nations. (America then refused to serve French fries in the congressional cafeteria; 'Freedom Fries' appeared on the menu instead.)

On February 15, huge anti-war demonstrations were held in major European cities. As many as three million people are rumoured to have taken to the streets of Rome; Madrid and London both probably saw a million protestors. The marches were notable for the wide range of people participating; not just political radicals but individuals from all walks of life felt an overriding need to speak up.

This mood was seized upon by philosopher Jürgen Habermas, who wrote a piece for the *Frankfurter Allgemeine Zeitung* entitled *What binds Europeans together: a Plea for a common foreign Policy, beginning in the Core of Europe*. It's a fascinating piece, suggesting some of Europe's strengths but also, possibly, revealing a fatal flaw. Habermas (the piece was co-signed by fellow philosopher Jacques Derrida, but Habermas was the author) outlined three values shared by Europe's core: religious faith as a private matter; a perception that the state has a 'civilizing' influence (in contrast to the marketplace); a distrust of violence (this lesson hard-learnt from colonialism and two terrible wars). The European project, he argues, is built round these, and as such is a continuation of the eighteenth-century Enlightenment, the 'Age of Reason'.

These are interesting points, but at the same time, the piece suffers from a potentially damaging arrogance. The piece is about 'Lugano 1956' Europe: it explicitly excludes Eastern Europe and Britain from its self-admiring 'core', because of their co-operation with America in Iraq. However one does not have to go back very far to see core Europe practicing violence, too: France's Algerian war, for example, or Germany's own dark twentieth century history. The piece's tone is uncompromisingly elitist: it contains sentences like 'The political-ethical will that drives the hermeneutics of processes of self-understanding is not arbitrary'. Both Habermas and Derrida are men of the far left, but they do not

253

deign to express themselves in language that European working men and women would understand. Surveys taken around this time show political Europe to be much more popular among the elite than among ordinary Europeans: this article helps us see why.

Whatever one feels about the piece (it can be seen as both informative in content and arrogant in tone), it is certainly a sign of its times. The war was making Europe ask: who are we, and what do we believe?

I very much doubt that Professors Habermas or Derrida watched Eurovision 2003. If they had, they would have seen an interesting show. After two years of rather samey (though fun) techno, contestants were looking to be different. Belgium's Urban Trad sang their haunting, Celtic-influenced Sanomi in a made-up language – and were rewarded for their imaginativeness with second place. Austria, as it often does, went left-field and produced joker Alf Poier making fun of the contest and also humanity's attitudes to animals. Others just turned off the synthesizers and just sang pleasant songs – I liked Malta's easy-listening *To dream again*, though not many other people did, as it came second last.

Media focus before the contest was on Russia's entrants, t.A.T.u.: two young women who arrived with a reputation for being shocking – a reputation that had sold a lot of records. Part of their 'shock' was that they claimed to be lesbians, though by 2003 this was hardly radical in Eurovision – and they turned out to be heterosexual, anyway. In Riga, they behaved like spoilt teenagers, turning up late to rehearsals then complaining about the facilities. They threatened to sing their song naked, but actually performed in some old jeans and T-shirts, thereby earning themselves the 2003 Barbara Dex award. The most shocking thing about t.A.T.u. turned out to be the quality of their performance. The crowd booed, partially no doubt because of Stalin but mostly because the duo had behaved like brats and put on a bad show. Their third place was a reward for pre-existing notoriety than for anything they brought to Latvia.

But perhaps they didn't want to bring anything to Latvia. There's a sense that t.A.T.u. was a giant V-sign from Russia to the West: "You think you're so liberal – well, put up with this then!" Fifteen years ago, that nation had been a superpower; now it was struggling to find its identity (and even its geographical boundaries: in 2003 it was at war with separatists in Chechnya). Fifteen years ago, it had claimed political and moral superiority to the west; now its old ideology had been discredited and it was recovering from a financial crash (its government bonds had been rated as junk from 2000 to 2002). To add to its pain, Russia's old arch-enemy was now trampling round the Middle East, unchecked. And in Eurovision, the last two winners had come from countries which had once been part of its inner empire and which now made no secret of their unmitigated delight at this being no longer the case. Ouch!

It is often said that the voting (which could, for the first time, be done by SMS) in 2003 was a European comment on the Iraq war. Britain, America's sidekick in the conflict, came last, getting *nul points* for the only time in its competition history. Turkey, which had resisted attempts to drag it into the coalition and had not allowed US forces an invasion route into northern Iraq, won.

However it wasn't purely political: Britain's entry was dire, with the singers, plucked from obscurity, hideously out of tune (to be fair, they had problems with the on-stage sound system, but one feels that a more established act would have overcome this). Victorious Turkey, on the other hand, pulled out all the stops. An established star, Sertab Erener, was chosen to represent them. She wrote the song herself, and insisted on singing in English – an unpopular move back home, until her song won, after which all was forgiven. A lush pre-contest promo video set *Everyway that I can* in a harem, and an imaginative choreographic routine was built around her for the live performance. After the contest, the song sold well round Europe, reaching Number One in Greece and Sweden as well as back home. It still does well in 'greatest ever Eurovision songs' polls, long after Turkey's stance on the Iraq war has been forgotten.

And yet… The 2003 contest does seem to come from a different, golden age, rather like that of 1956. In May 2003, most of Europe was distancing itself from America's adventure in Iraq. It was reaching out to an Islamic country, awarding first prize to a song steeped in that country's culture: *Everyway* might have been in English, but its music and dance were thoroughly Turkish. The most positive aspects of Habermas' and Derrida's message were sinking in: Europe has its own way. An exciting new future beckoned (2003 also saw new beginnings for Eurovision, with the first Junior Song Contest, for singers aged between 8 and 15, held in Copenhagen in November of that year.)

But poison was seeping out of Iraq. The victorious coalition was not greeted by cheering crowds and spontaneous order but by looters and bombers. Liberation began to turn into occupation. As 2003 progressed, reports of US treatment of prisoners in Abu Ghraib prison began to emerge. The coalition's attempt to control the conquered country became a recruiting drive for militant Islamist organizations, as young men watched videos of the war over the internet. The ugliness of these organizations would become ever more apparent. In early 2004, a few terrorists – it only takes a few – let off a horrendous set of bombs on Spanish commuter trains. Later that year, a school in the south of Russia would be attacked and nearly two hundred children killed.

The world, that had seemed to be coming closer together in liberal, democratic harmony, was suddenly becoming messy and scary again.

2004

Date of the final: 15 May
Venue: Abdi Ipecki Arena, Istanbul, Turkey
Debuts: Albania, Andorra, Belarus, Serbia/Montenegro.
Winner: Ruslana, Ukraine
Winning Song: *Wild Dances*

On May 1, ten new states joined the EU: Cyprus, the
Czech Republic, Estonia, Hungary, Latvia, Lithuania,
Malta, Poland, Slovakia and Slovenia. If Frankfurt's
philosophers wanted to concentrate on 'Lugano 1956'
Europe, political reality was pushing in the opposite
direction.

Eurovision was expanding, too. 2004 saw a record
number of entries: 36 nations, all eager to join in and thus
be European. A semi-final was held on the Wednesday
before the Big Night. The deal was that Saturday's final
would feature last year's top ten nations, the host, the 'Big
Four' (Germany, France, Britain and Spain), and the top
ten songs from the semi. Several Eurovision stalwarts
failed to jump this hurdle: Israel, Denmark, Portugal, as
well as new stars Estonia and Latvia.

The contest stayed peripheral, too – this time, it was
held in long-term EU aspirant, Turkey. The contest's
theme was 'Under the Same Sky', a hint to negotiators in
Brussels (and a quote from 1990's Euro-anthem winner,

Insieme 1992). The nation's Prime Minister, Recep Tayyip Erdogan, was among the enthusiastic, 12,500-strong audience: Eurovision mattered.

A better theme for the contest would probably have been the name of the eventual winning song, as 2004 was the year that choreography took over from singing. Much of that choreography was sexually explicit, with pawing and pelvic thrusting and plenty of thighs, cleavages, rippling muscles and six-packs on show. Several contestants seemed to have got their outfits from Ann Summers.

This might lead one to assume a certain dim-wittedness about the event, but, as usual, there is more to Eurovision than meets the eye or ear. The winner, Ruslana, who bounded onstage clad in (not a lot of) leather was a classically-trained musician, who later went on to become a serious politician and social activist. She wrote *Wild Dances* herself and plays the drums on the backing track; while she clearly had one eye on modern Eurovision trends, the piece reflects a long-standing interest in her country's traditional folk culture, especially that of the Carpathian mountains where she grew up.

Ukraine's Eurovision win coincided with its arrival on the European political stage. After breaking from the Soviet Union, it had suffered a major economic collapse in the mid-1990s, but by the end of the decade, things had picked up. Voices then began to be raised about its leadership. An investigative journalist was murdered in 2000. A tape of President Leonid Kuchma revealed him to be doing deals with Iraqi dictator Saddam Hussain. In the 2004 presidential election, Kuchma was not eligible, so his Prime Minister Viktor Yanukovytch stood. Yanukovytch's opponent was Viktor Yushchenko, a former finance minister who favoured closer links with Europe. During the campaign, Yushchenko developed a mysterious and debilitating illness – most likely a result of dioxin poisoning, which, if true, is almost undoubtedly the result of a deliberate attempt to kill him. The election appeared to be won by Yanukovytch, but few people apart from his core supporters believed the results to be fair. Ukraine took to the streets, despite the mid-winter weather. Huge rallies were addressed by opposition politicians – including Ruslana, who soon became a key figure in the opposition movement. The Orange Revolution was underway.

On December 26, Ukraine's Supreme Court declared the election void and ordered a fresh one, which was held in January 2005. It was won by Yushchenko and his Our Ukraine Party. Ruslana became a member of the Ukrainian parliament.

The Orange Revolution was at least partially about removing a corrupt administration. But it was also about belonging. A look at political voting patterns reveals trouble in store for Eurovision's 2004 winner. It shows a country facing two ways, its east towards Russia, its west towards Europe.

Another country placed on the European map by the 2004 contest was Serbia. We left this country having finally ousted Slobodan Milosevic. In 2003, now known as Serbia and Montenegro, it had begun its application to join the EU. In the same year, its Prime Minister had been murdered, as part of a conspiracy by old-guard loyalists and organized crime. However, the assassination made Europe-friendly liberals more determined than ever to move on from the past. The country's debut in Eurovision 2004 was a sign of this – and was rewarded with second place. Željko Joksimovic's *Lane moje (My Sweetheart)* was a powerful contrast to the winner, melancholy and gentle (though it shares with Wild Dances musical influences from its country's folk traditions).

Greece came third, courtesy of heartthrob Sakis Rouvas' Shake it. Later in 2004, that nation would host an impressive Olympic Games, another apparent triumph for Eastern Europe.

The other results from Eurovision 2004 reflected this new, eastern bullishness, too. Of the top nine countries, only Germany and Sweden were not located in or around the Balkans. Of the top fourteen, ten were Balkan/eastern Mediterranean. 'Old Europe' – France (despite featuring a bizarre lady on stilts), the UK, the Netherlands, Austria, Belgium, Ireland, Norway – languished at the bottom.

Old Europe was further embarrassed by the publication in November of a report by Dutch politician Wim Kok on the EU's progress towards the goals outlined in the 2000 Lisbon Agenda – or rather lack of progress. Europe was not becoming the world's most dynamic economy; instead, other economies were surging past it: China, India, even the EU founding fathers' old foe, America. More depressing still, the report didn't question the agenda or the realism of its goals, simply berated European governments for not fulfilling it properly.

Around the same time, Greece admitted to having fudged the figures that allowed it to join the Euro. It could hardly be thrown out, so nothing was done. Nothing was done, either, when France announced that it had broken the Maastricht rules. Europe's economy was doing OK. If a plan that hadn't been very realistic in the first place was being ignored, and past or minor infringements of club rules were forgiven, did that really matter?

Arguably a more pressing concern for political Europe was the continuing lack of public identification with it. While people generally approved of the EU, they felt little passion for it. Back in 1988, a survey had asked people around Europe how they saw themselves. Were they European, national, or a mixture of both? Few respondents (about 4%) had seen themselves purely European, and not many more as European first and national second. Instead, the vast majority had seen themselves as national first and European second (48%) or purely national and not European at all (38%). By 2004, these figures…

…were almost exactly the same. Nearly twenty years of European flags, anthems, a Treaty on European Union, the introduction of the Euro, the Lisbon Agenda (etc.) had had no effect at all on Europeans' perception of who, when push came to shove, they actually were.

The data (cited in Neil Fligstein's excellent book, *Euroclash*) can also be broken down into nations. Surprise, surprise, Britain leads the way in Euro-disinterest with 65% 'just national'. 27% of Britons say they are national first and European second, with just 8% preferring to be Europeans. But five other nations also have more than 50% of 'purely national' respondents: Finland, Sweden, Greece, Austria and Ireland. The Netherlands are knocking on this door, at 49%. And most of the countries that score relatively low in the 'purely national' score highly on 'national first/European second'. Over 50% of respondents in Spain, Italy, France, Denmark see themselves in this category.

On the other side of the chart, only the inhabitants of Luxembourg show any enthusiasm for being 'purely European', with 19%. In no other country does this figure get above 7% (Belgium, the next most European). It is only in the world of Lugano 1956 that more than 10% of a nation's population see themselves as either purely European or European first/national second. Five of The Six hit this rather unambitious mark, with the Netherlands falling short, only managing 7% in these two categories.

In other words, in peripheral European countries (old and new periphery) over 90% of the population see themselves as totally or primarily national. In the old core, this figure reduces, but only to around 85% – except in Euro-minded Luxembourg. But even here, over two thirds

(68%) of people say they belong to the Grand Duchy rather than to Europe.

Enemies of the European project will jump for joy at reading these figures. Friends of the project should feel humility. Eurovision, which is sometimes derided as being 'nationalistic', turns out to be an accurate reflection of the European mindset. Which, of course, is why over 100 million of us watch it.

2005

Date of the final: 21 May
Venue: Palace of Sports, Kyiv, Ukraine
Debuts: Bulgaria, Moldova
Winner: Helena Paparizou, Greece
Winning Song: *My Number One*

Ukraine's hosting of Eurovision 2005 was another example of the contest blazing a trail for 'European' modernity beyond the continent's traditional boundaries. A lasting legacy of this was the nation's visa policy. In order to make it easy for people to attend the event, Ukraine temporarily dropped its visa requirements for visitors from Europe and, while they were about it, North America. The plan was to reintroduce them once the circus had left town, but the removal proved so popular with local business leaders that it was made permanent. If you're travelling to Kyiv in 2016, you have Eurovision to thank for the lack of bureaucratic obstacles to your journey.

The theme for the contest was 'Awakening'. It was certainly very loud. Rock and punk found their way into the repertoire ("Rock is the new *schlager*," proclaimed Norway's glam-rock entrants Wig Wam). Most of all 2005 was the year of onstage percussion. This took an intriguing range of forms, from Romanian oil drums to a smiling elderly lady tapping a traditional *doba* during Moldova's anarchic entry. Over many of the beats, folk instruments twirled, taking Eurovision audiences to new Balkan and Middle-Eastern musical worlds. By contrast, a few balladeers stuck to their guns, standing and singing and being well rewarded: Chiara from Malta came second and Israel's Shiri Maimon fourth. Choreography triumphed in the end, however, with Helena Paparizou's stage show (literally, at one point) lifting her to being Europe's Number One.

Lyrically, much of what was on offer was bland – but there were some exceptions, mostly towards the end of the evening. Walters and Kazha, two young Latvians, sang *The War is not over*. The lyric contained a dig at the 'fairytale' theme of Estonia's 2002 Eurovision: the Cold War may be history, but life remains tough. France's Ortal Malka knew why: in the modern world, *Chacun pense á soi (Everyone thinks of themselves)*. Russia agreed: the dream offered by 'sweet America' has disappeared, according to Natalia Podolskaya – who then went on to reference the victim of a serial child killer; not usual Eurovision fare (but classic Russian stirring).

More obvious politics came from the hosts, for whom GreenJolly half-sang, half-rapped a street anthem from the Orange Revolution, *Razom nas Bahato (Together we are Many)*. This entry itself was controversial – aren't Eurovision songs supposed to be non-political? And another Ukranian singer, Ani Lorak, who happened to be a supporter of the old regime, had been pushed aside at the last minute to

266

allow GreenJolly to participate. *Razom* was, sadly, not very melodious, and finished way down the table – a disappointment, no doubt, for President Yushchenko, who at the end of the contest presented the winner with a special award (though he probably enjoyed kissing Helena Paparizou more than he would have Roman Kalyn, GreenJolly's stocky, crop-haired lead vocalist).

Perhaps the most intriguing thing about the lyrics of 2005 was their tendency to concentrate on the obsessional aspects of love: love as fantasy, love as a drug. Together with the pouting and posing of many of the acts, the spirit of Paul Oscar's 1997 *Final Dance* seemed to have won the day.

Was this a political comment, too? Europe was beginning to dope itself up with credit. Intended or not, Eurovision's metaphor is spookily apt. Within the Eurozone, countries that had traditionally had to pay high rates of interest on loans because they had been considered weak economically suddenly found themselves able to borrow in the new currency at low rates. So that's what they did. Governments such as Portugal and Greece borrowed, borrowed, borrowed to keep sleepy public sectors chugging along. Banks in Ireland and Spanish regional banks lent, lent, lent to property speculators.

Outside the Eurozone, British banks were perhaps the daftest of the lot, both lending irresponsibly and, intoxicated with 'sweet America's dream', trading new financial products that they did not understand in the misguided belief that these 'derivatives' would somehow automatically find realistic prices. (This belief, more bizarre than anything Eurovision could come up with, goes back to a PhD thesis written in 1965 by an American economist, Eugene Fama, who claimed to have proven that financial markets were efficient – in other words no matter how artificial the items traded, and even how ignorant the participants were of their nature, knowledge would in some way pool itself in the buying and selling and a fair price would establish itself.)

One exception to this folly was Germany, a nation traditionally obsessed with keeping its economic house in order. Perhaps as a punishment for not joining the credit-addicts club (or perhaps because their song wasn't very good), that nation was awarded the wooden spoon in Eurovision 2005 for *Run and hide* – to which the singer, Gracia, philosophically observed "Well, somebody has to come last". The German economy seemed to be in the doldrums, too, with slow growth and uncharacteristically low levels of investment. People were smugly talking about the continent's former economic leader as 'the sick man of Europe' – though in fact all it was doing was staying off the steroids. It would not be long before that tune changed. In September 2005, the person to bring that change about came to power, Angela Merkel, a former Chemistry student from the *Land* of Brandenburg in the old GDR. She would soon outshine even Helmut Kohl (and Helena Paparizou) in being Europe's Number One.

European leaders had been working on a European constitution since 2001; by the end of 2004 they had agreed on its contents and signed a treaty bringing it into being – once it had been ratified by member nations. Ratification can take several forms: usually a vote in that nation's parliament is enough, but seven European countries decided this was so important that a national public vote was required. Shortly after Eurovision 2005, the people of France went to the polls, and rejected the constitution by 55% to 45% (a relative of Ortal Malka's reportedly voted *'non'* because her song did so badly in Eurovision – it came second last). The Netherlands followed, even less enthusiastic (no, by 61% to 39%). Only one more vote was taken, in Luxembourg, where it of course won, but by that time the European constitution was dead. Federalists were shocked; if they had studied the figures cited in the last section they would have been less so.

Voting of a less political kind took place on October 22, when a special programme, *Congratulations*, was broadcast from Copenhagen to celebrate 50 Eurovision Song Contests (Euro-sulky Britain and snobby France didn't bother to broadcast it). Viewers were polled for their favourite Eurovision song of all time. To create a bit of suspense – well, a tiny bit, anyway – I've put the results in an appendix.

2006

Date of the final: 20 May
Venue: OAKA Olympic Arena, Athens, Greece
Debuts: Armenia
Winner: Lordi, Finland
Winning Song: *Hard Rock Hallelujah*

In Eurovision 2006, 37 nations competed, from tiny Andorra, who gave us four backing singers in stockings and suspenders, to vast Russia, with three ballerinas, one of whom seemed to have got stuck half-in, half-out-of a piano. In contrast with the previous two years, a wide range of musical styles was on offer. There was comedy from Iceland (even though it backfired: lots of people didn't get the joke and thought that Silvia Night, a caricature materialistic narcissistic young woman created by actress Ágústa Eva Erlendsdóttir, was genuine). There was acapella from Latvia, a football chant from Lithuania's LT United, country and western (plus Stetsons and onstage cacti) from Germany, a poppy girl-band from Spain, rap from Britain, techno from Romania, beautiful *sevdah* from Bosnia, and, of course, Gothic metal from Finland. Other nations went back to their Eurovision roots – a singer plus violins for Norway, ballads from Ireland and France, an Abba-like entry from Sweden. Greece put on a superb show, to match the extravaganzas of the late 1990s. It was all great fun.

Critics of Eurovision say it is 'formulaic', but looking through the varied entrants from 2006 shows that this isn't true: this contest was about Europe's diversity. It showed old traditions – the first record of a *sevdah* song goes back to 1475: the Bosnian genre, one of melancholy love songs, has influences from Turkey and both Jewish and Islamic Spain. (The word *sevdah* also means a particular feeling: that mixture of sadness and joy that comes from looking back at past happiness, especially in a relationship that has ended. It is untranslatable into English, though the poet Tennyson understood it when he wrote ''Tis better to have loved and lost than never to have loved at all'.)

It showed new traditions – metal has become a part of Nordic life, not to everyone's taste but a passion for some. It showed cross-cultural borrowing – Romania's Mihai Traistariu sang his catchy chorus in Italian: *Tornerò (I will return)* came fourth in the contest and became popular around Europe. (Traistariu is known as the 'male Mariah Carey' for his extraordinary vocal range, which extends five octaves.)

Russia took Eurovision at face value, and nearly won. It entered an established star, Dima Bilan, singing an attractive ballad, *Never let you go*. This reflected a new mood in the land of past European cultural giants, of Tchaikovsky, Tolstoy and Stravinsky; it seemed at last to want a place in modern political Europe. Geographers have traditionally split Russia in two, calling the 38% of the country west of the crest of the Ural Mountains 'European' – a minority of its space, but where 77% of its people live. The Russians themselves have been more ambivalent about being European, in both imperial and Soviet times often using the term 'European Russia' for subject states like Ukraine and Belarus. But in 2006, there seemed little ambivalence: the Bear wanted in, and a Eurovision win would help.

It didn't get one, however: its old adversary, Finland, pushed it firmly into second place. *Hard Rock Hallelujah*'s victory was seen as a national triumph. "Years of humiliation, frustration, and 'zero points' were wiped away," said one Helsinki newspaper (43 years to be precise, the longest time any nation has gone in the contest before winning). The Finnish prime minister suddenly announced he was a fan of heavy rock. An estimated 100,000 Finns attended a rally to welcome the winners to the capital (the city's population is half a million). A square was named after them in Rovaniemi, home town of lead singer Mr Lordi. Pepsi started marketing Lordi Cola. It was announced that the band would feature on a commemorative stamp (the odd, cloud-shaped stamps appeared in 2007, to celebrate the holding of that year's contest in Helsinki).

Who says Eurovision is just a TV show?

It wasn't just a win, either, but a very Finnish win. The band's monster outfits – and Mr Lordi's auto-biography (he is the son of a troll and a demon, and rides a sleigh pulled by vampire reindeer) – resonate with the great Scandinavian myths and their violent, mystical world. Finland had tried paying tribute to this tradition before in the contest, back in 1977, but *Lapponia* had pulled too many punches. Lordi did it the Eurovision way: go for broke! *Hard Rock Hallelujah* followed *Everyway that I can* and *Wild Dances* in presenting Europe with splendidly dramatized visions of its periphery.

Yet for one of those nations, the new sense of belonging was already beginning to decay. Negotiations about Turkey's accession to the EU stalled in 2006. The main reason was the continuing stalemate over Cyprus, but behind that was a lingering lack of political will in Europe. In 2007 French presidential candidate Nicolas Sarkozy would claim "Turkey has no place in the European Union". In Turkey itself, the old aims of Europeanization inherited from Kemal Ataturk – and celebrated (or was it parodied?) by Çetin Alp – were beginning to be questioned. Would Turkey be better off pursuing a 'neo-Ottoman' agenda, forgetting Europe and concentrating on its relations with members of its former empire?

Back in core Europe, a (relatively) old institution was notching up a success. The European Space Agency had been founded in 1975. Its founder members were the same nations who had been part of the third Eurovision Song Contest in 1958 (minus Austria) – Hilversum Europe, not Lugano. In 2006 its VEX spacecraft arrived at its destination and went into orbit, examining a planet's

273

atmosphere – it is still there, sending back information. That planet, appropriate given the subject matter of most Eurovision songs, is Venus.

2007

Date of the final: 12 May
Venue: Hartwall Areena, Helsinki, Finland
Debuts: Czech Republic, Georgia, Montenegro, Serbia (as solo nation)
Winner: Maria Šerifovic, Serbia
Winning Song: *Molitva (Prayer)*

This contest, more than any other, represented the Triumph of the East. The results table divides very simply. The top fifteen songs are all from the eastern half of the continent. The next three are classic Baltic bloc members. The bottom six are old Europe. This, many people argued, was the end of Eurovision as a song contest; the event had degenerated into an exercise in regional voting. A group of British MPs tabled a motion in their parliament, saying that the contest had 'become a joke' as countries voted on 'narrow nationalistic grounds' and called for the BBC to either renegotiate the rules or pull out (sound familiar?)

The trouble with this line is that if you listen to the songs, the Eastern ones are, by and large, much better. Old Europe offers cliché and/or rather soggy camp; it's the songs from the East that are (with a few grim exceptions) impassioned and imaginative. If you look at the performers, it is the ones from the East who have studied classical music, become big stars and gone on pre-

Eurovision tours to promote their songs; it's the West that wheels out the cruise-ship entertainers and thinks a little pre-contest PR will make Europe, old and new, love them. *Water*, a piece of tribal trance from Bulgaria's Elitsa Todorova and Stoyan Yankoulov, might not be to everyone's taste (I love it), but it takes risks and is performed with passion by two serious musicians. Compare that with the feeble and pointless *Flying the Flag for you*, from the nation that had once gifted Europe (and the world) The Beatles, Cream and The Kinks.

From elsewhere in the East, Hungary's Magdi Rusza gave us Janis Joplin-esque blues (and the first time the word 'evanescent' has appeared in a Eurovision lyric). Slovenia produced opera: Alenka Gotar was an experienced classical soloist – she had played Pamina in Mozart's *Magic Flute*, his most Eurovision-like opera. There was mighty Gothic rock from Moldova. The song that won, from Serbia, newly split from Montenegro and appearing for the first time as itself, was a beautiful ballad sung with great intensity.

Just like Lordi, winner Maria Šerifovic received a tumultuous welcome on her return to her home country. "This is a new chapter for a new Serbia," she told a crowd of 50,000 people. The old Serbia had not exactly been kind to Šerifovic, with the popular press criticizing both her Roma roots and her assumed sexual orientation (not exactly hidden by her stage show, although she did not come out until 2014), but she rose above this.

276

The old Serbia had also been rattling its sabre politically, with the speaker of the nation's parliament calling for an end to rapprochement with the West. Šerifovic's win changed the mood at once: the speaker resigned and the anti-western rhetoric abated. Europe welcomed the win, EU Enlargement Commissioner Olli Rehn commenting that it was "a European vote for a European Serbia". On June 13, the EU reopened its accession talks with the Eurovision winner, which had stalled over the issue of Serbia's apparent reluctance to arrest accused war criminals. Šerifovic was made an EU 'ambassador for intercultural dialogue' – possibly not the wisest appointment, as tact is not one of her virtues (she didn't exactly delight the Finns with her post-victory description of them as 'yellowish, see-through people' that she despised – though she later claimed this was a joke, as she was fed up with being asked how she liked Finland. The three-fingered salute she was seen giving in the Green Room as her votes ramped up was tactless, too: a relic of Milosevic-era Serb nationalism.)

However the new, European Serbia was soon in for a test: next February, the Assembly of Kosovo would declare independence. How would the province's old master react?

Second to Šerifovic's *cri de coeur* was a splendidly different piece, *Dancing Lasha Tumbai* from Ukraine's Verka Sedushka (a comically vulgar lady railway sleeping car attendant created by actor Andriy Danylko). The lyrics are essentially nonsense, though "Lasha Tumbai" sounds a lot like "Russia Goodbye" – the way Sedushka sings it, anyway. When questioned about this, Danylko kept a straight face and said the words are actually Mongolian for whipped cream. (Don't try asking for *Lasha Tumbai* in your coffee next time you're in Ulan Bataar, however. The actual phrase is *tashuurduulj tos*.)

Ukraine itself remained a divided nation: in a snap presidential election in September 2007, the eastern half of the country voted for the party of Russophile Viktor Yanukovytch, while the west voted *Lasha Tumbai* and supported Europhile Yulia Tymoshenko (who won by a narrow margin).

Whatever Viktor Yanukovytch wanted, political Europe was edging closer to Ukraine, with Bulgaria and Romania now members of the EU from the start of 2007. In Eurovision, Romania celebrated its new status by fielding a weak entry and came near the bottom of the 'eastern fifteen'. Bulgaria, however, came fifth: "We love you, Europe," called out Stoyan Yankoulov at the end of his piece.

While these countries were keen to join Europe, the EU was not totally loved by its existing members. In May 2007, Toto Cutugno was booed by an audience in Valetta when he announced he was going to sing *Insieme: 1992*. Brussels was slowly recovering from the rejection of the European constitution, and decided to place the changes, or some of them anyway, in a treaty. This was finally signed by leaders of most EU states – Britain's Gordon Brown missed the signing – in Lisbon in December. The treaty simplified voting and gave opt-outs from certain EU rules for more Eurosceptic countries like Poland and Britain. It got rid of the 'three pillar' model (something that nobody outside Brussels or Strasbourg had taken much notice of anyway). It created a European President and a 'High Representative of the Union for Foreign Affairs and Security Policy' (Euro-speak for Foreign Minister.) And it soon got into hot water: in 2008, Ireland refused to ratify it.

By contrast, the East was still eager to participate in political Europe. In December, the Czech Republic, Estonia, Hungary, Latvia, Lithuania, Malta, Poland, Slovakia and Slovenia all joined the Schengen border-free zone. Eastern Europe was becoming an integral part of Europe, and bringing gifts to the table. The 2007 Eurovision Song Contest had been a splendid celebration of this fact.

2008

Date of the final: 24 May
Venue: Belgrade Arena, Belgrade, Serbia
Debuts: Azerbaijan, San Marino
Winner: Dima Bilan, Russia
Winning Song: *Believe*

The 2008 final nearly had to be relocated, as in February of that year, rioting broke out on the streets of Belgrade in protest at the Kosovan declaration of independence. On February 21, a group from a mass 'Kosovo is Serbia' rally in the city broke off and attacked the embassies of some countries thought to support Kosovan independence, including near-neighbours Slovenia. It was felt that the Belgrade authorities had not done enough to prevent the attacks: the EU stopped the accession talks. However this was 2008, not 1999. The violence was brought under control: while discontent simmered in the north of Kosovo, where most of the province's Serbs live, the Serbian capital became peaceful again. Eurovision went ahead.

Instead of going to war, Serbia smuggled a reference to Kosovo into its rather beautiful *Oro* (*Oro* is a Balkan circle dance, similar to the Israeli *Hora* celebrated in that nation's 1982 Eurovision entry). "Wake me up on St Vitus' day," sings Jelena Tomašević. As every Serb, but no EBU official, knows, St Vitus' day, June 28th, is the anniversary of the Battle of

Kosovo in 1389, when a Serb army took on the invading Ottoman Turks. Serbia effectively lost – both armies were almost wiped out, but the encounter exhausted Serbia, while the much larger Ottoman empire was able to call on new forces and, after a pause, push west again. However the battle is seen as the event that created the modern Serbian nation. The location of the battlefield, a few kilometres north-west of Pristina, is a major cause of Serbia's determination to hold onto the province.

Politics also found its way into Georgia's entry, *Peace will come*. Diana Gurtskaya sang that her land was 'torn in half'. The two halves were Georgia itself and two breakaway regions, Abkhazia and South Ossetia, who wanted independence and close links with Russia. There had been a vicious war in 1992/3, especially in Abkhazia, where ethnic Georgian inhabitants had been massacred. Peace of a kind had then been brokered by international institutions, but it had remained fragile. In 2008, Russia began ramping up the rhetoric, insisting the two areas should have their independence.

By the time of the 2008 contest, Georgian drones had been shot down over the disputed areas and the issue was being discussed at the UN. Over the summer both Russia and Georgia massed troops to the north and south of the disputed areas. War would eventually break out on August 7, when Russian forces entered South Ossetia and Georgian forces attacked the area's capital, Tskhinvali. Needless to say, both sides argue that the other moved first; the truth is impossible to establish. Russia responded with airstrikes: the Georgians were quickly driven back, and soon after, Russian troops were in Gori and Poti, two cities in undisputed Georgian territory. They did not press on, however: they had got what they wanted.

The EU still regards Abkhazia and South Ossetia as Georgian, but the issue is complex. If the majority of the areas' inhabitants wish to be independent, why should they not be? To which one can answer 'if that majority has indulged in ethnic cleansing in order to create that majority'. But what does one do now to undo this past wrong? The two statelets remain in what political scientists call 'frozen conflict', unresolved issues left over from the collapse of the old Soviet empire, as does Transnistria, the russophile eastern part of Eurovision contestant Moldova, and, of course, eastern Ukraine.

Croatia produced the contest's oldest competitor to date, in the form of Laci, a 75-year-old singer who turned into '75 cents' for the competition. In *Romanca (Romance)* he bemoaned the modern world, especially the internet, which he didn't understand (he ended up 'scratching' an old 78 rpm record on a horn gramophone). The ageing of Europe's population is a matter of considerable concern among some commentators. We are living longer and having fewer children: many EU countries are expected to lose population in the next generation. By 2030 nearly a quarter of the EU population will be over 65, and by 2050, nearly a fifth could be over 80. There is an 80% chance that by that time, the 'old age dependency ratio' (the ratio of people aged over 65 to those aged between 15 and 64) will have fallen from one in four to one in two (these stats come from the Population Research Bureau, a respected global NGO based in New York, but there are many others, all telling a pretty similar story.) Looking at the bouncy, youth-obsessed Eurovision stage, these figures seem unreal, but they are not.

Optimists argue that these figures don't matter. We are getting healthier and can do productive work long after we reach 65. Machines can do ever more of the heavy manual 'support' work once done by the fit, strong young. If we are having fewer offspring it is because we are choosing to have smaller families, where children can be given more time and attention. At a deeper level, the optimists continue, reading too much into trends is dangerous, as the future is inherently unpredictable, despite what 'experts' tell us. Who, watching the first few Eurovision Song Contests, would have foreseen Sertab Erener, Lordi or Bulgarian tribal trance? Europe (and humanity in general) is nothing if not creative. Even if deep demographic trends are set in stone, our responses to them are not.

Pessimists point to the teeming, overpopulated world that demographers predict will surround our European island of ageing contentment. What will be the consequences of this imbalance?

Eurovision 2008 was won by Russia's Dima Bilan with *Believe*, a song based on Rhoda Byrne's bestselling, and quintessentially New Age, book *The Secret*, which argues that you can achieve anything you want through belief and positive visualization – a force called the Law of Attraction will bring this about. Critics of the book point out that visualizing a nice outcome doesn't always make it come true. Europe's 2000 Lisbon Agenda leaps to mind as an example.

Bilan, who comes from just north of disputed Abkhazia, had not been happy at coming second in 2006, and did more than just visualize success for 2008. He appealed to Western European taste by getting an American songwriter, Jim Beanz, who has worked with Britney Spears, Rihanna and Whitney Houston, to co-author *Believe*, then toured Eastern Europe in the run-up to the contest. An elegant stage show featured Evgeni Plushenko, an Olympic champion skater, floating round the singer. And he took his shirt off at the end. Intriguingly, Bilan also changed the last word of the song, which was supposed to say things would work out if he fully believed in himself ('me'), which is what *The Secret* preaches, to the more romantic, less New-Agey belief in an imagined listener: 'you'.

Ukraine's Ani Lorak made 2008 a Slavic double: having been elbowed out of the way in 2005 to let GreenJolly celebrate the Orange Revolution, she participated in this contest and came second with the steamy *Shady Lady*.

Meanwhile at the other end of the table, old Europe struggled. Germany's No Angels outdid Britain's 2003 Jemini in singing out of tune. Fed up with a string of poor results – largely due to their submitting a string of outdated ballads – Ireland cocked a snook at the contest via Dustin the Turkey, a satirical character from Irish TV: *Irelande douze Points* accused Eastern Europe of bloc voting, got booed at the semi-final and didn't make it to Saturday. Belgium, the Netherlands and Switzerland (the last of these with the pleasant *Era stupendo*) didn't make it through, either. France's Sébastian Tellier was an automatic qualifier, but caused a national scandal by threatening to sing *Divine* in English. A French MP raised the matter in parliament, asking the Culture Minister why France was 'giving up the defence of its language in front of hundreds of millions of television viewers'. In response, Tellier added some lines in French, but still struggled to get many votes. Only Norway bucked the trend, with Maria Haukass Storeng's *Hold on, be strong* coming fifth – but then Norway isn't really 'old Europe', just old periphery.

Old Europe had had enough. Britain's Terry Wogan quit the commentary box. Even the peace-loving Nicole wrote a shirty article in *Bild Zeitung*. We write out the biggest cheques, complained Old Europe, and we want to do better in the contest! A new system of judging the final was announced for 2009, based on the one that had been used in Sweden's Melodifestivalen selection process since 1999. Every nation's vote would be split 50/50 between televotes and 'experts', a panel of five national music-industry professionals. The latter would assess each piece on 'the originality of the composition, act, quality of the vocal performance and overall picture'.

The year 2008 did not give the world a vintage Eurovision. Some people say that the interval act, Goran Bregovic's gypsy-influenced 'weddings and funerals orchestra', was the most fun. It may, however, turn out to be a pivotal year in the balance of global wealth and power. On August 8, the Beijing Olympics opened with the most magnificent opening ceremony ever seen; a fortnight later, China was top of the medals table. And a fortnight after that, Lehmann Brothers bank collapsed in New York. Two days later, British bank HBOS collapsed, and had to be rescued by a rival. Another British bank, RBS followed.

Oh well, thought mainland Europe, that's Britain, enslaved to US-style neo-liberalism… Shortly after the collapse of Lehmann Brothers, Spain's Prime Minister, José Luis Rodríguez Zapatero, told Wall Street bankers that Spain "has perhaps the most solid financial system in the world. It has a standard of regulation and supervision recognised internationally for its quality and rigour."

On September 29th the Belgian bank Fortis had to be rescued by the three Benelux governments. On the same day, the Irish government agreed to underwrite the debts of its nation's banks. Iceland's banks crashed a week later, and could not be saved by the government of the tiny northern nation. A few days after that, the entire British financial system nearly went into meltdown.

2009

Date of the final: 16 May
Venue: Olympic Indoor Arena, Moscow, Russia
Winner: Alexander Rybak, Norway
Winning Song: *Fairytale*

In terms of the relationship between Europe and Russia, May 16 2009 seems an age away, as distant as those black-and-white images of Alice Babs or Margaret Hielscher. On that date, Russia put on a magnificent Eurovision finale, that cried out to the world that the mighty eastern nation wanted to be European. An estimated 30 million Euros were spent on the event, which involved creating a stage surrounded by LED screens – 30% of the screens in existence at the time were in the former Olympic Arena on that night. 20,000 people filled the auditorium to hear 25 songs from around the continent, from Lithuania to Spain.

However there were rumblings in the background. Lithuania, Latvia and Estonia nearly backed out in protest at the host's continuing support for the two breakaway republics in Georgia. (In the end, they came to Moscow, Estonia doing so as the result of a public vote: few countries have embraced democracy as passionately as the most northern of the Baltic states.)

And then there was the gay pride march. Attempts to

ban the event were foiled by protestors, who changed their venue, arriving at the garden in front of Moscow State University in limousines (the garden is a popular place for wedding parties). They then unfurled banners, chanted slogans and were arrested by riot police with what most observers agreed was unnecessary force: eighty or so people waving banners hardly represents a serious threat to public order.

Georgia had initially wanted nothing to do with the contest, given its recent mauling in its border conflict. But after it had won junior Eurovision (including 12 points from Russia), it relented. However the song that topped its domestic heats was a Trammps-influenced disco number called *We don't wanna put in* ('put in' being pronounced like the Russian leader, just in case anyone missed the joke). The EBU said this was too political: could the lyrics be rewritten, please. Georgia said 'no' – reasonably, as there is no other point to the song – and so didn't go to Moscow (which it probably didn't want to do anyway).

There was a rumour that Armenia planned to field rock stars System of a Down, four Armenian Americans whose song *Holy Mountains* had protested the Turkish genocide of Armenians in 1915. Turkey, which continues to deny the genocide, was not amused. In the end, folk duo Inga and Anush Arshakyan got the gig. Armenia then proceeded to annoy its neighbour, Azerbaijan, by featuring a statue on its semi-final 'postcard' that is in the disputed territory of Nagorno-Karabakh. The two nations had fought a war over this area in the 1990s, and control is still disputed (more post-Soviet 'frozen conflict'). After the contest, police in Azerbaijan contacted a number of their citizens who had voted for Armenia's entry by SMS. The Azerbaijani authorities later gave the Orwellian explanation that the people contacted had simply been 'invited to explain' why they had voted that way.

2009 was the first Eurovision final to be judged under the new half-and-half split between experts and televoters. The main beneficiaries from the new system were Britain, France, Denmark, Malta and Israel; the biggest losers from the new system were Azerbaijan, Turkey, Greece and Russia. This seemed fair. Britain, France and Denmark had all put special effort into their 2009 entries. Britain's *It's my Time* was composed by Andrew Lloyd Webber, who also played the piano for the evening, and American lyricist Diane Warren. France featured well-known *chanteuse* Patricia Kaas. Denmark's *Believe again* was co-written by Boyzone star Ronan Keating.

Both experts and public agreed on a runaway winner, Norway's violin-playing Alexander Rybak and *Fairytale*. Rybak (pronounced Ree-bak) was born in Belarus but brought up in Oslo. *Fairytale* was very catchy (rather clunky English lyrics let it down a bit) and well arranged: it had probably won the moment the accompaniment comes in on the fifth bar. Rybak performed with huge enthusiasm: like many winners – Abba and Katrina Leskanich leap to mind – he exuded a sense of simply loving being up there, and viewers couldn't help being caught up in it. Iceland's Yohanna pipped Azerbaijan for second place (Europe's televoters preferred the Azeris).

Outside the new-look Eurovision, the world's financial system tottered along. Despite difficulties with some banks, mainland Europe seemed to have suffered less than Britain or the USA. The 2008 crash was clearly the swansong for the pure form of Anglo-Saxon neo-liberalism, the idea that if financial markets were left to their own devices, resources would be efficiently allocated and we'd all be better off. This demise did not, of course, necessitate a return to 1970's-style Socialism, but it did restate the old, European wisdom that good government is a balancing act between market freedom and other social desirables – a balance that had been understood by Konrad Adenauer and Ludwig Erhard back when Lys Assia and Corry Brokken were winning Eurovision.

Europe's new currency seemed to have weathered the storm well. Germany's Finance Minister even admitted to being 'close to euphoria' about it (I doubt if his words influenced Loreen, three years later, but you never know). However in October, a new government came to power in Greece. A fortnight afterwards, the country's new leader, George Papandreou, admitted that the official figures for the nation's finances were completely wrong. The ratio of a Eurozone member's annual government borrowing to its annual GDP is meant to be 3%. Officially Greece had been being a bit naughty, running the ratio up to 3.7%.

Papandreou announced that the ratio for 2009 was actually going to be 6%. The rate on Greek government bonds went through the roof – leaving the nation that had to borrow most having to pay more for that borrowing than anyone else. The new government reluctantly admitted that it would have to cut back public expenditure – upon which Greek public sector workers went on strike. A grim cycle of events kicked in. More bad news would come out of Athens (usually a new set of figures showing the country to be in even more of a financial mess than had been previously admitted). Interest rates on Greek bonds would rise even more, making borrowing even harder for the government, which would then announce further austerity measures. Eurozone leaders would make funds available to bail Greece out, but by this time there would be public disorder in Greece as people protested the austerity. This would push bond yields up even higher and swallow up all the bailout funds ..

Just before Eurovision 2010, a 110 billion Euro rescue package was announced by the Eurozone nations and the IMF (the global fund that had saved struggling mid-seventies Britain. It, the European Commission and the European Central Bank (ECB), which started buying Greek government bonds at this time, make up the troika that now controls European finance). Relative calm seemed to settle. However rather than breathe a sigh of relief, financial markets started looking around to see who else's bonds were risky. Two veteran Eurovision contestants came into their sights: Ireland and Portugal.

As an oil producer, Russia could look on these events with some equanimity. Eurovision 2009 seemed to have been a triumph for it. However the triumph was marred. The arrest of the pride marchers did not play well with the rest of Europe. There was the business of those Georgian Republics – though Russia can argue that Europe was being hypocritical, insisting that Kosovo should follow its majority and become independent, but that Abkhazia and South Ossetia could not. One gets a sense that the nation was like an unpopular rich child, who throws a lavish party to win the other kids round but still ends up sitting alone in the kitchen at the end of the evening.

On October 14, Vladimir Putin proposed revamping the old Intervision Song Contest. This time it would involve members of the Shanghai Cooperation Organization, a body founded in 2001 consisting of Russia, China, Kazakhstan, Tajikistan, Uzbekistan and Kyrgyzstan. It did not say it would pull out of Eurovision at the same time, but the nation's leader was clearly hedging his bets. There are other gangs to join.

For the rest of Europe, the 'noughties' also ended on a sombre note, with the Euro project suddenly looking flaky and disagreement about how best to rescue it. The indebted countries, led by France, wanted money thrown at the problem; Germany and other financially sound nations such as Finland, Austria and the Netherlands insisted the old rules be kept to. By contrast, Eurovision ended the decade on a high, with a popular winner. A gentle tinkering with the rules seemed to have brought about a subtle rebalancing of the outcomes. The queue of nations wanting to participate was as long as ever. Roll on the new decade; roll on Oslo!

.

The 2010s

2010

Date of the final: 29 May
Venue: Telenor Arena, Oslo, Norway
Winner: Lena, Germany
Winning Song: *Satellite*

2010 was the first Eurovision of the new financial era. Europe's economies had stopped growing half way through 2008, and governments all over the continent were trying to cut back on expenditure. Traditionally, the way to counter recession had been that suggested by Maynard Keynes in the 1930s: governments should borrow money and spend it in order to get cash flowing round the economy again. But now, European nations were already up to their armpits in debt. This time it was agreed that the cure would have to be both nastier and slower: austerity.

The new mood was reflected in national selection procedures for Eurovision. Many countries stopped having special shows with public votes and just let 'experts' decide. Hungary was, apparently, warned off from participating at all by the IMF, from whom it was trying to secure a loan after its banks got into trouble. (Participants have to pay a fee to join Eurovision Exactly how much a nation pays seems to depend on the size of its home audience for the contest. My guess is that Hungary saved about 60,000 Euros. However for this, they would have got 8 hours of

TV: instead, they had to fill the time up with something else. A false economy?). The host broadcaster had to sell its rights to cover the 2010 FIFA World Cup in order to pay for staging the final – which was still an expensive business, costing them 211 million NKr (around 24 million Euros at current rates).

Eurovision was still a matter of great national pride for the hosts – in their own usual intriguing way. A set of stamps was issued to celebrate the contest. Three of them featured past Norwegian winners (Bobbysocks, Secret Garden and Alexander Rybak) and the public was asked to decide who should go on the fourth one. The winner, by a huge majority, was Jahn Teigen, of *nul points* for *Mil etter Mil* fame. Norway remains very happy to be outside the EU: a poll taken around the time of this contest showed 58% in favour of the status quo. As part of the European Economic Area, the country participates in a number of Europe-wide initiatives. Yet it values its independence hugely. Teigen is a symbol of this. We do things our way, thanks, Europe.

The semi finals removed long-time regulars Sweden, the Netherlands and Switzerland, as well as Lithuania's InCulto with *Eastern European Funk*, a song complaining about how Eastern Europeans were doing a lot of the hard work in Europe but not getting the respect they deserved. After 2004, when eight Eastern European nations (the 'A8') joined the EU, there had been a flow of immigrants to more prosperous Western Europe. It's hard to get full, accurate figures for the whole of Europe, but for Britain, by 2010 there were 472,000 Eastern Europeans working in the country (about 1.6% of the workforce). At least as many had already come to Britain, worked for a while, then returned home. Breaking these figures down by nationality, around seven out of ten were from Poland; Lithuania and Slovakia provided around 10% each. This influx did create some social problems, especially in eastern rural areas, but not as many as right-wing media enjoyed claiming: for example, these young, healthy people placed little 'burden' on Britain's health service. As usual with immigration, the big, unspoken story was one of energetic young people seeking opportunities, many finding them, the destination economy being boosted by hard-working newcomers and a few rotten apples giving the majority a bad name. InCulto's rather negative spin wasn't perhaps the best way of looking at this phenomenon.

The broadcast of the 2010 final began with a neat recreation of watching Eurovision back in 1956: a wife dutifully brings dinner for the family watching on a brown Bakelite TV which then conks out; her husband, who has chilled out for the evening by removing his jacket but not his tie, has to get up and give it a thump to get it to work. On comes the *Marche en Rondeau* – then we're back in 2010.

Several early songs – Azerbaijan, Spain, Moldova, Cyprus – set a timely tone of 'everything has gone wrong', as did Ukraine's dark, ironic *Sweet People*. Belgium's entry suggested the new cure: Tom Dice did away with backing

299

singers, fancy outfits or pyrotechnics; it was just *Me and my Guitar*. Eurovision has rarely seen anything so simple – and rewarded it (the judges ranked the song second; televoters like a bit of razzmatazz and only placed it 14th). Greece replied by singing about 'burning the past'. Ireland tried to recreate the past by fielding a previous winner with an old-style ballad, but did not prosper.

Its economy was faring the same. The former Celtic Tiger was now deep in trouble thanks to its government's promise to back its banks, and in November, it became the second EU member to receive a bailout. The glory days of the 1990s seemed a long way in the past, economically and in Eurovision.

Iceland created a model volcano in the Green Room, jokily reminding viewers of the eruption of Eyjafjallajökull the previous month. This had both given TV/radio commentators lockjaw and closed European airspace for five days. Many Europeans had been stuck in overseas destinations for that time (some Nordic holidaymakers in Spain had been taken home by bus, a journey of two and a half days, non-stop). The continent's skies were spookily empty. While the eruption caused some environmental damage, the flight cancellations are estimated to have prevented 2 billion kilogrammes of CO_2 being pumped into the atmosphere.

A few days before the eruption, air transport had been in the European news for a darker reason, the crash of a Polish military jet carrying many of the nation's leading figures to a ceremony to mark the Katyn massacre of 1940. This should have been a moment of reconciliation between Russia and Poland, but instead both sides blamed each other for the tragedy. As often with accidents, more than one factor seems to have been involved – including linguistic difficulties with Air Traffic Control: a reminder of the international nature of modern European life and the need for international protocols and practices.

Russia was represented in Eurovision 2010 by Peter Nalitch, a new kind of contestant. Forget talent contests; they're so 2000s. Nalitch had become famous on the internet. He had posted a home-made video of his song *Gitar* on YouTube. *Gitar* doesn't take itself too seriously, as he invites female listeners into his 'Yaguar' (clearly a beaten-up old Lada). The video became a hit, with over 2 million views, and Nalitch, an architecture student, assembled a band of friends and started gigging. The gigs proved popular. Russia, not forced into austerity, staged a full-on national selection TV show for Eurovision 2010, which the band entered and won by a large margin.

Social media were now a part of Eurovision life. A Facebook petition to get the orchestra reinstated was initiated in 2010 (given austerity, it had no chance). In Britain, a Facebook campaign to get the nation's Eurovision entry into its national charts failed. That didn't have much chance, either: the song got to number 179. In the contest, *That sounds good to me* was voted last by both judges and televiewers.

301

There was also unanimity about the winner. Lena, from the HQ of austerity, Germany, had discreet backing singers, a simple black dress, no props and minimal instrumentation on her backing track: no pounding techno beat or soaring strings. She simply sang her kooky *Satellite* in her idiosyncratic voice. This was Germany going back to traditions, both broadly cultural (Lena sounds like a modern version of those half-sung, half-spoken, 20s/30s songs from Bertolt Brecht and Kurt Weil) and specifically Eurovision (Germany's other winner, Nicole, had kept it simple, too). On returning home, she was greeted with the same enthusiasm that a peripheral nation would have given a winner in the previous decade. Germany was no longer the accommodating embodiment of that 1949 'European spirit' and was instead forcefully insisting on European austerity – but it still wanted to be liked.

2011

Date of the final: 14 May
Venue: Esprit Arena, Düsseldorf, Germany
Winner: Ell and Nikki, Azerbaijan
Winning Song: *Running scared*

Germany had to put on great show – and it did. The set, designed by Florian Wieder and lit by Jerry Appelt, featured a 1250 square metre LED screen backdrop (it weighed 30 tons) and 90 truckloads of lighting that created towers, wigwams, pyramids and cones of light, turning the vast hall of the former football stadium (36,000 people attended) into a magical, perpetually changing world. It is one of the great Eurovision stagings, the next generation on from the great RTE shows of the 1990s. It showcases the mastery of practical technology on which the host nation's economic success is built: the *Bundesrepublik* makes things excellently, and customers round the world want to buy them.

The semi-finals proved their worth by seeing off *Haba Haba, Boom Boom* and *Ding Dong*. It also got rid of the entry from Belarus, subtly titled *I love Belarus*, about how great it is to be young and free in that country. Politically, the most interesting non-survivor was Portugal's *Luta é Alegria (The Struggle is Joy)* from the colourful, fist-clenching, banner-waving Homens da Luta (Men of the Struggle – though two of the band are women). In the run-up to the contest, Portugal had become the third country to have its bonds savaged by international capital markets, and, after repeated denials that it needed help, a bailout had been organized, conditional on the usual austerity measures. Portugal, as is its tradition, found a way of putting political comment into Eurovision. A 'tight belt' is no use, complained Homens da Luta. Instead, let's bring bread, cheese and wine and have a half-protest, half-party! Germany did not enter a song called 'Who's going to pay for it, then?'

The final gave us a Moldovan lady on a unicycle plus musicians in crazy conical hats – the small nation (population 3.5 million) east of Romania has developed a reputation for off-the-wall entertainment in Eurovision. It gave us sign language from Lithuania. It also gave us Jedward: after 2010, Ireland modernized its act and featured John and Edward Grimes, identical twins from Dublin who had come to fame on Britain's *X Factor* talent show thanks to their exuberance, cockerel quiffs and ability to annoy lead judge Simon Cowell. *Lipstick* won the Marcel Bezençon award (awarded by the event's commentators) for best song, which perhaps says something about the other entrants: 2011 was not a vintage year. Maybe the songs were overwhelmed by the setting.

Iceland produced a touching entry: after the selected artist, Sjonni Brink, had suddenly died aged 36, his friends got together and performed *Coming Home* as a tribute.

Italy gave us some jazz, via *Madness of Love*. Jazz is

normally a recipe for failure in the contest, but singer/ pianist Raphael Gualazzi surprised everybody – including himself – by coming second. (The judges made him a runaway winner, giving him 251 points and the next song 182, the biggest majority ever. Televoters were less convinced, rating *Madness of Love* 11th, with 99 points.) Among the thudding synthesizers and chant-like backing vocal lines of 2011 it was good to see some real musicianship on display, both from Gualazzi and his trumpeter Fabrizio Bosso.

Italy was back in Eurovision after a 13-year break, and no doubt happy so to be after its near-triumph. Other kinds of attention proved less welcome. As 2011 progressed, it was the southern nation's turn to come into the markets' sights. This was particularly worrying for Europe, as Italy's economy was much larger – around 12% of the whole of Europe's – than that of Ireland, Portugal or Greece, which are all around a tenth of Italy's size. (In the EU's GDP stakes, Germany leads, comprising around 20% of the Union's economy, followed by France (16%) and Britain (15%). Italy is fourth. Behind it come Spain (8%), the Netherlands (5%) and Sweden, Poland and Belgium (all around 3%).) Italy's government debt was estimated at 1,800 billion Euros.

In November, rates on Italian bonds began heading towards 7%, a figure generally agreed to be unsupportable, as borrowing at that rate is crippling. Its alternately comical and sinister prime minister, Silvio Berlusconi, had to step down, and former EU commissioner Mario Monti took over: a 'safe pair of hands', but not democratically elected. Soon after, his new labour minister Elsa Fornero was in tears as she announced the inevitable austerity measures.

Meanwhile, Spain – for whom Eurovision 2011 meant the bouncy Lucia Perez telling viewers *Que me quiten lo Bailao (They can't take the Fun from me)* – was also in trouble. As with Ireland, the problem was indirect, not government-incurred debt but private-sector debt. In Spain, the villains were regional banks (cajas), which the government ended up having to guarantee to stop the nation's financial system collapsing. A month later Madrid announced massive cuts in government spending. Unemployment, already high, headed past 20%. In reply, the indignado protest movement took to the streets. A new anti-austerity political party, *Podemos (We can)*, would follow.

The Eurozone now had five troubled countries, which became known by the unflattering acronym PIIGS (Portugal, Italy, Ireland, Greece and Spain).

One place where austerity was not an issue was oil-rich Azerbaijan. Like Israel, Azerbaijan is not regarded as a 'European' country, but its geography makes it eligible to join the EBU, which it had done in 2008. Since then, it had enjoyed great success in the contest, and in 2011 it took that to the ultimate, by winning. *Running scared*, sung by Ell and Nikki (Eldar Gasimov and Nigar Jamal), was in many ways a Western European product. It was written by Stefan

306

Örn and Sandra Bjurman from Sweden and Briton Iain Farquharson. Singer Nikki has lived in North London since 2005. The four backing singers were Swedish. Such is modern Europe, where people move around – free movement of labour is a key foundation of the Single Market. Rather appropriately, Gasimov has recently quit music and now teaches International Relations at Baku Slavic University.

2012

Date of the final: 26 May
Venue: Crystal Hall, Baku, Azerbaijan
Winner: Loreen, Sweden
Winning Song: Euphoria

How do you follow the stunning production of Eurovision 2011? By an even more stunning show in a specially built stadium. When Ell and Nikki tearfully collected the trophy for Eurovision 2011, the site of the Crystal Hall, Baku, was a piece of waste ground near Azerbaijan's 162 metre National Flagpole. A year later, this astounding venue hosted Eurovision. It was covered in 9,500 LED lights, which were used to show the national flag of each participant as he or she sung. It seated 25,000 people. The Hall cost 105 million Azerbaijani Manats (about 120 million Euros) – though the Baku government spent much more than that on infrastructure (including upgrading the national football stadium in case the Crystal Hall wasn't ready on time) (This second stadium is names after Tofiq Brahamov, the linesman who awarded – quite correctly, of course! – the third goal to England in the 1966 World Cup. When Azerbaijan was a Soviet Republic, the stadium was named first after Stalin, then Lenin.)

A spokesman for the country's ruling party observed: "It is very important for Azerbaijan to make itself recognized in the world... There is no better opportunity than Eurovision to show the world that we are secular, not a radical Islamic country. We should demonstrate... that we have a developed economy, we have good infrastructure." He couldn't resist adding: "The world should see that we are a peaceful nation, not aggressive as Armenia describes us."

The builders of the Crystal Hall were German, as were Eurovision 2012's lighting designers (the same team responsible for 2011). As with its 2011 winning song, the 2012 hosts knew how to get the best from Europe.

The hosts got criticism for their politics: in 2011, *The Economist* magazine scored Azerbaijan 140th out of 167 in its Democracy Index. There was some debate about the ethics of setting the contest there at all, but the EBU's determination to be apolitical prevailed. Swedish entrant Loreen met opposition activists before the event. (Later in the year, she did the same when performing in Belarus.).

To be fair to Azerbaijan, it also got criticism for being too liberal. Iran withdrew its ambassador, disgusted that its fellow Shi'ite nation was hosting the event, which might involve a 'gay parade'. There were fears that terrorists from Dagestan, Azerbaijan's northern neighbour, would target the contest: a reminder that there are nastier people out there than the Baku government.

The semi-finals deprived us of Macedonia's Rambo Amadeus, a colourful performance artist whose other work includes hosting an erotic quiz show, writing a cadenza for a Mozart piano concerto and doing gigs backed by concrete mixers and vacuum cleaners. During his *Euro Neuro* banners were unveiled demanding a rescheduling of debt. A loss to the final.

They also weeded out San Marino's *The Social Network Song*, despite its having music by Ralf Siegel, now aged 66. Especially from 2008, the use of 'Web 2.0' online social networking tools had blossomed in Europe, especially in the north: around 50% of people now used Facebook, YouTube or Twitter in the Netherlands, UK, Scandinavia and the Baltics. Southern Europe (and, strangely, Germany) lagged behind, averaging around 30%.

The final was a classic, anyway. We had more fun from Moldova: you've not seen anything till you've seen the singer's trumpet. Albania, Azerbaijan, Bosnia, Estonia, Germany, Serbia and (my personal favourite) Spain all produced excellent ballads. Of these, Serbia's *Nije ljubav Stvar (Love is not a Thing)*, did best, coming third: singer/composer, Željko Joksimovic, already had an outstanding track record in Eurovision, having written songs that had come second, third (the lovely Lejla from 2006) and sixth.

Albania's Rona Nishliu pushed the boundaries furthest: an artist who works in areas from dance to experimental jazz, she produced something different, both musically and lyrically, for Eurovision with *Suus* (the title is Latin for 'his or her own': it's usually translated as *Personal*). Like a number of other recent Eurovision entrants, especially from the East, she is also a social activist: after the contest,

310

she campaigned against domestic violence.

Albania and Kosovo – where Nishliu had lived since aged 13 – were suffering from historical legacies in 2012. The unemployment rate in Kosovo was nearly 50%, and Albania was still recovering from both the terrifying Stalinist regime of Enver Hoxha, who had died in 1985, and a bizarre series of financial scandals that happened after the country had abandoned Communism (Albania was the last old eastern bloc nation to make this change. Multi-party elections were held in 1991 and won by the Communists. Their government collapsed the next year, and was replaced by Democratic Party.) In 1996/7 a billion Euros of the nation's savings had vanished in Ponzi schemes (at the time, Albania's GDP had been around 10 billion Euros). It is estimated that two thirds of the population lost money in one or other of these schemes, one of which was started by a former advisor to the prime minister.

Legacies of financial folly were stalking much of the rest of Europe, too – especially among young people (who had done nothing to bring these consequences about). Spain had joined Greece in having official youth unemployment figures of over 50%. Croatia would soon make it three nations. The figure for the three other PIIGS hovered between 30 and 40 per cent; Britain, France and Sweden were just over 20% and Belgium just under (by contrast, Germany's figure was under 10%.) In many parts of Europe, people began talking about a 'lost generation'.

The ultimate cause of this – in the Eurozone, anyway – was the Euro, in two ways. One was the irresponsible borrowing that Euro membership had allowed. The second was the removal of the traditional safety-valve for underperforming economies. Without a shared currency, the currencies of the PIIGS countries would have devalued. This would have made their exports competitive again, and their economies could have picked up. Without this valve, weak economies suffer 'internal devaluation', with economic activity stalling and jobs leaching away.

Eurovision 2012 had a clear winner, according to both juries and televoters: Loreen's *Euphoria* went on to be the most successful Eurovision song for decades, selling two million singles and topping charts all round Europe (except France, where it got to number 26).

Second place in 2012 went to Buranovskiye Babushki, six grandmothers from a village 1,000 kilometres east of Moscow (but still in European Russia), singing partially in Udmurt, a language spoken by about 500,000 people. Any proceeds from their participation were to go to the rebuilding of a church destroyed in the Second World War. The oldest of the *babushki* was Natalya Pugacheva; at 77 she had been born when Stalin's show trials were at their height and had grown up during the Second World War.

(Other minority languages were getting song contest exposure via the Liet International Festival, which in 2012 took place in Gijon in northern Spain. Songs were sung in Asturian (the eventual winners), Gallic, Catalan, Corsican,

Basque, Sami, Friulian (from north east Italy), Breton, Low Saxon, Udmurt and Frisian.)

As if inspired by an excellent Eurovision, political Europe finally began to sort out its financial mess. Estimates of how much it would cost to refinance the banks and governments of the PIIGS countries had been rising, and were now well past the 1 trillion Euro mark. The financial markets doubted Europe's ability to find this money, but on July 26 Mario Draghi, the President of the European Central Bank, made his definitive statement that the bank would do 'whatever it takes' to save the Euro. The markets finally believed him. The turmoil that had begun in October 2009 began to subside. But how long would it take to repair the damage? Was the damage even reparable with the single currency in so many countries where it seemed to be doing more harm than good? Still, a big step forward had been taken.

Even better things were still to come for European political institutions in 2012. In October, the EU was awarded the Nobel Peace Prize. On December 10 (the anniversary of Alfred Nobel's death in 1896), European Council President Herman Van Rompuy, European Commission President José Manuel Barroso and European Parliament President Martin Schulz travelled to Norway to accept the prize. The ghosts of Marcel Bezençon and Jean Monnet would have watched this with huge pleasure.

Eurosceptics argue that peace in Europe has been brought about by other factors, such as a distaste for aggressive nationalism since 1945, the need for greater co-operation in the face of the Soviet threat until 1991, the growth of multinational business and media, and simple technology: we can all telephone, travel and now email all round the continent. To this, Europhiles reply that it is exactly these changes that make the European Union both desirable and workable.

2013

Date of the final: 18 May
Venue: Malmö Arena, Malmö, Sweden
Winner: Emmelie de Forest, Denmark
Winning Song: *Only Teardrops*

After the extravagance of Azerbaijan, it was time for
Eurovision to calm down a bit. Eurovision 2013, in
Malmö, cost a mere 12 million Euros to stage, and seating
was only provided for 11,000 people.

The contest still managed spectacle, however. There
was an Olympic-style opening, where contestants
processed into the arena behind national flags, to a new
'Eurovision anthem', *We Write the Story*, composed by Bjorn
and Benny from Abba and Avicii, a young Stockholm-born
DJ. And once the show began, we had a man in a cage
mimicking the moves of Azerbaijan's Farid Mammadov,
and Aliona Moon from Moldova in a strange expanding
skirt that lifted her five metres off the ground.

Apart from the opening ceremony, nationalism took a
back seat. The postcards, which had of late become tourist-
board adverts for the home country, reverted to scenes
from the relevant participating nations. The interval act was
an affectionate self-parody of Sweden and Swedishness –
reserve, tolerance, industriousness, Abba… 1991 winner
Carola even took a deliberate 'pratfall' after a bar or two of

315

Fångad av en Stormvind.

The most controversial aspect of the contest was probably the brief kiss between Finland's Krista Siegfrids and her female backing singer. Controversial in some parts of the world, anyway: most of Europe took little notice, but Turkey quit the contest when it found out that was going to be part of the act. Chinese TV, which has broadcast the event since 2011 but does not do so live, edited it out.

Turkey's departure probably had other causes, too. The nation had been hammering on Europe's political door for decades, and was no doubt tiring of being told it could come in 'soon', especially since a horde of ex-Communist countries had been allowed in ahead of it. Europe, maybe, became tired of the hammering, too – though one can't help feeling its tiredness is that of a flirt who has suddenly found that the object of their attentions takes them seriously. In 2013, Turkey did its European ambitions few favours with a crackdown on demonstrators in Istanbul's Taksim Square. The old sticking points – Cyprus, the Armenian genocide – didn't go away. Perhaps the split was best for both parties.

Turkey signalled its new mood not by just quitting Eurovision, but by setting up an alternative televised international song contest, Türkvizyon. This featured countries or regions that either spoke Turkic languages or contained people of Turkish descent (or both). The net turned out to spread wide: amongst the 24 participants in the 2013 contest were Iraq, Kazakhstan, Bosnia, Northern Cyprus and parts of Siberia. The show was clearly modelled on Eurovision – a similar logo, his'n'hers presenters, shots of flag-waving spectators, postcards between acts and staging that tried to be as high-tech as possible (Türkvizyon did not have Eurovision's huge budget). The main differences were two long introductory speeches from the Turkish Minister for Education and the Governor of Eskisehir, the city where the contest was held. The tone was more restrained, too: some of the smaller participants just fielded solo singers in regional dress; the bigger acts featured backing dancers but ones that showed much more decorousness (except for the couple in the background in Gagauzia's entry) than we are used to in Eurovision. Eurovision experience clearly told in Türkvizyon 2013, however, with Azerbaijan winning, Belarus coming second and Ukraine third. But the point was made to Europe: we can do this, too.

Russia, Europe's other peripheral giant, was also creating clear space between itself and Europe – despite its 2013 Eurovision entry, Dina Garipova's *What if…* being on the popular contest theme of let's all be nice to each other. On September 20th, President Putin gave a speech to the Valdai Club, a leading national think-tank, where he argued that Russia was steering a middle course between its old totalitarianism and 'extreme, western-style liberalism'. In doing so, he was taking a time-honoured Russian position of a guardian of traditional moral values in the face of backsliding Europe, a position previously taken by Communism and before that by the Orthodox church.

Russia was also expanding its territory. Across its border in Ukraine, russophile Viktor Yanukovytch had become president in 2010. In November 2013, he refused to sign an Association Agreement with the EU, which would have provided financial and technological assistance and granted Ukraine privileged access to EU markets – with the ultimate goal of Ukraine joining the club. A month later, he signed a deal with Moscow, securing aid and cheap gas. These events brought crowds out onto the winter streets, especially the *Maidan* in Kyiv. Some flew EU flags. 2004 winner Ruslana threw herself into the protests, camping out with them and making speeches (and receiving death threats from opponents). In early 2014 she started touring Europe to raise awareness of the unrest, and met José Manuel Barroso in January. Matters came to a head in February: the world watched as police violence grew ever stronger in the face of continuing, determined protest. On February 22, Yanukovytch stepped down and fled to Russia. Four days later, his new hosts invaded Crimea. *Lasha hello.*

Crimea was, arguably, debatable land: traditionally part of Russia, it had been ceded to Ukraine by Khrushchev back in 1954. But the incursion did not stop there: after Crimea was secured, Moscow began to foment unrest in russophone eastern Ukraine. Two Eurovision contestants were effectively at war.

Elsewhere in Europe, the economies of Portugal, Italy, Ireland and Spain had stabilized. But that of Greece had not; unemployment kept rising and GDP kept falling. In contrast, Greece's 2013 Eurovision entry was one of its best for years. *Alcohol is free* featured *rebetiko* singer Agathonas Iakovidis and the group Koza Mostra. The group's leader, Elias Kozas, said that the song was simply about taking a positive attitude to troubles, but behind that one can't help spotting defiance towards the powers forcing austerity onto the Southern European country. 'We're going to party and you can't stop us.'

Safe from this turmoil thanks to monetary independence, the Nordic countries produced strong entries. Iceland's ballad *Ég á Líf (I have Life)* should surely have fared better than 17th. Norway's Margaret Berger came a powerful fourth, and the contest winner, Denmark's Emmelie de Forest with *Only Teardrops*, added to that small nation's list of well-crafted, well-performed Eurovision high-achievers.

2014

Date of the final: 10 May
Venue: B and W Hallerne, Eurovision Island, Copenhagen, Denmark.
Winner: Conchita Wurst, Austria
Winning Song: *Rise like a Phoenix*

In 2009, Russia had hosted one of the most extravagant Eurovisions ever. In 2014, announcements of votes for its entry were booed by the crowd, and one Moscow politician commented that the winning song marked 'the end of Europe'. Russia seemed ever more intent on turning away from the West. It was busy stirring and arming discontent in the eastern part of Ukraine. By August 2014, there would be virtual civil war in that region, and in September an airliner with 283 crew and passengers, 193 of them Dutch nationals, would be shot out of the sky near Donetsk, killing everybody on board. Evidence points to Russian-backed separatists being responsible.

Economically, Russia was looking for friends outside Europe: a new Eurasian Economic Union, consisting of Kazakhstan, Belarus and Russia, would come into effect on 1 January 2015. Talk of resurrecting Intervision as an east-facing contest continued, too, though no date had yet been fixed (it still hasn't, though the venue will be Sochi – if it actually happens). Bizarre anti-gay legislation seemed specifically designed to annoy western liberals. In December, a law was announced denying driving licenses to people with 'sexual disorders'. What a difference five years makes.

The 2014 contest took place on 'Eurovision Island', Refshaleøen. The district is a neat symbol of the changes in the continent's economic life over the last sixty years. Back when Lys Assia won Eurovision, Refshaleøen was home to docks and a large shipbuilding company, noted for the left-wing militancy of its workers. The company went bankrupt in 1996; the area was derelict for a while, but is now being rejuvenated as a location for small businesses and fashionable restaurants. After Eurovision, it became a symbol of the most recent chapter of Europe's economic life, financial ineptness, when it was revealed that the staging of the contest, including refurbishment of parts of the island, had gone way over budget.

The contest winner was Conchita Wurst, a female stage personality created by actor/singer Tom Neuwirth. When she appeared with her dress and beard to sing *Rise like a Phoenix*, many viewers probably thought she would be another in the long line of Austrian novelty acts, but she proceeded to show she was a fine singer with a strong song. Juries and televoters both gave her first place.

The results revealed a cultural split, however. Most of the traditionally liberal Western European countries voted enthusiastically for her: *douze points* from Greece, the Netherlands, the UK, Sweden, Israel, Portugal, Ireland,

Spain, Belgium, Italy, Switzerland and Slovenia. By contrast, Belarus gave her *nul points*, as did Armenia and Poland. (The split wasn't completely east/ west. She got *nul points* from San Marino and cinq *points* from Russia – thanks to its public, who ranked the song third. Russia's judges voted it down: an interesting sign that maybe Russia's macho, anti-western elite is less in touch with ordinary people than it likes to think.)

Conchita Wurst's victory proved popular. In October, she gave a concert outside the European Parliament at the request of a group of MEPs: several thousand people stood in pouring rain to watch the show. At a press conference in the Parliament she seemed uninterested in any controversy she had caused, and talked calmly about tolerance, respect and the need for people to agree to differ. A true modern European.

Second were the Netherlands' Common Linnets with the country-influenced *Calm after the Storm*. This was a quiet, well-crafted song that nobody really expected to get anywhere but which ended up selling more than the winner: a reward for one of Eurovision's most loyal participants (and, finally perhaps, forgiveness for Ding dinge dong).

Hungary's András Kállay-Saunders produced the darkest lyric of the evening. *Running* is about child abuse. Kállay-Saunders based his song on the real experiences of a friend. Getting figures on the prevalence of such abuse in Europe is notoriously difficult. The European Commission website suggests that between 10% and 20% of children suffer it – horrific if true. A survey carried out across Europe and published two months before the contest seemed to support this (though the sample, at 48,000, was rather small given Europe's population of 500 million). 10% of the women questioned had experienced 'some form of sexual violence' before the age of 15. The report went on to talk of other kinds of violence in the home, against adult women, and came up with shocking statistics here, too, with one in three respondents reporting some kind of physical or sexual violence. Even more scary, levels of reported violence were higher in 'progressive' countries like Scandinavia, the UK and France. Some people say this shows that violence is under-reported in other countries – but are they right? In defence of Europeans, the survey made no distinction between a one-off minor incident and the systematic, day-in-day-out cruelty that Kállay-Saunders is singing about. But the figures are still very unsettling. *Running* raised a deep and troubling issue for our supposedly liberal continent.

Less deep was Poland's entry, which featured a large-breasted lady doing an erotic dance with a washboard. The composers of *My Slowanie (We are Slavic)* claimed the piece was an ironic comment on sexual stereotyping. The song was the most popular with televoters in the UK, which either shows that that country's voters have an especially strong understanding of irony or that they don't take Eurovision very seriously. Irony-spotting televoters round

323

Europe rated the song fifth, while juries placed it 23rd.

Some commentators would link the last two paragraphs: do performances like *We are Slavic* demean women (if you miss the irony) and thus create a climate where sexual violence is more likely? This debate continues: when hemlines were rising in the late 1960s, the argument was the opposite; it was repression of matters sexual that created violence. Eurovision's liking for good-natured vulgarity sits easier with the latter approach.

On January 7 2015, Eurostat, the EU's official provider of statistics, announced that the price of goods and services in the Eurozone had fallen by 0.2% between December 2013 and December 2014. Deflation had arrived. Some historians were quick to remind us of the last major deflationary period, the Great Depression of the 1930s – though more optimistic ones pointed out that there had been brief periods of deflation in the 1950s, and that these had done nothing to harm the German *Wirtschaftswunder* or France's *trente glorieuses*. Midway between these two scenarios lies modern Japan, heavily in debt and with little growth, but still with a functioning economy.

On the very same day as the Eurostat announcement, two terrorists from Al Qaeda in Yemen burst into the office of Charlie Hebdo, a Parisian satirical magazine that had published cartoons of the Prophet Muhammad, and killed 11 people: 8 members of the team responsible for the magazine, a building worker and two policemen, one of whom, Ahmed Merabet, was a Muslim. Four people in a

Jewish supermarket were also murdered.

Around the continent people took to the streets to express their revulsion. On 11 January, up to two million demonstrators joined French President François Hollande and other world leaders in a march through the capital. 'Je suis Charlie' became a global slogan of solidarity; others added 'Je suis Ahmed'. From the point of view of this book, the most interesting thing about French reaction was that this was seen as an attack on France and French values: Europe didn't really get mentioned, except as an afterthought. In moments of pain and crisis, even core 'Lugano 1956' Europeans still revert to national identity.

2015

Date of the final: 23 May
Venue: Wiener Stadthalle, Vienna, Austria
Debut: Australia
Winner: Måns Zelmerlöw, Sweden
Winning Song: *Heroes*

Eurovision 2015 was a close-run contest, with juries and public voters disagreeing (the public preferred Italy's operatic *Grande Amore*) and Sweden's winner only pulling ahead from Russia, its nearest rival in the actual live voting, towards the end. At least part of the reason for *Heroes'* victory were the stunning graphics, where the singer seems to interact with the background – yet another technical first for Eurovision.

Russia's *A Million Voices* had reverted to the let's-all-be-nice-to-each-other theme of that country's 2013 entry. Singer Polina Gagarina appeared to mean it: she posted a picture of herself with Conchita Wurst on the net, in clear defiance of conservatives back home. Sadly, this didn't entirely silence the booing of her results, despite both the pleas of Conchita and the installation of Orwellian-sounding 'anti-booing technology' in the hall. Eurovision, as this book has argued, does not exist in a political and moral bubble – quite the opposite. So Russian artists will probably have to get used to this, as long as their homeland pursues its current policies on eastern Ukraine and LGBT rights. Gagarina did the best thing she could: sang well and appreciated the applause she got from most of the crowd. She made more friends in Europe on 23 May than enemies.

More specifically political was Armenia's *Face the Shadow*. The hook line is 'Don't deny', which had been the song's original title before the EBU insisted on a change. This was an obvious reference to the genocide of 1915 and Turkey's continuing refusal to accept the truth about this event. Historians continue to debate the death toll, but figures vary from half a million to two million people killed.

Romania's lovely *De la Capat (All over again)* dealt with that nation's diaspora: the song is sung by an émigré worker father to his son back home. It is estimated that around three million people have left the country (which has a current population of below 20 million) since 2002, creating concerns about immigration in some Western European countries and a skill shortage back home.

Ireland did not make it to Saturday, but on the Friday between the last semi and the final held a referendum on gay marriage. A 'yes' vote was expected – commentators found few people under 40 in favour of keeping the old ban – but the scale of the 'yes' victory, by 62% to 38%, surprised many.

If one anglophone nation was absent from the final, a new one was present: Australia. The country has long had many Eurovision fans, and the EBU agreed to let it participate as a special guest for the sixtieth contest. (It will be appearing in the 2016 contest, too, though Eurovision Executive Supervisor Jon Ola Sand recently said, 'It is yet to be decided whether Australia will become a permanent participant in the contest.') Guy Sebastian did Oz proud, providing an outstanding vocal for Tonight Again and coming fifth.

Britain, by contrast, struggled to get any votes at all, entering a chirpy novelty song that had little resonance with the modern contest, which has been about quality songwriting and emotionally moving performances since the 50/50 system was introduced in 2009. (Eurovision never was a novelty competition, anyway, despite the odd ding and the occasional diggi-ley). This was not what that nation's Prime Minister, just given an absolute majority by his electorate, needed as he set out on a tour of EU capitals to convince political Europe that Britain needed new terms of membership. A referendum on continued British EU membership will be held in June 2016. The nation's attitude to Eurovision does not bode well for the result – but maybe memories of Katrina Leskanich and Bucks Fizz will win the day in the end.

A 'Brexit' would not be good for political Europe (though federalists would no doubt be happy to see the back of the difficult northern island). The EU finds itself facing other challenges, too.

The first is Greece's continuing financial misery. A new government was elected in January, led by a new party, SYRIZA: the name is a semi-acronym for *Synaspismós*

Rizospastikís Aristerás, Coalition of the Radical Left. SYRIZA's platform was one of standing up to the EU/IMF/ECB *troika* and rejecting austerity. Tough negotiations began at once. At time of writing, Greece seems to have backed down enough to keep the troika happy, but there is concern that the difficulties have merely been pushed into the future. Commentators use metaphors like putting a plaster over a deep wound, papering over cracks in a wall or kicking a can down the road.

The second challenge is mass immigration. Migrants had been attempting to cross the Mediterranean for many years, but political meltdowns, first in Libya then in Syria, meant that the number began to accelerate in the new decade. These crossings were, and remain, incredibly risky. In September 2015, Europe was horrified by a picture of Aylan Kurdi, a three year old Syrian boy whose body had washed up on a beach near Bodrum in Turkey. However the EU seemed unable to stop such tragedies.

It seemed equally unable to cope with those who made the passage. A Commission recommendation that every country take a quota of refugees has, at time of writing, been accepted by some EU members and rejected by others. However, even if it eventually works, this is only a short-term fix. UNHCR reports a sharply rising trend in the numbers of people displaced by war or environmental degradation (a growing problem in sub-Saharan Africa). The figure for 2012 was 45 million; for 2014 it was 59.5 million; figures for 2015 are not yet available, but will almost undoubtedly be higher still. The issue is not going to go away, and challenges Europe to find a balance between its genuine desire to help displaced people and the practicalities of how to do so effectively.

Terrorism is a third problem. As this book shows, this has been part of European life since the early 1970s, but the threat is currently intensifying. On November 13, a set of attacks took place in Paris that were even more horrific than the January Charlie Hebdo murders. 130 people were killed in various outrages. Further such atrocities seem inevitable, given the rise of Daesh in the Middle East.

Unlike the two problems above, this danger does not divide Europe but draws us together. We have to co-operate to protect ourselves against it. But its threat has led to the quiet erosion of previously solid European ideals. The dissolution of national borders, exemplified in the 1985 Schengen Agreement, is one. Some argue that free speech is another. Governments are 'snooping' on private communications ever more. Most Europeans seem to feel that, in both cases, the loss of freedom is worth the security gain. So far, anyway...

Europe's story, as always, continues to evolve.

Conclusion

At the start of this book, I asked three questions about political Europe. What light has this story shed on them?

My first question was about European integration: how far should it go? The old federalist answer was 'all the way', ever closer union till we get a United States of Europe. Such an entity, federalists argued, would banish violent nationalism, be efficient economically and make us a world power to balance the USA and any other powers that might emerge.

This full-on view has become unfashionable (though the European Commission still makes comments on its website like 'the process of building Europe is one of progressive integration'). The mess over the Euro is the result of federalist political enthusiasm overriding economic prudence. Anti-EU voices are now being raised around Europe, as a result of this mess and as part of a resurgent nationalism spooked by terrorism and the increasing displacement of people outside our borders. And, of course, did we Europeans ever actually want 'ever closer union' anyway? Not according to the surveys.

Eurovision, it seems to me, offers a vision of a compromise between an integrated United States of Europe and the old fractured, nationalist continent of 1956. In this vision, the nation state still matters – but in a particular way. The song contest is a Europe-wide institution, European and proud of the fact (every fan's heart gives a leap when Charpentier's *Marche en Rondeau* begins; it's our European anthem). But within its European setting, Eurovision promotes nationalism *of a particular kind*. A gentle nationalism, a nationalism of enjoyment and participation, that does not seek to demean or disrespect others but welcomes other cultures and celebrates with them. We're there waving our flags, but so is everyone else, and we're really all there for a big party. Two things would destroy that party. One would be if some (or all) participants became aggressively, unpleasantly nationalistic. But another would be if national pride disappeared, if we all became cut-out model 'Europeans', ashamed of our different histories, traditions and identities.

To be European, in this vision, is to find a balance between belonging to something bigger than our nations (enjoying Balkan *sevdah*, French ballads, Nordic heavy metal, Bulgarian tribal trance and so on) and retaining a sense of national pride and identity (giving an extra cheer when our act appears, and even indulging in a bit of bloc voting). This is the balance that Europe-level government needs to find.

If such a balance were achieved, Brussels would still have plenty to do. It would have the job of creating and enforcing workable Europe-wide rules across the Single Market, to keep competition fair and to keep the free flow of capital, goods, services and labour. Europe-level government is the only way to take action on transnational

332

topics such as the environment, refugees, and taxing and regulating multinational companies and the financial system. Europe-wide institutions are essential to combat international crime, people trafficking and terrorism. Europe needs enough unity to speak with authority on the world stage (but enough diversity to truly speak for its wide range of citizens).

The work of Europe's two Structural Funds and the Cohesion Fund is, perhaps, more contentious, but should not be rejected on ideological grounds, especially as the ideology of the unfettered market is now as out of date as full-on federalism.

If the mood of Europe's citizens changes, we can integrate more. But the days of ever closer union being forced onto 500 million people, most of whom still consider themselves to belong either just to a nation or to a nation first and to Europe second, are hopefully over. The current legal insistence that EU members join the Euro sooner or later should be revoked. Federalists say such this would 'create a two-speed Europe', but Europe has never been one-speed anyway.

Right now it is multi-speed (European officials dislike this term, and prefer to speak of 'variable geometry'. The metaphor comes from aeronautics and engine design, where parts of a system, such as turbine vanes or aircraft wings, change shape according to conditions). The six 'Lugano 1956' nations remain firmly at its core, after six decades (Eurovision, by contrast, has undergone much more radical change: France once ruled, Britain then mastered the art of coming second, but where are those countries in the contest now?) Southern Europe battles on, its youth paying disproportionately for Euro membership. The east dissents over immigration. The north remains its old, proud half-in, half-out self.

None of this means that the European experiment has 'failed', merely just, like Eurovision, which is constantly evolving, that the experiment is ongoing.

My second question was what the extent of Europe should be.

Eurovision extends its boundaries to anywhere in the EBU – and for the moment, out to Australia. Maybe it is not the best guide to where political Europe should end. However the contest provides the interesting spectacle of nations on and beyond Europe's traditional boundaries testing the waters of European identity.

Some have leapt in with glee, mastering Eurovision: Israel and Azerbaijan spring to mind. Others continue to dance in and out of the contest. Turkey have been picked-on outsiders in the 1980s, a triumphant winner in 2003 but have not participated in the contest since 2012. Russia were eager Europeans in 2009, booed in 2014 and nearly won 2015.

And then there's 2004 winner, Ukraine. This is currently Europe's most debated border, with the west of the country eager to join the EU but the east more interested in ties with Russia. Behind this lies an old, deep, cultural conflict about identity and belonging – two things which, Eurovision reminds us, are important to people. Right now, a virtual war is raging in the east. Political Europe should be energetically leading efforts to sort this, but it doesn't seem to be doing enough – another sign of its current troubled status.

Some people, of course, argue that lines and borders cause more problems than they solve. Aren't we all Children of the Universe? Many Eurovision songs have made this point, and in the deepest sense they are surely right.

But a borderless world seems a long way away, right now. Europe is tightening its own. And everywhere, the world seems to be splitting into blocs. This was, perhaps, inevitable after the Cold War. We are in a new, 'multi-polar' world, with regional powers emerging, of which Europe will be just one. The job of the global idealist must be to make sure that the blocs don't start waging war on one another, as horrifically predicted in Orwell's *1984*, with his Eurovision-area Eurasia battling Oceania and Eastasia.

In this new multi-polar world, we need a confident, prosperous, liberal Europe, that knows what it believes and 'who it is'. Such a Europe will be best placed both to look after its citizens and to act as a force for peace, prosperity and progress everyway that it can.

Looking many years ahead – who knows, in fifty years' time, Eurovision may have gone global? Maybe, too, there will be some kind of world government (hopefully of the

335

right, inclusive kind; not domination by one of the blocs). Europe's evolving attempts to create transnational political institutions that respect national identities are a fascinating laboratory for what such an institution might look like. We must, surely, keep this laboratory going.

Thirdly, I asked what it meant to be European. What is a European set of values, a European way of doing things? Let's look at Eurovision.

The contest is technologically savvy: production values are superb, and continue to improve.

It flies the flag for openness and tolerance: Conchita Wurst's 2014 victory was seen in some other parts of the world as a sign of moral weakness (degeneracy), but for modern Europe it is a sign of moral strength (tolerance).

It is democratic, with its millions of televoters – though since 2008 it has backed off from pure democracy, thanks to its juries and their 50% vote. This could be seen as the return of elitism, but I see it as an intelligent, practical compromise. Interestingly, the two sets of decision-makers rarely disagree about the winner (they did so in 2011 and 2015): rather than bitter enmity, they seem to act as gentle checks on each other.

It promotes political liberalism. When artists like Loreen meet protestors in places like Azerbaijan or Belarus, they send a clear message about the European model of an open society.

At the same time, it fosters a *gentle* nationalism. To be European, Eurovision-style, is to have more than one

336

identity and to be at ease with and curious about other people's.

According to the philosophers who wrote to *Frankfurter Allgemeine Zeitung* in 2003, to be a modern European is also to reject violence as a way of solving problems. Cynics will point to the figures on domestic violence quoted earlier and say that this rejection is only skin deep, adding that our history (core and periphery) has been one of shocking violence, both in our imposition of empire on the rest of the world in the nineteenth century and in our own mid-twentieth-century internal struggles. But I'm an optimist. Europe's refusal, by and large, to participate in the second Iraq war is surely a positive sign. Eurovision was set up at least in part to ensure 'Never Again', and many of its songs continue to deliver that message.

The philosophers also claimed that there is a specifically European approach to questions about how much power is given to the market and how much to the state. Their solution – both are old-style Socialists – is outdated, but their general point is, surely, valid. There is a European tradition of balancing these forces. Eurovision, for example, remains essentially state-funded, via the various national broadcasters. Fans seem happy with this – would we really want sponsors' logos all over the stage and relentless product placement in the postcards?

This need for state/market balance was understood by the founders of Germany's hugely successful Social Market Economy back in the 1950s, at a time when others rejected it. Now almost everyone accepts it. The nations of Europe have different traditions on how that balance is struck, however. This diversity seems valuable, and it would be a shame to see it steamrollered by the remorseless one-size-fits-all logic of the single currency and political union. What suits Germany might not suit Spain. If Eurovision were just one type of song, it would be terribly dull.

So here is the Europe we see reflected in our song contest. It is technologically advanced (and continuing to advance); open and tolerant, a defender of human rights; liberal and democratic (though not demotic); gently nationalist (a mixture of diverse nations and enjoying that diversity). It also has a hard-learned disinclination to violence, and it is aware of the contributions of both state and market and is keen to find – and keep finding – the right balance between them.

If this list seems unremarkable, look around the world to see if exactly the same mix applies anywhere else. I don't see that.

If the list looks too self-congratulatory, we probably have to take another message from the philosophers, an unintended one: we Europeans, especially our elites, can be arrogant. Eurovision's populist, open-spirited playfulness is a welcome antidote to this.

Other people will, of course, argue that there is no such thing as 'European' culture, just a cluster of national and regional cultures, in turn now being overwritten by an efflorescence of subcultures. The wide range of music available in the best Eurovision contests hints at this.

I'd like to conclude these thoughts with a fourth 'big question'. Even before the shocks of 2015, there was a sense of a legitimacy crisis in Europe-wide political institutions. Voting levels in European elections had been falling since 1979: turnout in the first European Parliamentary election, in 1979, was 62%, but two decades later that figure was 43%.

2014's televised debates between the two *Spitzenkandidaten* for the presidency of the European Commission were watched by less than 500,000 people (Eurovision, remember, attracts over 100 million viewers). Can Eurovision and its enduring success offer political Europe inspiration to solve its legitimacy problem? I think it can.

The contest is 'transparent': people understand how it works and what the rules are. European government, by contrast, often seems deliberately opaque, with its legalistic language and confusing institutions (I still find myself getting mixed up between the European Council and the European Council of Ministers, sometimes just called 'the Council', not to mention the Council of Europe, though I know that's not an EU institution).

Eurovision is flexible: if an issue becomes pressing, solutions are implemented both quickly and with an understanding that they are provisional and remain open to change. By contrast European government seems unresponsive and incapable of self-criticism, clinging to its existing rule book, the *acquis communautaire*, like a child with a safety blanket.

Eurovision is financially accountable: costs may overrun, but at least we find out about it. European government has a poor history of getting its accounts signed off.

Above all, Eurovision is popular. Ultimately, Europe-wide political institutions will only have true legitimacy if the people of Europe embrace them, argue about them, start cheering and booing, and even bloc vote – bloc votes are better than no votes. Europe needs continent-wide political parties, more colourful candidates – more Theater – and a sense that the European Parliament really does reflect the diversity of opinion across the continent's hundreds of millions of voters, the way the best Eurovision Song Contests draw in musical styles from all corners of the continent (and beyond) Right now, the Parliament does not express this diversity. Surveys show that most EU citizens are politically moderate, not anti-EU but cautious about further European integration. But both the major parties in the European Parliament currently favour deeper European integration. If you want a party that is against this, there is no moderate option, only small, extreme, fringe ones.

In 2016, Eurosceptics argue that this discussion is becoming irrelevant. Political Europe is being pulled apart by centrifugal forces, they say, and the problems above don't need solving but will instead simply hasten its natural collapse. Europhiles point to earlier times in this book, such as the mid 1980s, when the European project got stuck but was rescued by the energy of people like François Mitterrand. They argue that it is in moments of crisis that European organizations find new structures and purpose, and hope that a stronger, less inward-looking Europe will Rise like a Phoenix from the current muddle.

Whoever is right, these are challenging times for Europe. Eurovision 2016 will be in Stockholm, from 10 to 14 May. I feel that its quirky, tolerant, heartfelt European-ness is needed more than ever.

Appendix A: Five Steps to Heaven (or is it Hell?)

There are five generally accepted steps that nations take from being separate entities to being parts of a 'United States of X'.

The first step is for them to join together in a *Free Trade Area*, where the tariffs (taxes on imports) that countries usually charge one another are removed, and goods move freely from one member state to another.

A *Customs Union* is the second: here, not only do area members charge each other no import duties, but they charge outsiders a common tariff. This was what was suggested for The Six in the 1957 Spaak Report.

The next step is a *Common Market*, within which there is free movement of not just goods but labour, capital and services. Standards, regulations and qualifications are harmonized to remove 'hidden' barriers to trade. The 1958 Treaty of Rome, while setting up a Customs Union, expressed a desire to proceed to this stage, as a result of which, the EEC became known as the 'Common Market'. Arguably a true Common Market did not come to Europe until 1993, with the formal introduction of the European Single Market (and arguably not even then, as Europe's legislators are still working on aspects of it).

Then it gets controversial.

It was traditionally argued that Step Four was *Monetary Union*, a shared currency – the Euro, at time of writing in use in 23 European countries (this figure includes Andorra, San Marino, the Vatican and Monaco).– and that Step Five was *Political Union*, where there is a new, single nation like the United States of America. However history, both ancient and modern, seems to show that these last two steps are not clear or distinct or even necessarily in this order. It tells us that a high level of political union needs to be in place before monetary union will work.

Maybe there should be six steps.

Step Four: Partial Political Union, to the extent where there is an 'Optimal Currency Area', with a high level of political and cultural unity – so, for example, the richer parts accept the necessity of supporting the poorer parts.

Step Five: Monetary Union.

Step Six: Completed Political Union. A United States of Europe.

Appendix B: Further Reading

On Eurovision, you can't beat John Kennedy O'Connor's *Official History* (2010 edition) for info, stats and pictures. There is also the wonderful Diggiloo Thrush website.

Academic work is now being done on the contest and its deeper meaning. A good example is *A Song for Europe* by Ivan Raykoff and Robert Deam Tobin (a collection of essays).

The video *The Secret History of Eurovision* is also recommended. Tim Moore's book *Nul Points* is a witty, very British look at the classic losers.

On the history side, there isn't really a standard volume on 'Europe since 1956'. There are many good works on aspects of the story however.

Academic/specialist texts first. Barry Eichengreen's *The European Economy since 1945* takes the (neo-liberal) economist's perspective, telling the story up to the mid 2000s. The baton is then taken up by Martin Wolf's 2014 *The Shifts and the Shocks*, especially chapters 2, 5 and 9. Hartmut Kaelble's A Social History of Europe 1945 – 2000 looks (unsurprisingly) at social history. Sociologist Neil Fligstein's *Euro-Clash* asks tough questions about who we Europeans think we are and where our project is going – not easy reading but very rewarding.

Andrew Moravcsik's *The Choice for Europe* and Craig

Parsons' *A Certain Idea of Europe* consider political decision-making. Parsons argues that you can't make sense of European history since 1956 without taking into account the European ideal. Moravcsik disagrees: in his view, what appear to be 'European' motives disappear under closer scrutiny and turn out to be national interest.

For more general readers, Hugo Young's *This Blessed Plot* berates the British political establishment for not getting involved in Europe earlier (sometimes, I feel, glossing over how difficult this was). Stephen Wall's *A Stranger in Europe* is a British Brussels insider's view of UK /Europe relations from 1982 to 2004. Johan van Overtveldt tells the story of the Euro (and predicts its demise) in *The End of the Euro*. The video on Estonia's Singing Revolution is very moving.

If you have any favourite books on the era or its major players – or the contest – please email me at chris@chriswest.info. I'm always eager to read more.

Appendix C: 'Fifty Years of Celebration'

This poll was done online in 2005 to find voters' all-time Eurovision faves. The method would have graced the most complex piece of Brussels bureaucracy. First, respondents chose their favourites from each decade of the contest. The top two from each decade went onto the list. Then four songs were added by the EBU. There were then two rounds of voting on these 14 songs. The end result was...

1. Abba, Waterloo
2. Domenico Modugno, Volare *
3. Johnny Logan, Hold me now
4. Brotherh'd of Man, Save all your Kisses for me
5. Helena Paparizou, My Number One
6. Olsen Brothers, Fly on the Wings of Love
7. Nicole, Ein bisschen Frieden
8. Cliff Richard, Congratulations *
9. Sertab Erener, Everyway that I can
10. Céline Dion, Ne partez pas sans moi
11. Mocedades, Eres tù *
12. Johnny Logan, What's another Year?
13. Dana International, Diva
14. France Gall, Poupée de Cire, Poupée de Son

Songs marked * didn't even win their years.

What's your Top 14? (Or Top 20. Or Top 17. Or Top 103 – it's Eurovision; chose your own number!)

Another, arguably even more enjoyable, exercise is to produce a list of personal Eurovision favourites that do not include the classics above. Most fans will put *Waterloo* and *Volare* among their faves, but when these disappear, a list can get a lot more idiosyncratic and interesting. One of the many pleasures of Eurovision is seeing how different these lists are. Almost every one will include at least one song that leaves most other people scratching their heads wondering why the hell that individual saw fit to include it. But that just shows how tastes differ, which in turn is a part of the subversive appeal of the contest.

Here's my 'bubbling under' Top Twenty. I have also excluded the two most obvious candidates for the decade 2005 to 2015, *Fairytale* (2009) and *Euphoria* (2012).

Floaty New Age, spine-tingling *chanson*, belted-out ballads, Cabaret camp, trance, wistful *sevdah*, a song nobody else likes – they're all here.

1. Nocturne (Norway, 1995)
2. Love shine a Light (UK, 1997)
3. Un premier Amour (France, 1962)
4. Quédate conmigo (Spain, 2012)
5. Theater (Germany, 1980)
6. Water (Bulgaria, 2007)
7. Su Canción (Spain, 1979)
8. Lane moje (Serbia and Montenegro, 2004)

9. Insieme: 1992 (Italy, 1990)

10. Un Banc, un Arbre, une Rue(Monaco, 1971)

11. Je suis l'Enfant Soleil (France, 1979)

12. Sanomi (Belgium, 2003)

13. Tornerò (Romania, 2006)

14. Dancevise (Denmark, 1963)

15. Rise like a Phoenix (Austria, 2014)

16. Lejla (Bosnia Herzegovina, 2006)

17. To dream again (Malta, 2003)

18. La Source (France, 1968)

19. I feed you my Love (Norway, 2013)

20. De la Capat (Romania, 2015)

Apologies to near-misses Judy, min Vän (Sweden, 1969), Mikado (Switzerland, 1976), Never ever let you go (Denmark, 2001), Madness of Love (Italy, 2011), Ég á Líf (Iceland, 2013) and…

Please feel free to email me your own list.

And as the Credits Roll...

Finally, I'd like to thank my lovely wife Rayna for helping make the writing of this book so enjoyable, for our many discussions about the contest we both enjoy so much and especially for putting up with my snarky comments about the Netherlands' 1975 winner.

Thanks, too, to Stephen Wall – a true British European – for support, interest and comments.

Thanks to the marvellous people who set up the Diggiloo Thrush website, which has been a gold-mine. There are some really rather good lyrics in among the dings and dongs, and I'd never have got to know them without this site.

Thanks to Robyn Drury, Diane Banks and the team at Endeavour Press for making the ebook happen, to Sally Jones for her excellent publicity work, and to Jessica Bell for her help with getting the book past the formatting guardians at IngramSpark.

And finally, thanks to you for reading this book. I hope you have enjoyed it as much as I enjoyed writing it, which was 'a lot'. If you did, please tell your friends and, if you fancy formal reviewing, amazon (I know it's rather sad, but authors' lives brighten up every time a nice review appears). And please email me (chris@chriswest.info) with any comments – it's always good to hear from readers.

Lightning Source UK Ltd.
Milton Keynes UK
UKOW02f1422230516

274832UK00002B/49/P